GOVERNING BY NUMBERS

Governing by Numbers
Delegated Legislation and
Everyday Policy-Making

by
EDWARD C PAGE
The Department of Politics
University of Hull

·HART·
PUBLISHING

OXFORD – PORTLAND
2001

Hart Publishing
Oxford and Portland, Oregon

Published in North America (US and Canada) by
Hart Publishing c/o
International Specialized Book Services
5804 NE Hassalo Street
Portland, Oregon
97213-3644
USA

Distributed in the Netherlands, Belgium and Luxembourg by
Intersentia, Churchillaan 108
B2900 Schoten
Antwerpen
Belgium

Hart Publishing is a specialist legal publisher based in Oxford, England.
To order further copies of this book or to request a list of other
publications please write to:

Hart Publishing, Salter's Boatyard, Folly Bridge,
Abingdon Road, Oxford OX1 4LB
Telephone: +44 (0)1865 245533 or Fax: +44 (0)1865 794882
e-mail: mail@hartpub.co.uk
WEBSITE: http//www.hartpub.co.uk

British Library Cataloguing in Publication Data
Data Available
ISBN 1–84113–207–1 (hardback)

Typeset by Hope Services (Abingdon) Ltd.
Printed and bound in Great Britain on acid-free paper by
Biddles Ltd, www.biddles.co.uk

For Edward C. Page
(1905–1998)

Preface and Acknowledgements

'It may be just a smear to you, mate, but it's life and death to some poor wretch' was the British comedian Tony Hancock's reaction when the doctor told him that the drop of blood he had taken by pricking his thumb was just a sample and that he would have to give a lot more for the full donation. Government activity is largely a series of pinpricks rather than grand measures such as Acts of Parliament implementing manifesto commitments or even annual budgets. The everyday process of government involves thousands of individual decisions about activities that might seem to concern trivial matters to any outside observer. Many of these decisions are formalised in legislation—regulations and orders—many others take effect through 'soft' law such as codes of practice and guidance or through simple administrative changes, only traceable through internal documents, if documented at all. The focus of this book is on Statutory Instruments (SIs), since they offer a way of studying the process of everyday government.

Like Hancock and his smear of blood, there might be a danger of exaggerating the importance of a Statutory Instrument. Why should *The Thames Estuary Cockle Fishery Order 1994* or *The N-nitrosamines and N-nitrosatable Substances in Elastomer or Rubber Teats and Dummies (Safety) Regulations 1995* be of interest to us? One reason for looking at them is that they really *are* a matter of life or death for the small group people involved in the shellfish and rubber dummy industries. Yet even though these particular measures may be of little obvious interest to those of us outside these industries, we are certain to be able to find some affecting us directly as employees, consumers, parents, drivers and taxpayers. In fact, while the chance of any individual regulation concerning any one of us is small, the vast number of SIs in existence—they are currently being produced at a rate of 3,000 a year—means that our everyday life is affected by them as a collectivity. We can find SIs to cover our daily lives from the alarm clock that wakes us up in the morning, the bread we eat for our breakfast, the car in which we drive to work, the roads we drive on, to the contents of the herbal tea that many of us take as a nightcap, the electric switch we turn off before we go to sleep, as well as the beds we sleep on, and everything in between all these.

A second reason for being interested in these small measures follows on from this: collectively they constitute the *process* of government. Politicians, civil servants and the interest groups with which they interact do not spend all, or even most, of their time concerned with what might be called 'major' policy changes such as new legislation establishing freedom of information or comprehensive reviews of the welfare state. Most of what can be termed 'government' appears to be a matter of dull routine, and unless we understand this, we cannot understand what government is about (see also Kerwin, 1999: 186). To put it as an analogy: anybody who learned English solely from the study of major texts, such as the works of William Shakespeare or the greatest speeches of US Presidents, would be familiar with some of the most exquisite uses of our mother tongue but would have difficulty understanding the everyday language of English speakers as they go about their daily lives. To understand government we need to look beyond the major case study, so dominant in the study of policy-making in Britain, and look at the bigger world of apparent routine that exists alongside it.

A third reason for focusing on these thousands of individual pieces of legislation is that they offer *windows* on this everyday process of government. From the simple act of picking up and examining an individual SI much information can be gathered—their texts outline the sorts of issues handled by this process, which departments are involved in it and how, in one specific area, government seeks to have an impact on society. It is a good idea for anyone wanting to understand the process of delegated legislation to spend a few minutes browsing through printed volumes of SIs or looking at them on the internet (http://www.hmso.gov.uk/stat.htm). A short SI is reproduced as Appendix A in this book to give an idea of what they look like. Going beyond the information about the everyday world of policy-making that can be found within the SI, it is possible to trace the origins, development and history of an issue through associated published sources including parliamentary debates, parent legislation, previous regulations, press releases and very occasionally newspapers. An individual SI also provides an excellent starting point for asking civil servants, politicians and members of interest groups about the process of government. Instead of addressing general questions about how government works, interviews can follow through how this process works in a specific case.

A fourth reason for looking at these small measures is that, on closer inspection, the world on which they offer a series of windows is often neither dull nor routine. For example *The Education (School Leaving Date) Order 1997* contains effectively just one line: 'The school leaving date for 1998 and for successive years shall be the last Friday in June'. It is not immediately apparent from these words that they (among other things) generated a flaming row between two of the most powerful government departments lasting nearly five years, which took a change of government to resolve. It involved a survey of school leavers, a new pilot scheme aimed at meeting school leavers' educational needs, a push against social security fraud, and (less directly) the popular singer Cliff Richard. The link between these things will be explained in Chapter 5, but the outline suffices to illustrate the major point that the closer you look the less dull and routine such issues become.

As it became increasingly clear that almost every one of the particular SIs looked at in detail held some points of interest by illustrating general questions about the character of British public administration, there was what one might term a 'Naked City' problem. *The Naked City* was a popular television programme of the late 1950s and early 1960s which took up, as the basis of a 30-minute drama, the story of someone who just appeared as another face in the crowd. The story usually involved some mixture of deceit, unrequited love, betrayal or murder and showed the seething pot of lust, dishonesty, ambition and greed that lay just below the surface in modern civilised life. It ended with the observation 'there are eight million stories in the Naked City, this has been one of them'. Pick any apparently ordinary person, and when you examine them closely they will have an extraordinary tale to tell. Similarly, any apparently ordinary SI had its own story with its own excitement. On most of the 46 SIs selected for more detailed analysis in this book, at least 3,000 words was written up in interviews and notes. So this book could have been nearly one and a half times as long as it is at present just setting out the 46 stories without anything else. Apart from this, there were two other aspects of the Naked City problem. One of these was getting across the richness of the cut and thrust of bureaucratic politics involved in many SIs without giving details and betraying the confidence of those who told you the story in the first place. The other difficult aspect of the Naked City problem was devising a method of presenting the material on these 46 stories as part of a general process of government rather than as 46 separate episodes.

This book takes these 46 episodes as well as the mass of other supporting information as a means of looking at a world of government that is highly political because of its collective impact upon the way in which Britain is governed and because, despite outward appearances, it involves conflict, controversy and the cut and thrust of politics. It is *government by numbers* because it chooses Statutory Instruments as a way into this world. Every year 3,000 or so Statutory Instruments reach the statute book. They outnumber Acts of Parliament by 40 or 50 to one. As the visible outward product of what Rose (1980) calls the 'ongoing Whitehall process', they are usually identified by a number and a year (e.g. SI 1998/1, SI 1998/2 and so on).

More directly, the metaphor in the title evokes the notion of routine and regularity. The notion of doing something by numbers (meaning following a specified sequence of prescribed routines) is associated with army life as it describes how soldiers remember and execute movements on the drill ground. The numbers metaphor thus highlights the commonplace notion that the 'ongoing Whitehall process' is about predictability and the routine execution of tasks. Yet while the title focuses attention on the apparent routine of decision-making in subordinate legislation, the central argument of the book goes on to challenge the idea that everyday policy-making is devoid of significant political action, discretion and creativity.

In another sense the numbers metaphor describes the underlying approach taken by this book. When painting by numbers, one fills each little patch of a canvas with paint of a distinct hue which, when viewed as a whole, generally reveals a still life or a landscape. Similarly, the small and diverse pieces of government action reflected in delegated legislation collectively offer a clear picture of the nature of government. The picture of government seen from the perspective of Statutory Instruments is somewhat different from that which can be gained either from general surveys or from studies of single, usually controversial and politically sensitive, cases. It is surprising how very little we know about everyday government, and the image created through the mosaic of SIs is remarkably sharp.

Although this study is based on an examination of a particular type of legislation, it looks at it from a political science perspective. The book arose from an interest in the obscure that started in the late 1970s with a Ph.D thesis that examined the role of government circulars in Scotland. Each one these obscure items had some history behind it, and this sparked the feeling that the altogether more important-looking volume of Statutory Instruments stored on the next set of shelves might also yield something interesting on closer inspection. My postgraduate supervisors at Strathclyde, Professor Brian Hogwood and Professor Richard Rose, had taught me that detail, when handled systematically and carefully, was often a good way of approaching a big issue. The problem at that time with any study of Statutory Instruments was that as there were so many of them, that analysing them systematically was likely to be prohibitively time-consuming. Now, to use another old television phrase, we have the technology. The availability of Statutory Instruments on CD-ROM in the late 1990s made the study of them possible. While there are limits to what can be gained by machine-based analysis of the texts of SIs, the ability to search, manipulate and quantify offered by digital technology was a *sine qua non* for this study.

The research was conducted between late 1997 and late 1999. It covered many SIs which had either been passed or begun life under the Conservative administration which was replaced by Labour in May 1997. The choice of time period was not wide. One could only look at recent SIs because the older the SI, the more likely that the people concerned will have moved to other jobs or out of the public service altogether, and the less likely they are to remember much about it. One impact of the timing is that I managed to look at the operation of the pre-devolution Scottish and Welsh Offices. In time I would like to go back and see how things have changed after devolution. Other impacts of the time period chosen for the empirical research are to be explored in the text. No single time period in politics can be considered 'typical', yet I do not believe that an examination of this particular time period gives a skewed or distorted account of everyday politics.

I am grateful to the large number of civil servants, politicians and representatives of interest groups who helped me in my research. The nature of the study was such that it required some familiarity with matters ranging from Industrial Training Board levies and load line regulations for small boats, to how optometrists are reimbursed for their services and the intricacies of labelling flour. All of my understanding of such matters came from the public servants and group representatives who helped me in this research. I enjoyed every single interview and felt a great loss when the interviewing stage of the research was finished. Very few of the SIs were remotely as straightforward as they looked. The earliest lesson I learned from the interviews was that it was impossible for the non-specialist to have much of an idea what an SI was really about even if all available published material on it (including the relevant Acts of Parliament, departmental press releases, parliamentary publications and occasional newspaper articles) had been consulted. The exciting thing about the interviews was that after the first few I knew that they were likely to take me into largely uncharted areas of government activity, often by an unexpected route. Those interviewed were without exception generous with their time and patience, explaining often rather technical issues to a non-specialist with clarity, precision and frequently humour.

The interviews with officials, MPs and interest group representatives lasted anywhere from ten minutes to two hours. These interviews were not recorded electronically. I took notes and wrote them up longhand as soon as possible after each interview—this usually meant in a fish and chip shop near Waterloo Station or on a GNER train back to Hull. If my understanding of particular areas is defective, then I alone take responsibility for that.

Occasionally I have attempted, where necessary, to make it difficult to identify precisely which individual is being quoted through modifying the quotations, without changing their meaning, as well as through other means, such as disguising the specific context to which they refer or ascribing quotes by male respondents to females and *vice versa*. Drafts of this book were sent to the departments where interviews were conducted. The most common suggested amendments were along the lines that the language respondents used in interview be toned down for publication. Thus words and phrases such as 'hacked off', 'slagged off', 'crap' and even 'fudge' were replaced by more anodyne expressions. The proportion of quotations thus affected remains small, but such amendments occasionally give the impression that officialese is more widely spoken than it is in reality.

This study would have been impossible without a grant from the University of Hull's Research Support Fund, and I would like to express my gratitude to Howell Lloyd and Peter Robson and members of the Committee. I am also grateful to HMSO and Context Ltd for permission to use their Statutory Instruments database on CD ROM for my purposes, to Peter Marks and Access Informatics for making available their excellent software *Transform Reports* without which the analysis of 27,999 Statutory Instruments would have been impossible, as well as to the 382 interest group representatives who responded to my questionnaire.

The project received intellectual support from colleagues including Terence Daintith (University of London Institute of Advanced Study), Bill Jenkins (Kent), George Jones (LSE) and Alan Page (Dundee) who helped me develop the broad approach to the question. Rod Rhodes (Newcastle) gave guidance on how to approach departments and their officials for interview, and some of the preparatory work was done while I was working on the ESRC Whitehall Programme which he directed (grant L124251008). I am also greatly indebted to several colleagues at Hull. Clive Norris' advice on interviewing techniques and on the use of interview material was invaluable. The quantitative analysis of the 27,999 SIs could not have been done without the help of Allan Reese. Gabbie Hayes' efficiency made it possible for me to conduct a large number of interviews in a short period of time, and handle the material they produced. Jack Hayward, Philip Norton and Philip Cowley went above and beyond the call of friendship by listening to me rattling on and on about Statutory Instruments, by commenting on ideas and issues as they arose, by suggesting ways out of holes and by looking at the manuscript at several stages of readiness.

Contents

List of Tables and Figure

1

Politics in Seclusion

The first general legislation passed under the Labour Government after it swept to power in the landslide of 1997 owed nothing to any manifesto commitment. While the legislation concerned the European Union, a matter which had split the outgoing Conservative Government so badly that it was generally regarded as one of the principal reasons for the scale of the Tory defeat, the law itself generated no controversy, did not appear in the newspapers and no mention of it was made on radio or television. *The European Parliamentary (United Kingdom Representatives) Pensions (Amendment) Order 1997* made a small change to *The European Parliamentary (United Kingdom Representatives) Pensions (Consolidation and Amendment) Order 1994* by tidying up the arrangements for complaints against the managers of the pension fund for United Kingdom Members of the European Parliament. It seems likely that few are aware of the existence of this law, even fewer care much about it and only a handful of people know why it was passed and who or what was behind the legislation. The Order was one of approximately 3,000 pieces of legislation passed every year, most of them more or less on the nod, without going through the active deliberative procedures of readings, committee and report to which Bills are subjected before they can find their way into the statute books as Acts of Parliament.

Statutory Instruments (SIs)[1] or, to use some of their other common names, orders and regulations, often appear to be about matters that are trivial or arcane. Their titles suggest a world of routine and detail. Among the first decrees passed in 1997 were *The Education (Recognised Bodies) Order 1997, The Bedfordshire and Hertfordshire Ambulance and Paramedic Service National Health Service Trust (Establishment) Amendment Order 1997, The Plant Protection Products (Amendment) Regulations 1997* and *The Channel Tunnel Rail Link (Qualifying Authorities) Order 1997*. Are such small pieces of legislation really politics and worthy of consideration as a major, or at least significant, aspect of our political system? If we think of a classical Aristotelian definition of politics as a *public* activity, then the answer may be that they are

---

[1] The term 'Statutory Instrument' is used here as a generic term for legislation produced by the exercise of powers delegated by statute and which is covered by the 1946 Statutory Instruments Act. The names given to individual items of delegated legislation vary and include 'orders', 'rules' and 'regulations'. This excludes Orders in Council issued under the royal prerogative or under the Crown's authority as an employer. Furthermore, not all delegated legislation is covered by the 1946 Act (see Daintith and Page 1999).

not. The obscurity of *The European Parliamentary (United Kingdom Representatives) Pensions (Amendment) Order 1997* is shared by most other SIs. Very few SIs are mentioned by name in the press: *The Beef Bones Regulations 1997* are a rare exception. More frequently issues covered by SIs are mentioned in vaguer terms such as 'new regulations', 'new measures' or simply as 'government decisions' or 'actions'—almost invariably after such regulations have been passed. Despite being the subject of a notorious parliamentary performance, few will have heard of *The Equal Pay (Amendment) Regulations 1983*.[2] Thus SIs are obscure and may not be classed as 'political' because they are not generally exposed to the glare of publicity. They are, however, public in the more profound sense of the term as it occurs in classical Greek theory—they reflect the use of public authority to govern common purposes.

The *prima facie* evidence suggests also that they are political in perhaps the central defining feature of politics: they reflect conflict and controversy. One person's routine and detail could be another person's battle lost or won, another person's livelihood wrecked or improved or opportunities substantially enhanced or limited. *The Education (London Oratory School) (Exemption from Pay and Conditions Order) Order 1993*, exempted this particular school, now famous as the school which Prime Minister Tony Blair has chosen for his children, from the legal obligation on other state schools to conform to nationally agreed measures on pay and conditions of service. At the time the measure was not opposed by the teaching unions as it was designed to allow the school to pay above national rates (*The Guardian*, 27 March 1993). Yet the measure was part of a broader strategy to secure greater independence for the school under existing (Conservative) legislation which did generate controversy. For any legislation, including secondary legislation, there is likely to be some beneficiary or beneficiaries and, equally likely, individuals or groups disadvantaged. In many cases, such as with drought orders (which restrict use of water so that water stocks may be preserved), the losers and winners cannot easily be defined; those who suffer today may gain from their sacrifices later.

Even if most SIs appear insignificant, some have been used to make major changes to policy and some can make front page news. In 1986 the Joint Committee on Statutory Instruments argued that SIs were capable of making major changes to policy:

---

[2] After having 'tasted' several bottles of wine, the Under-Secretary of State for Employment presenting the Order, Alan Clark, gave an ostentatiously cavalier reading of a text prepared by his civil servants to introduce the debate on this affirmative resolution and was accused of being drunk and of not supporting the measure he was introducing. His delivery made clear his disdain for his civil servants' work. He said of it later in his diaries:

> That fucking text! I'd barely looked at it . . . The purpose of the Order . . . was unchallengeable. But give a civil servant a good case, and he'll wreck it with clichés, bad punctuation, double negatives and convoluted apology. Stir into this a directive from the European Community, some contrived legal precedent and a few caveats from the European Court of Justice and you have a text which is impossible to read—never mind read *out*' (Clark 1994: 29–30).

Clark did not feel the need to give the name of the order in his diaries.

Instead of simply implementing the 'nuts and bolts' of government policy, Statutory Instruments have increasingly been used to change policy, sometimes in ways that were not envisaged when the primary enabling legislation was passed (quoted in Bradley and Ewing 1993: 625).

Moreover, SIs have been more or less directly involved in some recent political controversies, including, for example, the recent Bovine Spongiform Encephalopathy (BSE) issue, the development and sale of food with genetically modified ingredients, the outlawing of the use of imperial measurements in shops, the powers of the Home Secretary to detain dangerous paedophiles in custody, drink-driving laws, the Child Support Agency, highly contested road schemes, drought orders and cold weather payments to old age pensioners.

The Sierra Leone (United Nations Sanctions) Order 1997 was cited in the May 1998 uproar when Robin Cook, the Foreign Secretary, was accused of colluding with mercenaries to supply arms to the deposed leader of Sierra Leone in breach of a United Nations embargo. Quite rarely for an SI, it was quoted and a picture of it shown on the BBC's main evening news (11 May 1998). Indeed, whether one of the key actors had actually seen the SI concerned was a significant issue in the affair (see the *Financial Times*, 29 July 1998).

Deregulation as an initiative has paradoxically frequently been achieved in areas from charity organisation to fish farming by means of decrees (Shrimsley 1995). In 1996 the Conservative government generated substantial controversy when it tried to limit by delegated legislation the right of asylum seekers to social security benefits (and lost a court case, see p. 30). Collectively, Statutory Instruments are at the heart of the controversy about the over-regulation of industry: the volume of secondary legislation and the burdens it imposes was one of the main conclusions of the September 1996 Report of the Deregulation Task Force (1996) within the Cabinet Office,[3] and the *Financial Times* noted on 18 November 1999 that:

> like many previous Prime Ministers, Tony Blair declared 'war on red tape' by trying to 'stem the tide of new government regulations'. Statutory Instruments are likely to play a part in Britain joining the European Single Currency, should it decide to do so.[4]

Despite these prominent examples, it is undoubtedly true that the great mass of SIs remain obscure and escape major political controversy.

IT'S POLITICS, BUT NOT AS WE KNOW IT

The low visibility of the delegated legislative process means that SIs are part of a world whose *existence* is certainly well known, but its *character* has largely

---

[3] The powers granted to ministers under the Deregulation and Contracting Out Act 1994, including the power to amend primary legislation through ministerial order, also raise important constitutional issues (see Page 1995; Field 1995). The powers contained in this Act further serve to increase the political importance of delegated legislation.

[4] The 1998 Finance Act contained powers to make Statutory Instruments to make changes to the tax system to facilitate entry to the Euro.

escaped serious social scientific attention.[5] Instead, the study of policy-making has tended to concentrate upon less obscure processes of decision-making. This may be through looking at big issues, such as the poll tax or local government reorganisation, at larger interest groups, such as the British Medical Association, the Confederation of British Industry or the National Farmers' Union, or at significant landmarks in the development of sectoral policy in areas such as motor manufacturing, health or environmental protection. Despite its obscurity, the delegated legislative process is politics, but not as we know it since it may be expected to differ significantly from the process of policy-making over major issues.

Why should the obscure politics of delegated legislation be any different from the grand politics of the major public arena? This issue is central to the whole analysis of this book. Perhaps the best way of explaining this is to use Schattschneider's analysis of the scope and bias of politics. For Schattschneider, politics is conflict and, just like any fight, it attracts a crowd of onlookers:

> Nothing attracts a crowd as quickly as a fight. Nothing is so contagious. Parliamentary debates, jury trials, town meetings, political campaigns, strikes, hearings, all have about them some of the exciting qualities of a fight: all produce dramatic spectacles that are almost irresistibly fascinating to people (Schattschneider 1960: 1–2).

Not only is it a spectacle to observe, it is also contagious—people want to do more than watch, they often want to get involved. For Schattschneider, the crowd watching the conflict is crucial. If they get involved they can transform the conflict.

Schattschneider begins the exposition of his framework in *The Semisovereign People* with the analogy of a street brawl. This analogy can be made more effective if we change it from 1950s New York to the twenty-first century and a pub somewhere in northern England. If two soccer fans—one supporting Leeds United and the other Manchester United—are in a fight in a crowded bar, we may expect the development of the conflict to depend upon the nature of the watching crowd itself. If the crowd were all Leeds supporters we might expect them to come in on the side of the Leeds fan and the brawl would soon be over, with the Manchester United fan coming out of it worst. The opposite would be the case if the crowd were Manchester United supporters. If the crowd were evenly divided between Manchester and Leeds, then we would expect a harder fought and more protracted fight. Correspondingly, the character of the crowd affects the strategy of the original participants in the brawl: if the crowd is predominantly Leeds, then the fighting Leeds supporter will want to involve the

---

[5] Christopher Booker's regular *Notebook* page in the *Sunday Telegraph* is a major exception to the general rule that observers pay little attention to delegated legislation. Booker's column frequently deals with the substantive and procedural details of measures passed by the European Union and their implementation in the United Kingdom. See, for example, his 'Traders in revolt over metrication', *Sunday Telegraph*, 30 April 2000.

crowd. If the crowd is predominantly Manchester United, he will want to try to keep them out of the conflict. It would be exactly the opposite for the fighting Manchester United supporter. The nature of the crowd thus affects the character of the fight and its outcome.

This simple argument is the basis for the powerful hypothesis that the *scope* of a political conflict, i.e. the number and type of people who participate in it, affects the character and outcome of that conflict. If the bar brawl remained a brawl between two demented fans, the outcome would depend on the fighting skills of each of them. If it spread to involve the crowd, the outcome would depend upon the make-up of the crowd. Hence the scope of a conflict contains *bias*, and changing the scope of the conflict changes the balance of power between the parties to the conflict and shapes its outcome. In the political sphere, Schattschneider uses the extension of the franchise as a classic example of this principle—by bringing new voters into the political system, political reformers anticipate strengthening their own parties' electoral fortunes by involving new voters who they expect to vote for their party.

It can therefore be a key component of any political strategy to try to influence the scope of any conflict so that it maximises the involvement of people likely to support your side and minimises the involvement of people likely to support your opponent. Schattschneider argues that conflicts can be *privatised* (i.e. restricted to few participants) or *socialised* (broadened out to include many participants), and politicians will seek to privatise or socialise the conflict depending upon the perceived benefits such strategies will bring to their side of the conflict.[6] In an application of this to French education, Baumgartner (1989) shows that the teaching profession, opposed to educational reform in the 1980s, managed to move the issue of the curriculum reforms out of the narrow confines of the Ministry of Education to a wider public by managing to sustain the argument that the reform raised issues about the rights of man and the constitution.

We can use this approach to understanding the scope of conflicts to outline our expectations about the everyday process of government. We would expect the world of delegated legislation to be different from that of the major policy-making process for two main reasons. First we would expect items of delegated legislation to be more likely to contain issues which relate to privatised conflicts—conflicts in which participation is limited primarily to those most immediately affected by the issues it raises. Secondly, we would expect privatised conflicts of SIs to be capable of being socialised only in relatively few cases and with difficulty. Opening up a conflict to invite participation of those you believe to be on your side is, according to Schattschneider, one of the supreme tactics of politics. However, this tactic of seeking such support from a wider public or even a wider network of policy insiders can be used less frequently in the case of delegated legislation than with high profile primary legislation. This is not to

---

[6] While the terms 'socialised' and 'privatised' evoke debates about the ownership and control of firms and public services, and thus bring about some potential for confusion, greater confusion is introduced by seeking to invent new words for these phenomena.

suggest that socialisation of conflicts concerning SIs is unknown. *The Beef Bones Regulations 1997* (dealing with the BSE issue) and *The Food Labelling (Amendment) Regulations 1999* (dealing with the question of genetically modified foods) are clear examples of delegated legislation that has generated much opposition in Parliament and the mass media. For example on 23 April 1998 *The Times* ran an article with the title 'Bishop urges repeal of beef-on-bone law' and on 19 March 1999 a headline in the *Daily Telegraph*, 'Fines for failing to declare GM food attacked'. Other regulations have similarly made front-page headlines, such as the regulations which made motorcyclists wear crash helmets, *The Motor Cycles (Wearing of Helmets) Regulations 1973* or the regulations offering some protection to the countryside, *The Hedgerows Regulations 1997*. However, most delegated legislation remains, in Schattschneider's terms, privatised since it is extraordinarily difficult to socialise conflicts by appealing to a wider public due to the amount, content, language of regulations and because of the delegated legislative process itself. Let us elaborate on these four points.

The *amount* of legislation has an important bearing on the privatisation or socialisation of any conflict since, as Schattschneider reminds us, there is a limited appetite for conflicts among any public, whether bureaucratic élites, MPs or general public. If a new conflict arises, then generally it *displaces* an older one. Schattschneider's observation outlines a tendency and does not set out precisely how many conflicts can be sustained at any one time. However, with thousands of items of delegated legislation each year it is unlikely that many of them are capable of attracting significant attention.

The *content* of delegated legislation usually concerns a relatively small aspect of public policy, in many cases covering arrangements and procedures unknown outside a small group of people. *The Medicines (Control of Substances for Manufacture) (Revocation) Order 1997* (reproduced in Appendix A) deals not with general questions of animal feeding, but with the question whether 'certain substances having a hormonal or thyrostatic action and . . . beta agonists' should be permitted in stockfarming. In this sense decree legislation would resemble the *leggini* of the Italian parliamentary system since they can deal with highly specific issues (see Furlong 1994). This view is reinforced by the relatively large number of 'local' decrees compared with local Acts of Parliament (discussed in Chapter 3).

Where an SI involves a political conflict, the *language* of delegated legislation also makes it more likely to remain a privatised conflict. In part this results from the concentration upon legal detail which makes it difficult for non-specialists to appreciate what the regulation is actually doing. For example *The Town and Country Planning (Assessment of Environmental Effects) (Amendment) Regulations 1994* is a short decree containing a few clauses, incomprehensible to the non-specialist, along the lines:

3. In regulation 4(2), after 'consideration' insert 'and state in their decision that they have done so'.
4. In regulation 5(4), for 'of the request' substitute 'of receipt of the request'.

More generally the language of decrees may appear so abstruse that few are enticed into participating in debates or discussions about it. Writing about the Acts of Parliament that contain clauses enabling ministries to draw up decree laws, Hewart (1929: 77–8) argues:

> The obscurity of language of statutes is a matter for a separate treatise . . . It is not many months ago since a Judge expressed himself pretty plainly in Court upon the scandal of introducing Bills, or enacting statutes, in the complicated and unintelligible form of many of the statutes referred to in the particular case. If he was bewildered as an expert in that very breach of law, what must be the position of the ordinary tax-payer? The answer given by the Law Officer who was conducting the case for the Crown . . . was that it would not be possible to get Bills through the House of Commons in any other form. Now, this answer was not Machiavellian nor probably was it intended to be facetious . . . [T]he meaning appears to be that, if Bills . . . are to be got through the House of Commons within reasonable time, care must be taken that they shall not expose too large a surface for possible attack. Or, to put the matter more shortly, to be intelligible is to be found out, and to be found out is to be defeated.

Although Hewart is probably here, as elsewhere, overstating his case, it is quite possible that the technicality of the language of many SIs has the kind of effect he describes. They may be difficult to understand, even for the expert, and unlikely to arouse the interest of Members of Parliament, and possibly even of members of groups affected by the decree.

The *procedures* for processing SIs, and the reputation of regulations and orders for 'dullness' and 'routine' might further inhibit group participation as well as diminish public attention. The intention to legislate, or to develop legislation, is usually made known through processes of consultation according to which individuals and organisations are approached by government departments for their views. While there is, in principle, no general objection to groups thus consulted 'going public' and involving wider groups or the media, this happens only very rarely (see Chapter 7). SIs have a reputation for being uninteresting, even among politicians who have to scrutinise them (see Chapters 2 and 5) and they also lack the attraction of the fight as set out by Schattschneider.

THE CHARACTER OF SECLUDED POLITICS

It is not possible to characterise *all* Statutory Instruments, or rather the issues settled by SIs, as relatively obscure and likely to involve what have been termed 'privatised' conflicts. However, we have a number of reasons—deriving from the content, language and procedures of delegated lawmaking—for thinking that many of them can be thus characterised. If this is correct, then we may go on and explore what we may expect to be distinctive about the political process surrounding SIs by setting out the character of highly privatised conflicts. Such an exploration will not only allow us to discover why we would expect the delegated legislative process to differ from the politics surrounding major issues with which we are more familiar, but also allow us to approach the crucial question whether this process has any clear *bias* in favour of one set of participants and against another.

The participants

Many British political scientists since the 1980s have argued that British government involves 'policy communities' or 'policy networks'—bureaucratic actors and interest groups who share responsibility and expertise for distinctive aspects of public policy (see Richardson and Jordan 1979; Rhodes and Marsh 1992; Waarden 1992; Blom-Hansen 1997). There is a large literature extolling the virtues of subgovernment and related terms, and a number of often abstract metaphysical articles seeking, with little obvious success, to give them some sort of scientific precision (for example see Hindmoor 1998). For our purposes, discussions of subgovernment and 'policy networks' are, however, very vague on the crucial question of the range of issues that are handled by any one 'policy network'. According to a recent statement of the approach (Smith 1999: 19) a 'policy network' may embrace a whole sector (such as the 'agricultural policy network'), a whole genus of policy sectors (the 'economic network') or just a smaller distinct policy initiative (the 'welfare to work network'). While the policy networks literature is not much help to us here, the extreme privatisation of conflicts suggests patterns of interaction between very narrowly defined groups—between people who specialise in the particular subject covered by the delegated legislation. For example, the Mental Health Act administrators in the NHS speak to the specialists within the Department of Health responsible for the particular aspect of the Mental Health Act that concerns them. Let us revert back to the old analogy of human settlements that gave rise to the concern with networks and such like in the British literature (Heclo and Wildavsky 1981). If those involved in policy-making really are 'policy communities', then the communities one would expect to find surrounding SIs are more likely to be isolated hamlets rather than bustling villages, towns or cities.

The degree of specialisation involved in SIs has implications for both government departments and the interests concerned. For government departments, this form of interaction between narrowly defined groups would imply a *locus of power and authority at a much lower level in the hierarchy* for the delegated legislative process than for the process of primary legislation or for the process of decision-making involving more publicly visible issues. We would expect the specialised subdivision of a ministry to be where the action takes place in delegated legislative decision-making if it conforms to the expectation of a highly privatised set of conflicts. Ministers would be expected to become involved in such matters only exceptionally and rarely. While ministers must give their approval to all proposed SIs, in so far as SIs deal with privatised conflicts with no recognisable impact on wider publics, the involvement of ministers remains limited and formal. As far as pressure groups are concerned, such a narrow focus suggests not only the possibility that within a large interest organisation, as within government, the relevant units concerned with lobbying may be at a relatively low level in the hierarchy. It also suggests the possibility that groups with very small memberships and/or very specialised and narrow concerns will be highly active participants in the policy process. We would, on the interest group side, expect the world of privatised conflicts to be one of the *specialised group* or the *specialised subunit of a larger group*.

Strategies

The ability to extend or limit the scope of conflict—to involve more people on your side, as it were, or to exclude those against you—is a fundamental strategy of politics. It is a strategy which is closely linked to democratic decision-making since it is based upon the ability of participants in the policy process to mobilise the potential of support for their side of the conflict from significant portions of a wider public. This support was mobilised directly by, for example, the pro-hunting lobby who successfully managed to link the damage that would be experienced by the relatively small number of people who hunt foxes and earn their living from it with a wider attack on the 'countryside'. It gave birth to a significant protest movement, one of the high points of which was a rally in 1997 attended by an estimated 100,000 people and which was deemed so important by the Labour government that it sought to lend its support to the rally despite the apparent commitment of the Labour Prime Minister to supporting anti-hunting legislation. The attempt to link hunting to more popular pursuits (such as fishing) as well as to portray proposals to ban it as an attack on the country-side and the rural way of life by an urban Labour élite is a classic strategy of conflict socialisation and remains an important strategy of the pro-hunting movement.

In the world of privatised conflicts, this ability to invoke political support through a direct appeal to a wider public, as in the case of the pro-hunting lobby, is simply not there most of the time. It is, of course, conceivable that almost any issue could have consequences that might possibly involve a wider public—a health scare might give front page status to a planned regulation covering the composition of dummies for baby feeding bottles or a strike by court reporters might put the regulations governing their pay and conditions of work into the front page headlines. However, in practice, in the world of privatised conflicts, such direct appeals are likely to be limited. Under these circumstances we would expect the strategies of groups to invoke a wider public only indirectly—through pointing out the wider consequences of government actions or persuading ministers of the unpopularity their decisions are likely to generate at some stage in the future. It might not be possible to mobilise public support for a minor technical amendment to a set of forms required to detain people under the Mental Health Act. Yet it might be possible to persuade a minister or a civil servant that any imprecision or errors in the existing unamended forms could be interpreted by a wider public as negligence in the event of some publicised incident—such as an abscondment, wounding, murder, suicide—involving a detainee to whom the form was meant to apply.[7]

Rather than through the direct appeal to public support, we would expect public opinion to be rather indirectly involved in this world of privatised conflicts. Proposals which lead to 'good government' either improve the standing of government or avert the possibility that it is left looking bad. One would expect government departments to be especially susceptible to such good government approaches by groups since the professional reputations of civil servants are likely to be shaped by their ability to make things run smoothly and without embarrassment or mess. As Finer (1958: 30) pointed out, 'the basis of smooth administration is a favourable public opinion [so] it is prudent to consult affected publics in advance of final decisions'.

On what basis would we expect a group to prevail in the deliberative process surrounding privatised conflicts? The world of privatised conflicts is not one where one can expect majorities or votes to be mobilised because, by definition, the option of socialising conflicts is absent. In fact, simply on the face of it, there is no real compulsion apart from 'good government' considerations that would lead a department, which has the authority to pass a regulation, to pay any attention whatever to any group critical of its proposals. We know, however, that government departments do pay attention, at least sometimes. So what is it about a group that gives it the ability to be heard in this privatized world? At the heart of this relationship is trust. As Finer (1958: 35) puts it:

> Ability to keep confidences is . . . a very good touchstone of the general principle underlying the relationship [between groups and government departments] . . . As Sir Norman Kipping [then Director General of the Federation of British Industries] put it 'confidence on the part of government in one's *bona fides*'. The rule might be expressed, very simply, thus: both parties are assumed to trust one another and one another's intentions and if either party wants to be treated responsibly, it must act responsibly.

---

[7] The frequent appearance of stories in the newpapers in the 1990s covering shortcomings, including defective administration, in the care of those detained under the Mental Health Act shows that such detail in the implementation of the Act can become the subject of potentially highly embarrassing press coverage (for a discussion of some of these see Sheppard 1996). See, for example, the scandal following security lapses in the Personality Disorder Unit at Ashworth Hospital which generated headlines such as 'Child left to play with sex offenders' (*Daily Telegraph*, 28 April 1998) and 'Ministers refuse to close secure hospital hijacked by paedophiles' (*Independent*, 13 January 1999) and was the subject of a major inquiry (see Fallon 1999). One tragic incident in 1998, the murder of Christopher Edwards in Chelmsford Prison, involved the failure by police to fill out a form that would have alerted magistrates that he and his murderer suffered from mental illness, presented a special risk and, even if no bed in a psychiatric hospital was available, should not have been forced to share a prison cell together (see *Guardian*, 16 June 1998).

In a similar vein, Heclo and Wildavsky's (1981) *Private Government of Public Money*, which presents the relatively closed world of bargaining for public spending within the executive, points out the centrality of trust and the building of confidence in the relationship between government departments and the Treasury.

Bias

In the privatised world of policy-making, then, the strategies of those involved are likely to be dominated by the building up, maintenance and mobilisation of trust. Precisely how trust is established, how it can be mobilised and to what effect, are empirical questions that cannot be answered in abstract terms without evidence. However, it is possible that the strategies of groups and government introduce a bias in the process—a tendency for certain participants, or certain types of participants, to enjoy advantages in the policy process associated with privatised policy-making that are different from those they enjoy in broader socialised policy processes. In fact this precise issue has dominated the discussion of Statutory Instruments in the social science and legal literature. The critics of delegated legislation have emphasised the ability of the process of delegated legislation to allow the executive to legislate unchecked by the normal constraints of politicians, parliamentary majorities and interest groups. Others have pointed to the increased flexibility offered by the process of delegated legislation, allowing broader participation in the policy process away from the glare of publicity than is likely to be possible among more socialised conflicts that engage newspaper and television headlines. For many of the critics of SIs, the process is a means for the executive, or more specifically the bureaucracy, to increase its power. Lord Chief Justice Hewart (1929: 14) wrote, in a celebrated polemic in defence of the legislature and judiciary against the executive, of the 'new despotism' that emerged after World War One. There was, he argued, a:

> mass of evidence [that] establishes the fact that there is in existence a persistent and well-contrived system, intended to produce, and in practice producing, a despotic power which at one and the same time places Government departments above the sovereignty of Parliament and beyond the jurisdiction of the Courts. If it appears that this system springs from and depends upon deep-seated official conviction, which in turn it nourishes and strengthens by each successive manifestation of its vigour, that this, when all is said and done, is the best and most scientific way of ruling the country, the consequences, unless they are checked, must be in the highest degree formidable.

The bureaucratic expert 'clothe[s] himself with despotic power' since he can

> (a) get legislation passed in skeleton form; (b) fill up the gaps with his own rules, orders and regulations; (c) make it difficult or impossible for Parliament to check said rules, orders and regulations; (d) secure for them the force of statute; (e) make his own decision final; (f) arrange that the fact of his decision shall be conclusive proof of its

legality; (g) take power to modify the provisions of statutes; and (h) prevent and avoid any sort of appeal to a Court of Law (Hewart 1929: 20–1).

While Hewart acknowledged that consultation and 'elasticity, promptness and technical knowledge' may be introduced into the legislative process, he argued that the tendency to 'administrative lawlessness' results from the genuine:

> belief . . . in certain quarters . . . that Parliamentary institutions and the Rule of Law have been tried and found wanting, and that the time has come for the departmental despot, who shall be at once scientific and benevolent, but above all a law unto himself (Hewart 1929: 14).

The delegated legislative process allows the bureaucrat to dominate.

On the other hand, one cannot simply assume that the bias works in favour of the executive; the bias may actually be in favour of the groups which seek to participate in the policy process. The fact that government does not have to place the legislation within a parliamentary timetable means that there is no deadline for the consultative process. Since secondary legislation does not generally involve party political commitment to the same degree as primary legislation, consultations with groups can challenge the basic principles of legislation without any direct threat to the governing party. Consultations are carried out in seclusion and deal with issues that appear technical and rather uninteresting to the outside world, including MPs. In consequence, dialogue between ministries and outside interests can carry on without the potential embarrassments to the government that could come from the glare of publicity accompanying full parliamentary debate. Delegated legislation is a matter which may be expected to be handled by *subgovernment* rather than by the core institutions of government. The notion of 'subgovernment' recognises that collective institutions of government—Cabinet, the Prime Minister, the civil service, Parliament—often have little direct role in formulating policy. Instead, ministries, or sections of ministries, with or without involving interest groups, are prime movers in the policy process.

The classic example of subgovernment is the shift to comprehensive education in 1965, arguably one of the single most radical changes in British education since the 1944 Education Act—given effect to not by an Act of Parliament but by what might be termed as an administrative action: Ministry of Education Circular 10/65. This measure was mentioned in Cabinet (although hardly discussed) only after it had effectively been finalised within the Ministry of Education. We might expect a diminished role for the central institutions of *government* and a larger role for *subgovernment* in making SIs. In part this expectation arises from the characteristically specialised nature of delegated legislation. Moreover, with Acts of Parliament there is a single timetable of legislation for which time has to be negotiated at Cabinet level. With decrees, individual government departments have greater flexibility to develop their own priorities and timetables and consult in their own way. Relieved of pressures from the collective institutions of government, we may expect British civil servants to consult widely and in earnest. Consultation is, after all, the 'preferred' policy style of the British civil servant (Richardson and Jordan 1979; Richardson 1982; Jordan and Richardson 1987). The views of the critics of delegated legislation such as Hewart were not universally accepted, even at the time, among scholars of constitutional law and public administration (for a critical view of the Hewart argument see Jennings 1932; 1933). Several critics allude to the fact that Hewart himself had 'advised and defended the departments' as Attorney General between 1919 and 1921, 'during a period when exceptional powers were being exercised' (Carr 1952: 232). The most potent critics of the 'administrative despotism' thesis point to the flexibility of delegated legislation (see, for example, Willis 1933). The flexibility argument is an exceptionally old one. For example, in the early nineteenth century, Sir Edwin Chadwick's desire to use delegated legislation for the protection of public health raised substantial criticism. Chadwick was described as '[b]orn in a Lancashire farmhouse in 1800 where the children were washed all over every day, he made it his life's business to wash everyone in England all over by Executive Order' (see Carr 1952: 234). Chadwick's argument in favour of delegated legislation was that even a small change in primary legislation could take a year or more, while a 'central authority' with delegated legislative powers 'might make the alteration or supply unforeseen omissions in a day or two' (Carr 1952: 234).

More recent literature has shown that the flexibility which delegated legislation brings with it may operate to the benefit not only of the executive but also to other participants in the policy process. Rather than excluding people from the policy process, decree legislation may allow for greater participation in its formulation. Walkland (1968: 44–5) identified these arguments in 1968 when he wrote:

> Consultation plays a greater role in the preparation of statutory instruments than in the preparation of Bills. Once the main lines of legislative policy are laid down in an Act, the task of putting it into operation, and making the machinery work, becomes, in practice, the joint responsibility of a Department and its clientele of groups. The existence of a strong political commitment on the part of the government may prevent negotiation with interested parties on matters of principle, as may strong inter-Departmental pressures and the control exercised by the Cabinet over major legislative projects; once the principles have been secured, a Department is generally allowed a free hand in administration, and may be ready to concede a great deal in the course of implementing a statute.

The evidence on which he bases this argument is somewhat limited—the submissions by different ministries to the 1952–3 House of Commons Select Committee on Delegated Legislation (1953). These submissions generally suggested that no regulations are passed without full consultation of relevant interests. It is possible that departments might simply have been espousing a superficial allegiance to a principle that they believed MPs wanted to hear. However, even allowing for this, the fact that wide consultation is a norm to which lip-service must be universally paid is itself significant. It suggests that the bias in the delegated legislative process cannot be simply be assumed to be a pro-executive bias.

In so far as groups participate in the privatised policy process of delegated legislation, the process may itself contain bias in favour of certain types of groups and to the disadvantage of others. It is impossible to set out any clear expectations of which particular groups may be advantaged or disadvantaged with any degree of confidence. However, it is quite possible to hypothesise that since we may expect power to derive from trust in the world of privatised conflict, some groups are better at developing trust than others. It may be that highly professionalised organisations tend to have particularly strong influence over government in delegated legislation since they can mobilise expertise acquired in the course of professional training and experience often lacking in the civil service. Commonly cited as a professionalised group are the medical professions, but we could add many more including, for example, specialist branches of actuarial professions as well as insurance, road-building, farming, surveying, telecommunications, international law, among many others. In this sense trust may develop from necessity—where people with necessary expertise to shape legislation are outside the civil service and therefore must be listened to. Alternatively, it may be the style in which a group conducts itself that affects the trust and therefore the bias inherent in this privatised policy process. The classic distinction in the literature of policy-making in Britain is the distinction between 'insider' groups which seek to influence through cultivating contacts with civil servants and providing useful technical advice to them, and 'outsider' groups (Grant 1995).

MOVING OUT OF SECLUSION

Setting out what the character of politics may be in this secluded world, shrouded in obscurity, allows one to point to a set of expectations about how the 'ongoing Whitehall process' which we are looking at through Statutory Instruments differs from other policy-making processes about which we already know more. However, while obscurity and seclusion are likely to be features of most of the 3,000 SIs passed each year, we have already seen that we cannot assume that they characterise all of them. Some SIs cannot become obscure because they relate to issues that have already become socialised conflicts—regulations on food safety around the time of a food scare, or regulations governing the holding of ballots to end the practice of selection in grammar schools, for example. Some SIs gain publicity for reasons that are not easily predictable. The tabloid *Mail on Sunday* (6 September 1998) under the heading 'Actors win dole U-turn' covered a regulation giving 'resting' actors the right to claim social security benefit, linking the issue with 'Labour Luvvies' (evoking a perceived link between an effete acting profession and the New Labour administration) and the Prime Minister's father-in-law (who was a famous actor in the 1960s and 1970s). It also interviewed actors from popular soap operas such as *Eastenders* and *Brookside* and topped the report with a picture of the acting union's vice-president, Tony Robinson, dressed as an eighteenth century peasant (in his character as Baldrick from the comedy series *Blackadder*) holding up a dead bird.

Some SIs are potentially obscure, and some of those involved in the policy process may succeed in socialising the conflict in order to gain the support of a wider public. Thus, for example, a change in council tax benefit relief which affects relatively few people may be cast as an attack on the vulnerable poor in order to maximise opposition. Socialising conflicts to achieve support is not the sole preserve of interest groups. The Labour government defined, for example, a change in pensions regulations as part of its attack on 'fat cat' businessmen to minimise the effect of opposition to the changes. Civil servants may also seek to socialise conflicts as a means of countering opposition, whether this comes from other parts of the bureaucracy or indeed from politicians. Because of the constitutional norms of political neutrality and of loyalty to the minister, civil servants working on delegated legislation are constrained in how they may socialise issues involved in delegated legislation since it is an overtly political activity. Clear instances of such activity are consequently difficult to come by. However, more subtle means were mentioned by some of the officials interviewed for this book. Consultation documents may be couched in terms that maximise outside support for departmental proposals. Research can be commissioned safe in the knowledge that its results, likely to strengthen the case for a proposed regulation, can only with difficulty be kept out of the public domain. Ministerial as well as group opposition to proposed regulations can in this way be weakened.

Thus, in addition to understanding the nature of secluded decision-making— the participants, the strategies they employ and the bias of the process—we need also to understand the possibilities for, and consequences of, moving issues out of obscurity. It might be possible to counteract bias in the 'ongoing Whitehall process' by taking items out of seclusion and into a wider arena, either in Parliament or before the public.

ILLUMINATING THE OBSCURITY

This central purpose of this book is to explore the impact of the obscurity of the 'ongoing Whitehall process' on the conduct of policy-making and, in particular, to look at the effects this has on the nature of the participants in the policy-making process, the strategies they use in the process and, above all, the bias of the process. Before the everyday world of government can be investigated, we must understand the nature of the instruments chosen to serve as windows on this world. Chapter 2 describes the broad character of delegated legislation. Description of the formal procedures involved in the passage of Statutory Instruments is important not only as background to understanding subsequent chapters; it also allows one to pinpoint the type of distortion that may be expected when we look at the world of everyday government through these particular windows.

While the formal procedures described in Chapter 2 may explain how SIs come about, they do not explain what they do. If SIs are truly matters of monotonous detail, peppered only occasionally by the odd important or politically contentious regulation, then we may discount the whole enterprise of studying them as nerdish self-indulgence. So Chapter 3 looks at 28,000 SIs passed between 1987 and 1997 in order to give an impression of the sorts of things covered in them.

Chapters 2 and 3 cover material which is essential background for understanding the detailed examination of particular items of delegated legislation that follows. SIs are frequently not what they seem on the surface to be. Chapter 4 is the first of three that look at 46 recent SIs from major government departments and describes what they do, where they came from and the procedures involved in making them. Chapter 4 concentrates on the origins of SIs, Chapter 5 examines the role of politicians in the development of delegated legislation and Chapter 6 the role of the civil servants who draft SIs.

Consultation is an important component of many, although not all, SIs. Chapter 7 looks at the process of consultation on SIs from the perspective of interviews with interest group representatives and a large survey of interest groups. Chapter 8 explores the role of Parliament both as a participant in the routine world of decision-making through the work of, above all, the Joint and Standing Committees on Statutory Instruments.

Chapter 9 directly answers the question of the distinctiveness of the politics of seclusion. It argues that the view of the British political process that it offers differs quite substantially from generally accepted descriptions of policy-making in Britain. 'What on earth do you people teaching government in universities actually tell your students?' was the reaction of one civil servant to a question about one of the less well understood features of the world of everyday politics: the policy role of junior ministers in making SIs.

In developing our understanding of the politics of seclusion, this book also offers an empirical description of the world of everyday policy-making. This world has been almost entirely ignored by social scientists. For all the models of policy-making, all the case studies of British government in action and all the grand theories that have emerged along with the massive growth in the number of social science researchers and their publications since the 1950s, we still know very little about how government actually works on a day-to-day basis. The concentration of many scholars upon major and interesting policies and issues certainly casts light on how these particular policies and issues are handled. But the real process of government contains very few policies and issues that are patently major and interesting, and very many that are not. It should therefore be no surprise to us that the type of big issue that comes up a few times in a decade in any particular ministry—the sort on which researchers like to base their case studies—is rather atypical of the process of government.

The focus on SIs allows us to see more of the everyday process of government that usually remains obscured from public and scholarly view. By ignoring this world we are effectively in the dark about the way most of government works. There is no good reason for such neglect. The language used to describe the type of thing that goes on in this world—'low politics', 'secondary legislation', 'implementing regulations'—seems to imply that little is lost if we do not bother with it. Yet to claim that subordinate legislation is of subordinate significance is to be taken in by the formal terminlogy of law-making. The measures adopted and issues raised in the process of everyday government are often highly significant. Moreover, this everyday world is remarkably well documented—parliamentary and other committees publish investigations and reports on regulations and proposed regulations, government departments issue consultation documents and press releases about them and, of course, every general SI and many local ones are published. They can now be consulted free of charge on the internet. The everyday world of government stares us in the face as citizens and as social scientists, and we need to look back at it more closely.

2
Examining the Instrument

Statutory Instruments are the focus of this study because they represent incisive tools for investigating a world we know very little about—the twighlight world of everyday government. But what are Statutory Instruments? While this book is not about delegated legislation in general, or the legal and constitutional issues surrounding it (see Daintith and Page 1999), the question cannot be avoided here. Statutory Instruments are a type of law which governments can pass only under specific circumstances. Governments cannot freely pick and choose what they do through Statutory Instrument and what they do by Act of Parliament or some other method of shaping public policy. The consequence of this is that only some policy issues can be addressed by Statutory Instrument. Therefore one reason for setting out what Statutory Instruments are is that such a discussion helps us understand precisely what features of everyday government we are seeing, and what is likely to remain out of sight. A second reason for describing Statutory Instruments arises from the distinctive procedures governing how these particular laws reach the statute book. These procedures help shape the process of delegated legislation and thus the world of everyday government presented in this book is to some degree structured by the specific arrangements for Statutory Instruments.

This chapter is primarily concerned with describing what Statutory Instruments are and the rules according to which they are made and challenged. The focus is on understanding their characteristics as far as they influence the resulting picture we get of the world of everyday government through them, rather than setting out a definitive account of all the historical, constitutional and legal issues surrounding them. After discussing the nature of SIs, this chapter goes on to look at the development of delegated legislation and its increasing use in the twentieth century. The chapter then moves on to look at the formal procedures for passing delegated legislation and the possibilities for parliamentary scrutiny and judicial review associated with it. The conclusion addresses the question of how these characteristics may affect the picture of everyday government we get through viewing the process of everyday government through Statutory Instruments.

Statutory Instruments are a form of law. Governments can make two broad types of domestic law—*primary* and *secondary* legislation.[1] *Primary* legislation in Britain refers to laws which derive their authority directly from the Crown or the Crown in Parliament. According to the traditional principle of the sovereignty of Parliament (Dicey 1952), government is free to pass whatever Acts it chooses, as long as they pass through the formal stages of parliamentary approval and receive the Royal Assent. Acts of Parliament can, for example, limit or extend personal freedoms, create or abolish democratic institutions such as local governments and nationalise or privatise industries. Accordingly, Acts of Parliament are supreme laws which cannot be challenged in the courts. In practice the traditional notion of the sovereignty of Parliament no longer applies in the same way since the United Kingdom joined the European Union, but this does not detract from the fact that primary legislation is, in principle, a higher form of law which can be challenged through the courts only if it conflicts with an even higher form of law in the shape of European Union legislation.

Statutory Instruments are *secondary* (also termed *subordinate* or *delegated*) legislation. They are not the only type of secondary legislation, but rather the form most commonly associated with the term.[2] Secondary legislation refers to laws which derive their legitimacy from powers given to a minister or a department in primary legislation—that is, in an Act of Parliament. The provisions of many Acts of Parliament contain clauses along the lines that a Secretary of State or a minister may make provisions by order to bring a particular clause into operation or to specify, amend or adjust how the clause is to be interpreted or applied. For example, the Government of Wales Act 1998, which set up a devolved assembly for Wales, contains the provision (at Section 22(2)) that:

> The Secretary of State shall, before the first ordinary election, lay before each House the draft of an Order in Council . . . making provision for the transfer of functions in each of the fields specified in Schedule 2 as the Secretary of State considers appropriate.

Secondary legislation can only be made where there is an explicit provision in primary legislation to do so; that is to say, where government has the legal powers or *vires* to issue delegated legislation. Consequently every Statutory Instrument must contain reference to specific clauses in Acts of Parliament that give governments *vires* to draw up subordinate legislation. All secondary legislation has 'parent' primary legislation. Moreover, provisions within delegated

---

[1] Not all law is statute law. For a discussion of the common law powers of ministers see Daintith and Page (1999: 34–5).

[2] Some bodies are given law-making powers which are exercised through other means, such as under the Financial Services Act 1986 (Daintith and Page 1999: 280). In addition the law-making powers of the Scottish Parliament are delegated through the 1998 Scotland Act.

legislation can be declared invalid by courts if, for example, they are judged not to be consistent with the powers granted in the parent legislation or if the procedures used to draw them up are invalid (discussed more fully below).

NOT NEW, BUT INCREASINGLY IMPORTANT

The term 'Statutory Instrument' is a generic term applied to secondary legislation although SIs also go under other less precise names[3]—'Rules', 'Orders', 'Orders in Council', 'Regulations'. The term 'Statutory Instrument' is itself a legal term since it is defined in the 1946 Statutory Instruments Act:

> When by this Act or any Act passed after the commencement of this Act power to make, confirm or approve orders, rules, regulations or other subordinate legislation is conferred on His Majesty in Council or on any Minister of the Crown then if this power is expressed
> a) in the case of a power conferred on His Majesty, to be exerciseable by Order in Council
> b) In the case of a power conferred in a Minister of the Grown, to be exercised by Statutory Instrument
> any document by which that power is exercised shall be known as 'Statutory Instrument' and the provisions of this Act shall apply thereto accordingly (HMSO 1946).

While the term was fixed in 1946, the phenomenon of delegated legislation is much older (see also Craig 1946). Scholars have traced the development of some forms of delegated legislation back to the medieval period (see Allen 1950: 24; Sieghart 1950: 305). It was used in the eighteenth century to introduce quarantine arrangements to cope with a plague outbreak in the Baltic (Carr 1952). However, the systematic use of delegated legislation as a routine tool of government is associated with the development of public services such as health, education, police, social policy and labour law in the nineteenth century.

The common argument in favour of delegation in the nineteenth century, to which authorities such as Dicey (1952) subscribed, was that Parliament could not be expected to get involved in the level of detail required for the regulation of the services of the modern state. For Edwin Chadwick, termed Britain's 'Prussian Minister' because of his approval of hierarchically structured state administration:

> legislators in Parliament could hardly be asked to devote their attention to the amount of the pauper's butter ration or the length, width and material of the old women's under-petticoats, and yet on such details the successful management of the whole scheme would depend (Carr 1952: 241).

---

[3] These names are less precise because, for example, not all 'rules' are set out in the form of Statutory Instruments, and some Orders in Council, issued under the Royal Prerogative, can be primary legislation.

Unless the burden of detailed regulation were delegated to executive bodies, the administration of modern public services would be at best slow and at worst impossible.

One sign of the increasing use of delegated legislation was the move to systematise the arrangements for their publication in the late nineteenth century. At the time, arrangements for publication were haphazard. Items of delegated legislation were published in different places and some were not published at all. In consequence, one observer commented, 'they have been hidden away in all sorts of holes and corners' (M.D.C. 1893: 165). The Statutory Rules Committee published an *Index to Statutory Rules and Orders* in 1892 in an attempt to bring some form of systematisation into the rules and the 1893 Rules Publication Act aimed to make the mass of subordinate legislation available through routine procedures of publication and sale.[4] Another sign of the increasing use of delegated legislation was the growth in criticism of the reliance of government on this method of law-making.

The central problems raised by critics were that the amount of delegated legislation was increasing and that the executive was becoming too powerful since it could pass laws without submitting them to full parliamentary scrutiny. Such arguments were raised in the nineteenth century. Toulmin Smith, the opponent of Chadwickian centralisation, argued that delegated legislation served 'the ends of centralisation . . . more effectively . . . than any other means that ingenuity can devise' (Carr 1952: 242). Yet the critics became more vociferous in two major periods of the twentieth century—the interwar years and the years immediately after World War II.

The fact that these two periods witnessed significant debates about the desirability of delegated legislation underlines the fact that the two world wars were widely viewed as being major landmarks in the development of the use of delegated legislation. The Defence of the Realm Act of 1914 (DORA) gave delegated powers to the government to deal with wartime emergencies. Carr (1952: 244) argues that the regulations issued under DORA were at first military but later extended to 'any field of government activity . . . people found themselves forbidden to hold dog shows or to whistle for a taxi cab in London'. With the end of World War I most DORA laws lapsed with the exception of 'a few which had filled conspicuous gaps in our peacetime law' (Carr 1952: 244) such as the control of guns and narcotics. Emergency legislation empowering government to make regulations across a broad range of issues was introduced several times in the first

---

[4] Arrangements for the publication of delegated legislation remained a major feature of legislation on the topic after the late nineteenth century. In 1996 a loophole in the law emerged, highlighted but not caused by the privatisation of Her Majesty's Stationery Office (HMSO). According to the 1946 Statutory Instruments Act SIs had to be printed and sold by HMSO. HMSO had been contracting out the printing of SIs since at least the early 1960s (see Ganz 1997). In principle such SIs might be challenged on the ground that they were not printed by HMSO. As one civil servant interviewed commented, 'I think that a judge would have been happy to have ruled that an SI would not be valid without HMSO publication. If I were a practising solicitor, I would have had a go at that one . . .'. For a discussion of the role of HMSO in delegated legislation see Tullo and Pawsey 1998.

half of the century to deal with strikes and war. Carr argues that each 'blank cheque precedent was remembered' for the next piece of emergency legislation. The 1939 Emergency Powers (Defence) Act raised similar criticisms of overbearing delegated legislative powers being exercised by the state to those generated by DORA in the World War I. Gordon (1943: 121) writes of the inability to 'wave a handkerchief at an aeroplane or drop a tram-ticket without infringing the law'.

The use of emergency powers highlighted a more general tendency for the amount of delegated legislation to increase. As Carr (1921: 31) points out in his discussion of the late nineteenth century, 'delegation is frequent in the statute law of the period'. In the last five years before 1900, an average of 1,000 Statutory Rules and Orders were passed. In the early twentieth century the average number of Rules and Orders grew to 1,300 a year before the World War I, 1,500 during World War I, 'in the years 1919, 1920 and 1921 it reached the unprecedented figure of 2,275 and in the inter-war period it remained in the neighbourhood of 1,500'. The figures for the early years of the twentieth century are, however, difficult to compare with subsequent figures since they exclude some types of regulation (e.g. temporary regulations) which are included under the system set up following the 1946 Statutory Instruments Act (see Figure 2.1).

Most prominent among the critics of the inter-war period was the former Solicitor General and Attorney General and (at the time of his famous critical book) serving Lord Chief Justice, Lord Justice Hewart. The arguments of his *New Despotism* (Hewart 1929) which alleged an 'administrative lawlessness' and an overmighty executive have been outlined in Chapter 1. Hewart's criticisms provided an impetus for the government to set up the Committee on Ministers' Powers (1932), under Lord Donoughmore 'to consider the powers exercised by or under direction of Ministers of the Crown by way of a) delegated legislation and b) judicial or quasi-judicial decisions'. The Committee reported in 1932 and accepted the need for delegated legislation: to save parliamentary time, to deal with technical issues, with unforeseen contingencies and emergencies, for 'flexibility' and 'experimentation'.[5] The Committee expressed its general satisfaction with the way in which departments went about drafting and presenting delegated legislation but made a variety of specific proposals.[6]

[5] Two members of the Donoughmore Committee, Labour supporters of a more interventionist government, Harold Laski and Ellen Wilkinson, argued even more positively that delegated legislation was desirable and should be expanded 'as the only way to grapple with the functions now performed by modern governments' (Committee on Ministers Powers 1932: 138). Elsewhere Laski mocked the 'irresponsible Lord Chief Justice [Hewart] whose hatred of change is even greater than his persuasive rhetoric' and who led a battle against a purely imagined 'phantom army of bureaucrats . . . lusting for power' (Laski 1938: 42).

[6] They included: a standardisation of nomenclature for different types of legislation, change in standing orders of both Houses of Parliament requiring all Bills to be accompanied by a memorandum explaining what powers of delegated legislation they contained, an end to 'Henry VIII' clauses by which delegated legislation could be used to change primary legislation, the addition of an 'explanatory note' to allow Parliament and public to understand the general purpose of the delegated legislation and a Standing Committee in each House to look at items of delegated legislation as well as clauses in primary Bills which delegate powers.

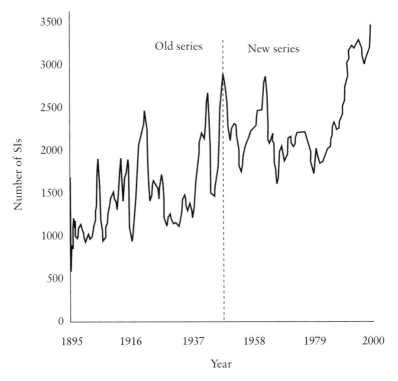

Figure 2.1 Volume of delegated legislation: number[†] of regulations 1895–1999

[†] numbers reflect last serial number published each year.
Sources: *Annual Catalogue of British Official Publicatons 1894–1909* (Bishop's Stortford:
    Chadwick Healey, 1975); *Annual Catalogue of British Official Publications 1909–1919*
    (Bishop's Stortford: Chadwick Healey, 1975); *Annual Catalogue of British Official
    Publications 1920–1935* (Bishop's Stortford: Chadwick Healey, 1975); *Table of
    Government Orders 1671–1990* (London: HMSO, 1992).

Parliamentary pressure to reform the system of delegated legislation persisted
throughout the 1930s and 1940s and led to the 1946 Statutory Instruments Act.
In the early years after 1947, there was further substantial debate about
Statutory Instruments. The Select Committee on Delegated Legislation (1953)
produced a major report on the subject, and authors such as Allen (1950),
Sieghart (1950) and to some degree Carr (1952) echoed, albeit with greater
restraint and moderation, some of the Hewart criticisms (some of these arguments are revisited in Ganz 1997).

But in its main contours, delegated legislation has since 1946 developed along
the lines established earlier in this century. Figure 2.1 shows that there have been
periods of relative stability in numbers punctuated by periods of increase: a
decline in the immediate post-war years followed by an increase in the late

1950s, a general decrease in annual rates of legislation until the early 1980s, but a sustained and rapid increase thereafter until the present (see also Select Committee on Procedure 2000: para. 24). Several observers have commented on the tendency for governments to give themselves broad delegated legislative powers. For example the former Conservative minister Lord Rippon (1989: 205) argues 'although our Bills get longer and longer, increasingly they are merely skeletal legislation, leaving vital details to be settled by orders and regulations'. Reid (1987: 685) makes a similar point when he argues that Parliament 'appears willing to delegate more and more power, subject to fewer and fewer restrictions, to ministers of the Government'. The Select Committee on Procedure (2000: para. 26) saw:

> no reason to dissent from [the] overall conclusion [of the 1996 Select Committee on Procedure] that 'there is . . . too great a readiness in Parliament to delegate wide legislative powers to Ministers, and no lack of enthusiasm on their part to take such powers. The result is an excessive volume of delegated legislation.' The Clerk of the House described the current position as 'on a high plateau in terms of numbers'.

Scott (1996: 73), investigating the scandal over sale of arms to Iraq, showed how governments could use very old laws, passed in a different era, as a basis for issuing delegated legislation when he stated:

> The criticism that I have felt bound to make falls, if it is justified, collectively on the successive administrations that made use of the 1939 [Import, Export and Customs] Act emergency powers long after Parliament, in enacting those powers, had intended.

Others (Daintith and Page 1999) have suggested that there has been an increasing tendency for governments to use delegated legislation as a means of dealing with matters of principle and policy rather than with detail. Moreover, the *portmanteau* grant of powers to make delegated legislation for a broad range of largely unspecified purposes, associated with wartime emergencies, is now used in peacetime to enable European Union law to be given effect to in UK legislation. The European Communities Act 1972 allows 'any designated minister or department' to make regulations (with some specified exceptions[7]) 'for the purpose of implementing any Community obligation of the United Kingdom'.

HOW SIS ARE MADE: THE FORMALITIES

In order to become law, Statutory Instruments do not have to pass through the same sets of parliamentary procedures as Acts of Parliament, but almost all SIs are subject to some form of parliamentary control. These procedures are generally grouped into three types: affirmative procedures, negative procedures and 'other' procedures. Which procedure any one particular SI has to follow is a

---

[7] It excluded taxation, retrospective provisions, creating major new criminal offences or rules of procedure for courts.

matter stipulated in the parent primary legislation.[8] Statutory Instruments subject to *affirmative procedures* require positive parliamentary approval—10 per cent of SIs made between 1991 and 1999 were affirmative SIs. These affirmative procedures fall into three different types. One type involves the laying of the SI in draft before Parliament before it is made. It can then be made only if it is approved by Parliament. Usually it has to be laid before the House of Commons alone, but can require the approval of both Houses. A second type of affirmative procedure involves the laying of the instrument after it has been made, but it cannot come into effect until it has been approved by Parliament. According to a third type of affirmative procedure, the instrument is made and laid before Parliament, and may come into effect immediately, but cannot remain in force after a specified period (often 28 days but also sometimes 40 days or one month) unless approved within that time.

When subject to *negative procedures* an SI will reach the statute book unless Parliament resolves to vote against it. 68 per cent of SIs made between 1991 and 1998 were negative SIs. There are two types of negative procedures. According to one set of procedures, the SI is laid in draft and cannot be made if, within 40 days, Parliament votes its disapproval. The other procedure involves the laying of the instrument after it is made, and the instrument can remain in effect if Parliament passes no negative resolution within 40 days. In the case of both negative and positive resolutions, the differences among sub-types lies in the distinction between making legislation and coming into effect. The draft procedure (positive and negative) requires parliamentary approval in order that the legislation can be *made*; the other procedures (positive and negative, with some exceptions) require parliamentary approval or acquiescence so that the legislation can *come into effect*, although in practice there is little difference between draft and non-draft procedures in this respect (Boulton 1989: 546).

There is a third variety of SI—those that require no parliamentary approval, active or passive, either because they do not need to be laid (19 per cent of SIs made between 1991 and 1999), or because once they are laid, there is no specification of any type of parliamentary approval procedure (2 per cent of SIs).

Many but not all Statutory Instruments have to be laid before Parliament (on laying see Campbell 1987). The Joint Committee on Statutory Instruments and (less frequently) the Commons Select Committee on Statutory Instruments play a key role in the parliamentary scrutiny of Statutory Instruments (Boulton 1989). The Joint Committee is composed of seven members from the House of Lords and seven from the House of Commons, chaired by a member of the opposition party. The function of the Joint Committee is to scrutinise those SIs that require positive or tacit approval of both Houses and to draw to the attention of Parliament those SIs which are problematic on one or more of several grounds including defective drafting, unexpected use of powers, *ultra vires*, or· being unjustifiably delayed before presentation to Parliament.

---

[8] Statutory Instruments passed under authority of section 2(2) of the European Communities Act 1992 can use either affirmative or negative procedures.

The Joint Committee examines the SI for largely *technical* defects, 'not on the merits of or policy behind the instrument' (Boulton 1989: 552). Moreover, the 'drawing to attention' by the Committee does not imply any further action by either House. Of the 703 items of delegated legislation reported by either the Joint or the Select Committee between 1973 and 1983, 574 or 82 per cent were not debated (Hayhurst and Wallington 1988: 564). Where the SI requires only the active or tacit approval of the House of Commons, the seven MPs on the Joint Committee form the Select Committee on Statutory Instruments and draw those instruments to the attention of the House of Commons on the basis of the same criteria as are employed by the Joint Committee. The House of Lords can consider an SI only after the Joint Committee has reported; the House of Commons can consider the SI at any time. Where there is a pressing issue, the Government may ask the House of Commons to approve an SI before the Select Committee has met to discuss it. Motions to approve or object to SIs 'prayers' are debated between 10.00 am and 11.30 am in the House of Commons, and in the House of Lords debates on SIs can be initiated by various devices: prayers (as in the House of Commons), motions, and 'unstarred questions' (i.e. questions to the Government).

In addition, the House of Lords Delegated Powers Scrutiny Committee, established in 1992, has the responsibility of looking at Bills before Parliament which contain clauses delegating powers to ministers and is to report 'whether the provisions of any bill inappropriately delegate legislative power, or whether they subject the exercise of legislative power to an inappropriate degree of parliamentary scrutiny' (see Himsworth 1995). There is no equivalent House of Commons committee looking at proposed ministerial delegation contained in bills. Since 1994 both Houses of Parliament have had additional functions with respect to delegated legislation under the Deregulation and Contracting Out Act 1994 (Page 1995). This legislation was passed as part of the Conservative Government's long-expressed desire to get government 'off the back' of industry by removing unnecessary regulations. It gives any minister the power to make orders which would repeal legislation deemed to be superfluous and burdensome. Since this was in many cases likely to involve repealing primary legislation by delegated legislation, the government made special provision for the parliamentary consideration of secondary legislation issued under such a 'Henry VIII' clause. The legislation led to the creation of the House of Commons Deregulation Committee specifically to look at SIs issued under this Act. In the House of Lords this function is exercised by the Delegated Powers Scrutiny Committee.

COURTS AND DELEGATED LEGISLATION

Lord Chief Justice Hewart condemned SIs on the grounds that they gave powers to administrative bodies which were potentially outside the purview of courts and therefore represented a potential infringement of basic liberties. In fact, it is not accurate to regard secondary legislation as operating outside the scope of courts and judicial review. In a 1931 case, *Minister of Health v. R., ex parte Yaffé* ([1931] All ER 343), the court dismissed an appeal by the Minister of Health that the courts were unable to adjudicate on a case involving a conflict between the minister and a local authority over the disposal of land, since the minister was acting in accordance with powers delegated to him by the parent Act of Parliament. Lord Tankerton was of the opinion that:

> Parliament has delegated its legislative function to a Minister of the Crown, but in this case Parliament has retained no specific control over the exercise of the function by the minister, such as a condition that the order should be laid before Parliament and might be annulled by a resolution of either House within a limited period. In my opinion, the true principle of construction of such delegation by Parliament of its legislative function is that it confers only a limited power on the Minister, and that unless Parliament expressly excludes the jurisdiction of the court, the court has the right and duty to decide whether the Minister has acted within the limits of his delegated power.

As Bradley and Ewing (1997: 729) point out, 'the essential difference between statute and Statutory Instrument is that, unlike Parliament, a minister's powers are limited' (see Bates 1998 for further discussion). Courts can challenge and have challenged the validity of SIs. Courts can declare parts of SIs, or even the whole of an SI, to be invalid.[9] The use of delegated legislation is among the most important in the range of executive activities over which judicial review can be exercised (see Daintith and Page 1999). The area of judicial review has developed a significant body of technical legal analysis and scholarship which cannot be summarised here (see for example Gordon 1996; Jowell and Le Sueur 1999; Ganz 1997; for an introductory discussion see Carroll 1998: 260–95; Papworth 2000: 215–42). Nevertheless, it is possible here to give some examples of the types of reasons courts give for ruling that parts of delegated legislation are invalid.

Courts can declare SIs *ultra vires* where the primary legislation does not delegate the authority to legislate in the manner claimed by a regulation. All SIs are based on at least some claim that they are derived from primary legislative *vires*. Yet courts have challenged whether these *vires* actually do constitute a lawful basis for the specific actions taken in the SI. Courts can, for example, argue that the relevant primary legislation had a more limited range of uses than those implied by the SI. In *R. v. Divers (Saul Andrew)* ([1999] 2 Cr. App. R (S) 421) parts of *The Crime (Sentences) Act 1997 (Commencement No.2 and Transitional Provisions Order) 1997* were declared invalid. The Order was made following a part of the Crime (Sentences) Act 1997 which allowed the Home

---

[9] Moreover, where deletion of an unlawful provision in a Statutory Instrument affects the sense of the remainder, the whole of the relevant regulation can become void. See *DPP v. Hutchinson* [1990] 3 WLR 196 and *R. v. Inland Revenue Commissioners, ex parte Woolwich Equitable Building Society* [1989] 63 TC 589.

Secretary to make *transitional* provisions, but it did not empower the Secretary of State to amend the text of an Act, in this case the 1967 Criminal Justice Act, in the way the Order sought to do. The Court of Appeal found that 'these were no transitional provisions or savings and the amendment should have been made by Parliament'. The Secretary of State was therefore acting beyond his authority and the amendment of the text of the Act by commencement order was *ultra vires* and ineffective.

It need not necessarily be the wording of the SI that is important in defining whether the SI is *ultra vires*, but the intention behind the parent legislation can also help define whether the government is acting lawfully in making an SI. In *R. v. Secretary of State for the Environment, Transport and the Regions, ex parte Spath Holme Ltd* ([2000] 1 All ER 884), Spath Holme applied successfully to have *The Rents Acts (Maximum Fair Rent) Order 1999*, issued under The Landlord and Tenant Act 1985, quashed. The Court of Appeal argued that 'where it was not clear that Parliament had intended to confer an unlimited and unrestricted power, the court was entitled to consider the legislative history of that power'. It found that from the relevant section of the 1985 Act it 'was clear . . . that that power had been conferred for a limited purpose, namely the countering of inflation. The 1999 order had been introduced for another purpose', in this case 'to alleviate hardship suffered by regulated tenants faced with large rent increases following a change in the methods of determining fair rents'. The SI was therefore '*ultra vires* the powers conferred by . . . the 1985 Act'.

A challenge to an SI on the basis of its impact on fundamental rules of natural justice can also involve interpretation of the intention behind the primary legislation. In *General Mediterranean Holdings SA v. Patel* ([1999] 3 All ER 673) one of the rules set out in *The Civil Procedure Rules 1998* issued under the 1997 Civil Procedures Act was declared *ultra vires* on the ground that 'the language of the 1997 Act . . . did not suggest that Parliament had in mind the abolition or limitation of the right to legal confidentiality'. The court held that, 'if that had been the intention of Parliament, then the use of delegated legislation would not have been a satisfactory means of achieving that aim'. This highlights the fact that while it may be possible under some circumstances for primary legislation to limit such rights, courts may regard secondary legislation as an inappropriate instrument for this, unless Parliament has clearly expressed its intention to use it in this way. *The Supreme Court Fees (Amendment) Order 1996* was declared unlawful in *R. v. Lord Chancellor, ex parte Witham* ([1997] All ER 779) on the ground that it restricted access to justice. A citizen wanted to sue for defamation, but could not because he was on Income Support, there was no Legal Aid for the case and he could not afford the fees set out in the Order. The Order was declared *ultra vires* since:

> the common law has clearly given special weight to the citizen's right of access to the courts. . . . Nothing has been shown to displace the proposition that the executive cannot in law abrogate the right of access to justice, unless it is specifically permitted by Parliament.

In R. v. *Secretary of State for Social Security, ex parte Joint Council for the Welfare of Immigrants* ([1996] 2 All ER 385) the Conservative Government's attempt to reduce the eligibility of asylum seekers to social security benefits in *The Social Security (Persons From Abroad) Miscellaneous Amendments Regulations 1996* was challenged. The Court of Appeal declared the SI *ultra vires* because it was 'so uncompromisingly draconian' and Parliament could not have intended 'a significant number of genuine asylum seekers to be impaled on the horns of so intolerable a dilemma. The need either to abandon their claims to refugee status or alternatively to maintain them as best they can but in a state of utter destitution'. It added 'so basic are the human rights here at issue that it cannot be necessary to resort to the Convention for the Protection of Human Rights and Fundamental Freedoms to take note of the violation'. The limitations of the court's scrutiny is also highlighted by this case—the Secretary of State for Social Security promptly gave himself clear powers in new primary legislation, the Asylum and Immigration Act 1996, to make such changes in social security provision for asylum seekers (see also R. v. *Secretary of State for Social Security, ex parte T* [1997] COD 480).

Many Acts of Parliament impose statutory duties of consultation on the minister before delegated legislative powers are used, and SIs can be challenged on the basis of the alleged failure by the Department to fulfil its obligations to consult those affected. In *Agricultural, Horticultural and Forestry Industry Training Board* v. *Aylesbury Mushrooms Ltd* ([1972] 1 WLR 190) the court found that the minister had a duty to consult the mushroom growers before issuing *The Industrial Training (Agricultural, Horticultural and Forestry Board) Order 1966*. Since he did not, the court ruled that 'the order has no application to mushroom growers as such'. To find that the principle of statutory consultation has not been observed does not necessarily lead courts to declare an SI invalid. In R. v. *Secretary of State for Social Services, ex parte Association of Metropolitan Authorities* ([1986] 1 WLR 1) the court acknowledged that '[t]he Secretary of State had failed to consult the Association with regard to the making of the regulations before making them' and granted a declaration to that effect. Yet because the complaint was about the procedure rather than the content of the Order, and because the regulations 'had been acted on for some time' the regulations would not be quashed. In a later case, R. v. *Secretary of State for Social Services, ex parte Association of Metropolitan Authorities* ([1992] 25 HLR 131) the court argued that it would not declare *The Housing Benefit (General) Amendment Regulations 1992* unlawful since:

> there is a public interest in not upsetting regulations which have been made unless good reason can be shown for doing so; it would be disruptive and lead to uncertainty and delay; these were regulations which . . . [the Secretary of State] was perfectly entitled to make and no useful purpose would be served in quashing them.

Conformity with European legislation is another basis for challenging an SI. The landmark *Factortame* cases, which established substantial qualifications to the traditional doctrine of the supremacy of Parliament, involved an SI—*The Merchant Shipping Act 1988 (Amendment) Order 1989*. More recently, and less spectacularly, in R. v. *Secretary of State for Social Security, ex parte Taylor* ([2000] 1 CMLR 873) the European Court of Justice gave a preliminary ruling that parts of *The Social Fund Winter Fuel Payment Amendment Regulations 1998*, which set receipt of state retirement benefit as a qualifying condition for receipt of Winter Fuel Payments benefits, were discriminatory. The state retirement pension was payable to women at the age of 60 and men at 65 and this constituted unlawful sexual discrimination in breach of Council Directive 79/7.

In European law cases, the principle of proportionality has also served as a ground for a successful challenge to an SI. In R. v. *Ministry of Agriculture, Fisheries and Food, ex parte National Union of Farmers* the plaintiffs were challenging *The Sheep Annual Premium and Suckler Cow Premium Quotas (Amendment) Regulations 1993*. Macpherson J. held that 'what the UK Regulations have done is . . . to add a legislative pre-condition which is no part of the EC Regulation'. Moreover these conditions were 'out of scale and unnecessary to achieve the purposes' of the EU regulations that they offend 'against the principle of proportionality' ([1996] COD 94).

CONCLUSIONS

So what kind of window on the world of everyday government do SIs offer? One characteristic of SIs likely to shape our picture of everyday government is that we can only see issues which are covered, in some form, by legislation. Anything that does not involve a change in the law seems likely to remain obscure. How strictly does this limit our vision of the world of everyday government? Of course, in outlining expected features of everyday politics which are likely to be exaggerated or otherwise distorted by viewing it through the window of delegated legislation, one cannot say with any confidence how distinctive such a view is. We have virtually nothing by way of empirical studies covering sufficiently broad aspects of everyday government with which to compare with the world of delegated legislation. However, at first glance viewing this world through Statutory Instruments appears to be rather limiting.

If we consider all the tools government uses to shape its environment then, adapting the categories developed by Christopher Hood (1983), we may expect legislation to be only one of four instruments; *authority* (the power to make laws, to confer legal rights, permissions, duties, obligations and commitments on others). In addition government may use *nodality* (broadly the power to persuade and give advice), *treasure* (the influence that can be gained through offering financial incentives and disincentives) and *organisation* (the ability to do things directly through state employees in networks of government offices).

However, it would be mistaken to believe that everyday politics surrounding other tools of government—nodality, treasure and organisation—are unrelated to legislation and therefore remain hidden within a study that takes Statutory Instruments as a window on the world of everyday government. Hood points out that tools of government are likely to be used in conjunction with each other. Legislation is a particularly important and pervasive tool of government. Legislation sets out the framework within which the other three can be employed. Treasure, whether as financial transfers to individuals (e.g. in social welfare benefits or housing grants) or taxation or grants to organisations (such as local authorities) requires legislation. Direct action by state employees (organisation in Hood's schema), whether these are, for example, police officers, customs officials or social workers, requires that these officials have legal powers to, say, arrest, search or detain citizens. The power to persuade and give advice (nodality) probably has the least direct relationship to legislation. Nevertheless, as we shall see in Chapters 4 to 7, government issues advice and guidance on legislation, and some SIs give legislative force to what was formerly advisory and make advisory what was formerly set out in statute.

Nevertheless, the picture of everyday government offered by delegated legislation is likely to be somewhat distorted by giving greater prominence to law, legal issues and lawyers than might be expected if other methods of examining this world were used. Central to the development of SIs is the existence of legal powers to act, how these powers are interpreted, and how they may be used to frame new laws in a manner that will withstand possible scrutiny through legal specialists in Parliament and through the courts. Government lawyers are a major presence in the world of everyday government viewed through delegated legislation. While this probably reflects their more general importance in government, we need to be aware that the method of analysis is likely to exaggerate their role in other spheres of everyday government.

A second feature of SIs, the formal procedures for their passage into law, is likely to give us a distinctive view of the world of everyday government. SIs involve a series of procedures that make them more likely to involve politicians than other instruments. Decisions leading to the issue of an advisory circular, the award of a capital development grant or the merging of two divisions within a ministry may or may not involve the direct approval of a minister. Ministers *have to be* directly involved in the approval of SIs because, for the most part, the delegated powers in the primary legislation are delegated to them. At a minimum, ministers are required to sign them, and, as we shall see, in many cases their involvement extends beyond this. Not only are ministers involved in delegated legislation, but the procedures for passing SIs also mean that Members of Parliament have a more prominent role in this part of the world of everyday government than we might expect elsewhere. Since delegated legislation must normally be notified to Parliament, MPs have at least the possibility of objecting to and debating proposed SIs and in some cases their actual approval is required before they reach the statute book.

The analysis of the status of SIs as delegated legislation has gone only some way to answering the main question of the distinctiveness of the view they give us on the world of everyday government. At the beginning of Chapter 1 it was argued that governments cannot always choose what they do by SI and what they do by other forms of instrument, legal and non-legal. The status of SIs tells us very little about what type of issue is handled by SI.

The next chapter seeks to answer this question.

3

The stuff of everyday politics

Do SIs handle anything important or are they concerned with the dull things in life? While instances of politically important SIs have been cited in earlier chapters, it is quite possible that these are big exceptions to a morass of otherwise uninteresting detail. As was seen in the last chapter, SIs are *subordinate* legislation. If the issues settled by SI are narrowly circumscribed by the primary legislation passed by Parliament, or if these issues are routine matters of detail, they become interesting only to those with, in Oakeshott's words, the curiosity of the *concierge*. They can be of no earthly importance to the political scientist or the democratic theorist. So while it might be clear to the casual observer that SIs are largely about detail, is this detail uninteresting or is it the stuff of politics? Do governments use subordinate legislation merely to handle subordinate and uninteresting political issues?

The purpose of this chapter is to look at the nature of political issues handled through delegated legislation. It examines three aspects of the nature of delegated legislation. Two of these aspects are relatively straightforward. The types of *areas of public policy* for which SIs are used is a simple matter of categorising and listing the subject areas covered by SIs. *The types of things SIs do*, what they ban, prohibit, mandate, permit and so on, can also be presented through studying the text of SIs. However the third aspect, *the political importance of the issues handled by delegated legislation* raises more complex problems of analysis. This issue forms the central focus of this chapter, and the other two aspects of the nature of delegated legislation are answered in the process of examining the third. Before the central question of political importance can be answered it needs to be developed further in theoretical terms.

The idea of political importance raises two separate questions. First, how much is actually decided in the process of delegated legislation? We know, for example, that many Acts of Parliament are the result of a highly political process in which groups, politicians and officials have discretion to shape the character of the legislation. For example, the Scotland Act 1997 resulted from a manifesto commitment by the Labour Party and its precise shape resulted largely from deliberations within the Labour Party and within government. Governments do not always have the same amount of discretion in framing secondary legislation. Let us compare the Scotland Act 1998 with two SIs.

The Local Government Reorganization (Representation of the People) Regulations 1997 make no amendments of any substance. Their main effect is to change references to old local authorities ('non-metropolitan counties') in the

original legislation to references which fit the changed local government structure ('non-metropolitan areas for which there is a county council'). *The
Environmental Protection (Prescribed Processes and Substances) (Amendment)
(Hazardous Waste Incineration) Regulations 1998* implemented European
Council Directive 94/67 on the incineration of hazardous wastes. In both these
cases the Government had far less discretion to shape the legislation than it did
with the Scotland Act. Even if we argue that the Labour Government had little
discretion to leave a Scotland Bill out of its legislative programme, it still had far
more scope to decide what was in it than did those drafting the two Statutory
Instruments. There was substantial political action in drafting the Scotland Bill;
in so far as the two rather routine SIs reflected any political action, this action
was played out in other arenas long before anyone thought of drafting them.

The level of discretion of the legislator helps define, then, the degree to which
political *choices* are made through Statutory Instruments; no choice means that
Statutory Instruments truly do live up to their reputation of uninteresting routine since everyone, including the legislator herself or himself, is excluded from
making choices. It is likely that in almost all Statutory Instruments there is at
least some minimal degree of legislator choice—if not over the *content* of the
legislation, then over the *timing* of its introduction.

However, the political importance of delegated legislation is not simply a
function of the amount of legislator discretion embodied within it. It is quite
possible for a legislator to have enormous discretion over the timing and content of legislation, while the legislation itself appears relatively insignificant.
The Imitation Dummies (Safety) Regulations 1993 or *The Excise Duties
(Hydrocarbon Oil) (Travelling Showmen) Relief Regulations 1989* appear to the
casual observer inherently trivial, and even if the legislator had enormous freedom to shape these regulations (and we have no easy way of finding this out) it
is difficult to imagine classifying such SIs as politically important. Thus the
political significance of delegated legislation may also be a function of the *content* of the legislation itself.

Determining what makes legislation trivial or important in the abstract is
exceptionally difficult, and the idea that the content of an SI can make it inherently trivial should not be accepted uncritically. The importance of the content
of a regulation neither reflects the number of people affected (by this criterion
the SI that transformed early retirement schemes for teachers would be politically less important than an SI that allows for the creation of a new exit from a
busy motorway), nor the amount of money involved in its application (by this
criterion the SI that establishes an experimental workfare scheme would be
politically far less important than an increase in line with inflation of the exchequer grant to local authorities). Moreover the importance of legislation changes
over time: while animal health and hygiene regulations attracted little attention
in the 1960s and 1970s, later in the 1980s and 1990s they became politically
important, in part because of increased public attention to animal rights and in
part because of major animal-health related food scares such as BSE and

Salmonella. Some years ago the title of an SI such as *The Heads of Sheep and Goats Order 1996* would probably have raised a smirk and the measure dismissed as trivial,[1] yet in the late 1990s it became politically sensitive because of its relationship to issues about animal health.

If we bear in mind the fact that there are nearly 3,000 Statutory Instruments issued each year, the simple question of how much of political importance takes place through the delegated legislative process becomes immensely hard. To read 3,000 would be a Herculean task, to evaluate how much political action there is in each one would require near omniscience. One cannot tell simply by the physical characteristics of a Statutory Instrument, such as its length, or even necessarily by reading its content, how significant are the political issues immediately behind it. Nevertheless, it is possible both to convey an understanding of the character of the body of delegated legislation as a whole, as well as to approach an answer to the question of its political importance, by examining the content and characteristics of delegated legislation.

In this chapter the question of the political importance of Statutory Instruments is pursued in part by a process of elimination. It is possible to describe and enumerate different types of Statutory Instrument which are overwhelmingly politically unimportant. 'Overwhelmingly' is added here since it is quite possible that an SI that, say, simply corrects an error in a previous SI could raise important political issues, but none that I am aware of would fit this category. The first part of this chapter eliminates just under one half of Statutory Instruments from our consideration as relatively insignificant politically. The basis of this analysis is the 27,999 SIs issued between 1987 and 1997 contained in the JUSTIS CD-ROM (for details of the data and how they were analysed see Appendix B). The process of elimination of a body of SIs that is overwhelmingly politically unimportant, however, is not enough to establish the political importance of what remains. The second part of the chapter takes those SIs that are left after one has discounted those which are overwhelmingly politically unimportant and looks at what they do and whether any generalisations can be made about their political importance. While it is possible to classify different types of SI fairly accurately, it is more difficult (with some exceptions) to ascribe any political importance to any one category of SI. The third part of the chapter approaches the question in a different way and asks whether there is much evidence of highly contentious issues being handled by SI on anything other than an occasional basis. The final part seeks a direct answer to the question posed at the beginning: how much political action is there in Statutory Instruments?

---

[1] In much the same way as *The Baking and Sausage Making (Christmas and New Year) Regulations 1985* appear to have been a recent frequently cited example of a trivial if not ridiculous-sounding law (see Loveland 1996).

SIs come with labels attached. Headers on them tell you what part of the wide world of government and public policy we are dealing with—the brief SI in Appendix A (*The Medicines (Control of Substances for Manufacture) (Revocation) Order 1997*) is clearly labelled 'Medicines' even if we could not deduce what it is about it from the title. There are many clues in the title of the SI about what it does. The one in Appendix A, for example, revokes legislation. We can further find out which departments are involved in the legislation and we can look at the 'Explanatory Note' at the end and find out that it is related to a particular EU directive. In short, the text of SIs can give valuable information which allows us to describe in broad outline certain types of delegated legislation. Since these labels are standard across all SIs, it is possible to use computer software to scan large numbers of machine-readable SIs and give precise numbers falling in each category. What are these categories and can we say that some are more politically important than others?

Humdrum SIs

The categories of delegated legislation are presented in Table 3.1. They are not exclusive categories. SIs can and do belong to more than one of them. SIs falling in one or more of the first five categories—42 per cent of the SIs issued between 1987 and 1997—cover the most humdrum and least important SIs. A large number (10,829) of SIs are local rather than national (termed 'general') SIs.[2] The most common form of local SI is the road order. Roads orders are usually 'local' SIs, accounting for 8,397 of the 10,829 local SIs. These are required to build roads, to classify them, and to regulate traffic on them (for example *The M1 Motorway (Junctions 28–30) (Temporary Prohibition and Restriction of Traffic) Order 1991*).

---

[2] 'Local' in this case is a technical term defining the legal status of the SI, and contrasts with 'general' legislation. It refers to a distinction made in the 1893 Rules Publication Act according to which 'general' rules had to be printed and put on sale, while 'local' rules need not be. This distinction has carried through to modern legislation. The distinction between 'general' and 'local' is related to the same distinction made between local and public and general Acts of Parliament. Yet the status of an SI is not determined by the character of the enabling legislation: 'local' SIs may be issued under powers granted in general Acts, and general SIs may even be issued under powers granted in local Acts (see Cabinet Office 1987: 40). The formal rule for classifying SIs as local or general is that 'Statutory Instruments must be defined as local or general according to their subject matter . . . [A]n instrument is to be classified as local if it is in the nature of a local and personal or private Act, and general if it is in the nature of a public general act' (Cabinet Office 1987: 40). That this principle is by no means clear is suggested by the host of legislation classed as 'general' which appears to have a very limited local application such as *The Sealink (Transfer of Fishbourne Terminal) Harbour Revision Order 1991* and *The Road Traffic (Special Parking Areas) (London Boroughs of Camden, Hackney and Hounslow) (Amendment) Order 1994*.

Table 3.1 Type of SIs 1987–1997

	All SIs		Excluding humdrum SIs	
	N	%	N	%
Local†	10,829	38.7	na	na
of which roads	*8,400*	*30.0*	*na*	*na*
De facto local	2,863	10.2	na	na
Errors	261	0.9	na	na
Non-UK territories	259	0.9	na	na
Ecclesiastical	60	0.2	na	na
Iterative	11,746	42.0	7,492	56.1
Serial-numbered	3,950	14.1	2,497	118.7
European	2,220	7.9	2,095	15.7
Commencement	769	2.7	754	5.6
Consolidation	318	1.1	253	1.9
Appointed day	125	0.4	102	0.8
Deregulation order	45	0.2	42	0.3
Others	6,699	23.9	4,049	30.3
N	27,999	179.6‡	13,355	129.4‡

† identified by the absence of an explanatory note. Includes some recent SIs for which information other than the name and serial number was unavailable on CD ROM at the time of data extraction (August 1997).

‡ percentages add up to over 100 since multiple codings are possible.

Source: see Appendix B

It may at first appear odd to discount such SIs as having less political importance than others since the location of roads has been one of the major areas of public concern over the past twenty years. From the 'Nimbyism' of the 1980s to the green road protests of the 1990s, roads have generated substantial controversy including major and sometimes violent public protests, campaigning by national and local interest groups as well as pressure from the European Commission. In addition one roads SI, *The M4 Motorway (London Borough of Hounslow) (Bus Lane) Order 1998*, or rather the issue raised by it, became front page news in summer 1999 as it was taken to signify a rift between the Prime Minister, Tony Blair, and his Deputy Prime Minister, John Prescott.[3]

However, it is possible to discount the SIs that allow road schemes to go ahead as being the subject of political controversy, since they do little more than

[3] The dedication of one lane of part of the M4 motorway near Heathrow Airport as a bus lane had been causing many traffic jams since the scheme started in June 1999. The Prime Minister, Tony Blair, was caught in one such jam; his bodyguards decided to drive in the bus lane barred to other drivers. He was reported to have been embarrassed by the incident 'especially as he could see thousands of voters fuming as he drove past' and to have carpeted the Deputy Prime Minister, John Prescott, who, as Secretary of State for the Environment, Transport and the Regions, was closely associated with the experimental scheme. See 'Blair says "No" to life in the Bus Lane', *The Times*, 23 June 1999.

formally announce the outcome of a process of deliberation, including in many cases a public consultation, conducted *outside* the process of drafting and redrafting an SI. If there is political action associated with roads SIs, the action takes place around the planning process connected with the road scheme; the SI is a result of this process rather than itself a focus for consultation and bargaining.[4]

Since the term 'local' is a technical-legal one, it does not embrace all SIs that would be considered local by any commonsense definition (based on the notion that they have a limited local application), such as *The Stanswood Bay Oyster Fisheries Order 1988*. We might also class these 2,863 *de facto* local SIs as humdrum. In doing so, however, we have to recognise that we might also be throwing out some which have national significance—the dissolution of NHS Trusts, for example, is a major national political issue carried out by local SIs.

There are three further generally humdrum categories. Some 261 SIs simply correct errors in earlier SIs. For example, *The National Health Service (Travelling Expenses and Remission of Charges) Amendment (No. 2) Regulations 1989* correct a few sums in *The National Health Service (Travelling Expenses and Remission of Charges) Amendment Regulations 1989*. We may discard these as having no real political importance: in so far as they remedy SIs which have any importance they will be included in the analysis anyway. Slightly fewer, 259 Statutory Instruments, are regulations made for territories governed, or partially governed, by the United Kingdom Parliament within the British Isles (e.g. *The Copyright, Designs and Patents Act 1988 (Guernsey) Order 1989*) as well as outside (e.g. *The Virgin Islands (Constitution) (Amendment) Order 1994*). Finally changes in ecclesiastical law, many concerning the pay and conditions of work of clergy and related occupations, are also made through Statutory Instrument. These account for 60 SIs.

Less humdrum SIs

Once we have eliminated those which are more likely to be humdrum, we are certainly not left with a set of laws which reflect pressing matters of public inter-

---

[4] One ex-official in interview indicated that the procedure of delegated legislation might be used to overcome opposition to road schemes. He said:

The Ministry of Transport highways side had a new road construction programme. This was entirely national. The process of securing legislative approval was by SI. There were some procedures of public consultation. There was also a lot of dissatisfaction. People felt the Department had made up its mind and was not going to change things after consultation and it was not going to have an effect. There was a feeling that with a lengthy motorway project the job was to be spread over a few years, so there is no way it could be planned in one go. It would take several Instruments. Objections by some environmentalists would be raised, but the Department would get its way piecemeal. It gets ten to twelve miles length, and that bit of motorway is authorised. They might have even started work on it and that preempts where the next bit is. You need to know the whole plan, [the environmentalists] said, rather than being driven to stage two by stage one.

est. Assessing the degree of political action requires a detailed knowledge of each of the 13,355 SIs still in our analysis. However, it is possible to make some generalisations about the broad types of legislation since they tend to fall into distinctive groups of legislation, and some of these groups can be associated with different forms of political action. The numbers of SIs falling into each type is set out in Table 3.1.

Iterative regulations

SIs sometimes come in large sets—i.e. they are very similar in name to SIs issued before or after. For example, there are 59 SIs with the title *The Road Vehicles (Construction and Use) (Amendment) Regulations* in the ten-year period between 1987 and 1997 and 179 *The Food Protection (Emergency Prohibitions)* orders. Many tend to do similar things: *The Food Protection (Emergency Prohibitions) (Dounreay Nuclear Establishment) Order 1997* aimed to protect the public against the dangers of consuming seafood caught around the nuclear reactor in Dounreay, and SIs in this series make similar provisions for potential food contaminated by oil and chemical spills and radioactivity (including the fallout from the Chernobyl disaster in 1986).

As an approximate measure of how many SIs look the same, at least from the perspective of their titles, a regulation was classified as an iterative regulation if the first thirty characters of its name (stripped of dates and sequence numbers) was identical to at least two other regulations issued over the period. According to this measure, over one half of the 13,355 SIs look similar to other SIs. However, just because an SI is part of a set, even a very large one, does not mean that it is uncontroversial. As with Dounreay shellfish and Chernobyl sheep, some can handle sensitive political issues. *The Social Fund Maternity and Funeral Expenses (General) Amendment Regulations 1995* have an identical name to seven other regulations issued between 1987 and 1997. Most of them place new limits on the conditions under which the government will pay for funerals of people on benefit, and most have generated controversy. Moreover, names are not always a good guide to content—similar names can be given to SIs that do very different things. *The Firearms (Amendment) Act 1997 (Commencement) (No. 2) Order 1997* which brought into effect the ban on handguns in the wake of the Dunblane tragedy was different from *The Firearms (Amendment) Act 1988 (Commencement No. 2) Order 1989* which introduced greater controls on the movement of ammunition to Northern Ireland. Just because a regulation looks the same as a previous regulation does not mean that they both do the same thing. Still less does it mean that both are humdrum and uncontroversial.

Serial-numbered regulations

A large number of SIs are numbered as part of a series. It is possible to have, as some of the examples have already shown, an SI with the same name as another in the same year, but designated as No. 1 or No. 2 Order—the recent record for high numbers being *The Offshore Installations (Safety Zones) (No. 71) Order 1987* (designating specific areas around oil platforms that craft cannot enter without permission). Around one in six (14.1 per cent: see Table 3.1) of non-humdrum SIs are in such series. While the designation of a serial number might suggest repetitive routine, it would be wrong to discount such SIs as having no political interest. For example, it was *The Housing Benefit (General) (Amendment) (No. 2) Regulations 1996* that threatened to remove Housing Benefit support to elderly people in sheltered accommodation (see Chapter 5), and *The Crime (Sentences) Act 1997 (Commencement No. 2 and Transitional Provisions) Order 1997* that was used by Labour to implement only some of the Conservatives' 'tough sentencing' policies.

One indicator of the political importance of some such serial regulations is the fact that they constituted 37 per cent of SIs considered by the Social Security Advisory Committee between 1991 and 1995, which tends to report only on important and contentious secondary legislation in the field of social security (see Chapter 6). Serial regulations cannot as such be categorised as routine and politically uncontentious.

Regulations implementing EU legislation

In some SIs, much of the major political action has taken place elsewhere—in the European Union. While this is not to suggest that implementation of EU legislation does not involve substantial discretion in interpretation and timing by British government officials and ministers, this discretion is bounded by the requirement to implement EU law. Statutory implementation of EU legislation most commonly takes the form of legislation by Statutory Instrument. Of the 1,369 provisions for which the CELEX (1997) database (the digital version of all legislation enacted by the European Union) cites the United Kingdom's implementing legislation, 1,253 (92 per cent) is given effect to by SI. It is possible to tell which SIs are implementing EU legislation through the text of the Explanatory Notes as well as the footnotes of the SI. These should, if implementing EC or EU laws, contain explicit references to European legislation.[5] Of the 13,355 SIs, 2,100 (15.7 per cent) contained references to European legislation.

[5] The document produced by the Cabinet Office to guide the drafting and handling of SIs sets out that the European legislation on which the SI is based should be cited in footnotes and mentioned in the explanatory note. See Cabinet Office 1987: 30 and 135–6.

As discussed elsewhere (Page 1998) there is no evidence of a secular increase in the impact of EU legislation on domestic legislation; a large increase in EU-related SIs in the early 1990s, associated with the implementation of the European Single Market, subsided in the mid-1990s. Leaving aside the pre-devolution Scottish Office and Welsh Office, European delegated legislation is most prominent in MAFF, the Department of Trade and Industry and the (former) Department of Transport (see Page 1998 for details).

Although the political action is likely to be bounded by the EU legislation they implement, such European SIs are not without political controversy. British newspapers frequently carry stories which outline the damage that EU legislation, usually implemented by SI, is doing to British business, agriculture, consumers and citizens. For example, the *Sunday Telegraph* of 25 April 1999 carried three articles by Christopher Booker whose headlines convey the nature of the controversy: 'Firms cut jobs as law on working hours bites', 'Vets costs bleed meat plants dry' and 'Fishermen caught out by cod quotas' (see also Booker and North 1996). The EU has set up a rebuttal unit which specifically seeks to answer such allegations made in the British press, described as 'euromyths', via its *Presswatch* series available on the internet (http://www.cec.org.uk/pubs/prwatch/).

Commencement and appointed day orders

In some SIs the political action concerns the *timing* of the enactment of legislation already done and dusted. Acts of Parliament do not always come into effect straight away, or at times defined within the text of an Act—they are subject to *commencement orders*. *The Security Service Act 1996 (Commencement) Order 1996* brought all the provisions of the Security Service Act 1996 into force on 14 October 1996. Or the commencement order may bring in only part of the legislation as with *The Planning and Compensation Act 1991 (Commencement No.16) Order* which brings into effect parts of two sections of the Planning and Compensation Act 1991. The Cabinet Office's (1997) guidelines suggests that 'as far as possible' dates of coming into force should be specified in the primary legislation, and the number of separate commencement orders kept to a minimum. Slightly different are the appointed day orders[6] which name a day for a specific legal provision to come into effect. For example, *The Crown Agents Act 1995 (Appointed Day) Order 1997* specifies 21 March 1997 as the day on which all the property, rights and liabilities of the Crown Agents is transferred to The Crown Agents for Overseas Governments and Administrations Limited. 856 (6.4 per cent) of the 13,355 SIs are commencement or appointed day orders.

Can we regard these as simply routine matters which involve little political action? To do so simply on the basis of their often brief contents and their apparently anodyne wording (typically 'Section A of Act B, insofar as it relates

---

[6] Also included are Scottish 'specified day' and 'specified date' orders.

to paragraph C of Schedule D, shall come into force on 8 April 2001'), would be guesswork. We will see in the next chapter that it is possible for the commencement of a particular clause of legislation to generate significant political conflict: the decision to commence a costly piece of primary legislation, the decision by a Labour government to bring into effect some parts of Conservative legislation on law and order, were highly political. In another case, as the *Independent* put it (1 December 1999), 'One brief debate' on *The Northern Ireland Act 1998 (Appointed Day) Order 1999* 'transfers Ulster back to its people'. The devolution arrangements of the Good Friday Agreement which brought peace to Northern Ireland, restored self-government to the Province and put Republicans in government were in this case brought into effect by an appointed day order after a year and a half of hard bargaining between the parties to the Agreement. We must, therefore, be wary of dismissing commencement and appointed day orders as raising no significant political issues.

Consolidating regulations

Some SIs *consolidate* existing legislation: they tidy up, by bringing into one item of legislation diverse existing SIs. Consolidating SIs generally do more than tidy up. Their genesis, as described in interview by officials across all government departments, appears to be similar. An official in the legal office of the government department is asked to draft an SI. In doing so he or she realises that the existing legislation in the field is rather untidily spread among a variety of instruments. This untidiness is widely perceived to be frowned upon by the Joint Committee on Statutory Instruments, so if time is available a consolidating SI will be drafted by the legal department containing the new provision as well as the larger compilation of existing SIs.

Generally, since consolidation is generally prompted by a request for a new law, consolidation is almost invariably associated with minor substantive revisions. *The Air Navigation (General) Regulations 1993*, for example, consolidate existing legislation and add some minor changes such as excluding police helicopters from specified flying restrictions; *The Cereal Seeds Regulations 1993* which, in addition to consolidation, bring 'naked oats' within cereal regulations and make a series of other minor changes. Consequently, while we cannot discount all consolidating legislation as devoid of political action, we would not expect to find many of the 253 consolidating SIs (out of the 13,355 or 1.9 per cent) covering significant political issues.

Deregulation regulations

Since 1994, under the Deregulation and Contracting Out Act, it has been possible for primary legislation to be changed by Statutory Instrument for the purpose of reducing regulatory burdens on business. There were 42 such SIs up to spring 1997. These SIs pass through a special parliamentary procedure. Parliament considers deregulation orders in two stages. At a first stage a proposal is discussed by the Deregulation Committee, and at this stage it can be recommended that a deregulation order be laid along the lines of the proposal, or with amendments or not at all. Then a draft deregulation order is laid and debated in the House.

Examples of this type of legislation include *The Deregulation (Football Pools) Order 1997*, a 'Henry VIII' SI which removes some restrictions on football pools, including lowering the age of participation from 18 to 16, and *The Deregulation (Friendly Societies Act 1992) Order 1996* which makes a series of changes to arrangements for administration of friendly societies, including reducing the number of copies of altered rules which a society must send to the central office of the Registry of Friendly Societies from four to three. These are not necessarily contentious. In 1996–7, while two proposals (i.e. first stage) were 'disapproved' by the Committee, all 14 draft deregulation orders were approved without division in the House. The continuation of deregulation orders under the New Labour administration suggests that this thrust of legislation is not associated only with Conservative governments.

SUBJECTS COVERED AND MINISTRIES CONCERNED

Functional areas of SIs

The discussion so far has given some account of what many SIs do. Are there any particular policy areas more likely to be the subject of SIs than others? Table 3.2 sets out the policy areas of SIs over the ten years from 1987 excluding the humdrum SIs. The largest number of SIs concern education (743), social security (709), local government (561), the National Health Service (527) and income tax (451).

One must, of course, be careful when evaluating the significance of the policy areas of SIs. Part of the reason for the apparent prominence of education lies in the division of territorial responsibilities for education in the United Kingdom. Since there is separate legislation for education in England and Wales, Scotland and Northern Ireland, one would expect more legislation in this area than in policy areas, such as Value Added Tax, which are generally covered by UK legislation. Similarly inflated by the division of territorial jurisdictions in the UK is the number of SIs on local government, the NHS, rating and valuation, legal aid and public health among the most numerous SIs.

Table 3.2 Subject Areas of SIs 1987–1997 (covered by over 100 SIs only)[†]

Subject	N	%
Education	743	5.47
Social security	709	5.22
Local government	561	4.13
National Health Service	527	3.88
Road traffic	475	3.50
Income tax	451	3.32
Housing	361	2.66
Pensions	349	2.57
Agriculture	344	2.53
Rating and valuation	288	2.12
Legal aid and advice	282	2.08
Merchant shipping	235	1.73
Public health	226	1.67
Food	225	1.66
Customs and excise	220	1.62
Value Added Tax	217	1.60
Sea fisheries	181	1.33
Animals	178	1.31
Criminal law	178	1.31
Town and country planning	175	1.29
Contamination of food	170	1.25
Health and safety	169	1.25
Medicines	153	1.13
Police	152	1.12
Civil aviation	146	1.08
Terms and conditions of employment	136	1.00
Water	136	1.00
Representation of the people	134	0.99
Betting gaming and lotteries	131	0.97
Offshore installation	129	0.95
Building societies	128	0.94
Supreme court	125	0.92
Children and young persons	123	0.91
Environmental protection	120	0.88
Companies	116	0.85
County courts	116	0.85
Sheriff court	112	0.83
Council tax	110	0.81
Financial services	108	0.80
Court of Session	105	0.77

[†] Available for all but 38 of the 13,355 SIs; many had several subject headings; 12,201 had 1, 1,238 had two, 113 had three, 9 had four, two had five, four had six and four had seven. Percentages expressed as a percentage of 13,571 SIs with at least one valid subject area
Source: See Appendix B

Ministries and SIs

The British territorial ministries (the Scottish and Welsh Offices) before devolution were the most frequent signatory departments to delegated legislation (Table 3.3). Statutory Instruments are signed by one or more ministers, whether of Cabinet rank or junior ministers, or on occasion (usually with local instruments) by an official from the ministry. By coding the names of ministries at the foot of the SI, we get a picture of which ministries are *involved* in the issue of delegated legislation, although this does not necessarily mean that they played a leading role in drafting it. The broad functional responsibilities of the Scottish and Welsh Offices means that they are involved in over one-fifth of all delegated legislation after discounting local and ecclesiastical legislation. The role of the territorial ministries in education also accounts for the strong divergence between the large number of education SIs (Table 3.2) and the relatively small number of SIs issued from the ministry responsible for education (Table 3.3) since many education SIs are issued by the Scotland, Wales and Northern Ireland Offices. The Northern Ireland Office itself is one of the less frequent signatories to delegated legislation, with under one in 20 SIs (4.95 per cent). This is because the delegated legislation of the Northern Ireland Office, Statutory *Rules*, is handled by separate procedures and much delegated legislation in Northern Ireland is thus excluded from the data in this chapter.

Table 3.3 Signatory Ministries to SIs†

Ministry/Department	N	%
Scottish Office	2,538	22.00
Welsh Office	2,514	21.79
Treasury	2,293	19.88
Health and Social Security	1,983	17.19
MAFF	1,358	11.77
Environment	1,288	11.17
Transport	1,059	9.18
Trade and Industry	1,033	8.96
Home Office	793	6.87
Education and Science	674	5.84
Lord Chancellor's Departments	650	5.64
Northern Ireland Office	571	4.95
Employment	509	4.41
Defence	161	1.40
Heritage	71	0.62
Foreign and Commonwealth	27	0.23

† Available for all but 1,820 of the 13,355 SIs. Percentages expressed as a percentage of 11,535 SIs with at least one ministry mentioned.
Source: See Appendix B.

The Treasury's wide range of responsibilities, cutting across many functional areas, also gives it prominence in Table 3.2, with just under one in five SIs (19.88 per cent) naming it as a signatory. Of the functional ministries, Health and Social Security (currently two ministries) and the Ministry of Agriculture Fisheries and Food (MAFF), the Departments of the Environment and Transport (currently one ministry), and Trade and Industry are the most common signatories to SIs. The Foreign Office and the Ministry of Defence, along with the recently formed Department for National Heritage, are involved in the least SIs.

POLITICAL ACTION AND SIS

We have categorised SIs on the basis of a variety of criteria. Over half were excluded as belonging to categories unlikely to reflect significant political action. Of the remainder, it is extremely difficult to say with any certainty how much political action is involved. Consolidation legislation appears to be the most clearcut candidate for exclusion from any list of types of SI reflecting political action since it, for the most part, simply repeats legislative provisions already in existence. Commencement orders may be assumed to reflect little political action since they merely put a date on the implementation of legislation resulting from battles already fought and won or lost. However, not only is the ability to bring into effect (or not bring into effect) provisions of legislation through an SI an important power which could engender controversy, such regulations may also include details about how a statutory provision is to be interpreted. European Union legislation may, under many circumstances, be automatic and leave little room for national discussion. In many other cases the timing and interpretation of EU rules in national contexts could provoke intense controversy. By comparison with other member countries the British government has been accused of being over-zealous in its application of EU rules and over-restrictive in how it chooses to interpret them (see Booker and North 1996; Select Committee on Agriculture 2000: para. 16).

Some serial-numbered and iterative regulations are profoundly routine, yet others can be intensely political. One good example of this is the Teachers Pension Regulations, an annual event which generally appears to pass without major controversy. In 1997 the regulations were changed significantly with the effect that they made it exceptionally difficult for teachers to take early retirement. The Regulations provoked major hostility from the teaching unions, the Association of Teachers and Lecturers took the matter to court (and was represented by Cherie Booth, the barrister wife of the then Labour opposition leader) and eventually forced a concession from the government that the introduction of the changes would be postponed from April to October 1997 in order to avoid a 'mad rush' of retirement applications during the exam period (as the headline in the *Observer* of 12 January 1997 put it, 'Teachers scramble for the exit door'; see also the *Guardian*, 6 January 1997 and 22 February 1997).

We might have carried on looking at, for example, whether SIs which seem to effect regular updates of amounts of money to be allocated by way of subsidy tend to reflect significant political action. Yet here again, there are examples of the worthy and uncontentious (e.g. the annual SIs governing uprating of government compensation to small employers for statutory maternity pay) while others generally raise significant controversy, such as the annual grant settlement to support local government services.

HIGH POLITICS, LOW POLITICS AND SIS

In short, we have made some progress towards answering the central question posed at the start of this chapter: how much political action is there in Statutory Instruments? We can say that there is little political action in over half, and for the remainder we have a mixed bag, with few significant categories of SI equating neatly with high or low levels of political action. We can take things a little further, however, if we approach the question from the other side, as it were. Instead of asking how many SIs engender political controversies, we may get a better understanding of the political character of SIs by asking what sort of issue is decided by Statutory Instrument? With 28,000 SIs to choose from over ten years one can always find examples of contentious SIs and examples of non-contentious SIs. What we need in order to establish the political importance of SIs is some evaluation of the degree to which they are used on *a regular basis* to legislate for issues of major controversy. In order to do this, we need to look at a broader range of Statutory Instruments in some detail.

A random sample of 100 was selected from the 'other' category in Table 3.1. These are one-off SIs which do not fit any of the categories in Table 3.1 and cannot be viewed as a representative sample of all SIs. The sample was selected from this group partly because they form a group about which nothing is known. They were also chosen because if there is any grain of truth in the expectation that SIs in any of the categories discussed above (apart from deregulation orders) are more likely to be routine and uncontentious, we are less likely to find evidence of substantial political action. Thus when interpreting the results of the analysis of this sample, it has to be remembered that it is skewed, as far as is possible on the basis of outward appearance, towards providing evidence of SIs which involve substantial political action. If we cannot find evidence of such political action here, then we are unlikely to find evidence that SIs are used on a regular basis, as opposed to the odd example plucked from 27,999, to legislate for issues of substantial controversy. The results of the analysis of this sample are presented in Table 3.4.

Table 3.4 Contents of 100 SIs[†]

Local/Commencement	3
Consequential SIs	4
Definitions and forms	14
Procedures and machinery of Government	22
Permissive	5
Regulatory	37
Distributive	13
Public services	2
Total	100

† See text for sampling details, full list of SIs in Appendix C

Local and consequential SIs

Of the 100 in the sample, only seven were clearly very limited in the kind of political action they involved (see Table 3.4). Three of the 100 SIs turn out to be SIs of the sort that the analysis had tried to exclude so far although this could not be detected from the name of the SI: two local SIs (*The Protection from Eviction (Excluded Licences) Order 1991* and *The Harbour Authorities (Variation of Constitution) Order 1993*) and an appointed day order (*The Employment Code of Practice (Picketing) Order 1992*). Only four further SIs were clearly consequential, i.e. rather formal changes in regulations made to accommodate prior changes in legislation. *The Local Government (Magistrates' Courts etc.) (Amendment) Order 1994* repeals legislation rendered obsolete by changes in the law and *The Local Government (Transitional Election Arrangements) (Scotland) Order 1994* as well as *The North Eastern Sea Fisheries District (Constitution of Committee and Expenses) (Variation) Order 1996* are both changes following local government reorganisation in Scotland, Cleveland and Humberside in the mid-1990s. *The Land Registration (Charges) Rules 1990* can likewise be classified mainly as consequential since they tidy up Land Registration procedures following changes to mortgage documentation. This small amount of relatively very minor legislation was to be expected since the sample was drawn from those SIs one would expect to display signs of political action.

Definitions and forms

Fourteen of the SIs in the sample were categorised as defining legal obligations created in other forms of legislation (see Table 3.4). Four of them do this by setting out or amending forms which have to be completed in conformity with an Act of Parliament. The other ten give definitions to legislation; for example, how 'low' a rent has to be before it is exempted from assured tenancy arrangements, how Child Support Agency assessments of the maintenance contributions of an absent parent impact upon maintenance orders and agreements, or what is a 'connected flight' for the purposes of liability to air passenger taxes.

Procedures and machinery of government

Twenty-two SIs are classed as 'machinery of government' SIs since they make arrangements for government institutions and their personnel (see Table 3.4). This includes the abolition of District Advisory Committees on disability discrimination, regulations governing potential conflicts of interests in local government over housing allocation, the transfer of staff from the Polytechnic and Colleges Funding Council to the Universities Funding Council, the procedures for consultation on water extractions in the Norfolk and Suffolk Broads, the transfer of immigration appeals from the Home Office to the Lord Chancellor's Department, the judicial treatment of tax appeal cases and the giving of Welsh names to police authorities in Wales.

Permissive

Five SIs are permissive (see Table 3.4) since they give legal powers to individuals and organisations including those giving power to the Secretary of State for Education to pay grants to bodies other than local education authorities, enabling the Ministry of Agriculture to order the destruction of animals under specified circumstances and allowing the Residuary Body for Wales to levy income from local authorities.

Regulatory

Thirty-seven of the SIs have been classed as 'regulatory' (see Table 3.4). By this is meant that the behaviour of those outside government is regulated. These are, on the face of it, likely to be the most politically contentious of the 100 SIs examined here. However, relatively few, less than a quarter, cover obviously major political issues—the prohibition of fishing for angler fish, the reform of education in Northern Ireland, the regulation of prescriptions by nurses and midwives in Northern Ireland, the arrangements for the testing of poultry flocks, the meat and animal hygiene inspections, referral of milk businesses or (in a separate instruments) water businesses to the Monopolies and Mergers Commission, the classification and labelling of video recordings, overhauling the rules on patenting inventions.

The remainder of the regulatory SIs appear at face value relatively less likely to be controversial as they cover: the insurance liabilities of landowners in

Northern Ireland for rock-climbers on their land, the Northern Ireland law of limitations in libel actions, the keeping of mink,[7] the application of UK law to offshore installations, amendments to the list of prescription-only medicines, the transport of poisons in emergencies, the use of explosives and equipment in coal mines, definition of hazardous substances, bankruptcy in Scotland, the extension of social security provisions to service personnel in Cyprus, interest on awards made by industrial tribunals, anti-money-laundering legislation, determining damages against mine-owners for damage caused to the property of others, the placement of children outside the British Isles by voluntary adoption agencies, the administration of Friendly Societies, the discipline of senior Scottish police officers.

Distributive

The 13 distributive SIs (see Table 3.4) affect financial arrangements between individuals and organisations. They include changes in arrangements for paying pensions to dependents of police cadets killed while on duty, the taxation of costs awarded in the High Court, increasing the number of Marshall (university) scholarships from 30 to 40, provisions for costs incurred by building contractors in public works schemes and regulations covering compensation for homeowners whose houses are blighted by mining subsidence.

Public services

Two SIs (see Table 3.4) define the nature of public services; one applies general school regulations to self-governing schools and the other regulates the running of bail hostels.

HOW MUCH OF POLITICAL IMPORTANCE IS INVOLVED IN DELEGATED LEGISLATION?

In this chapter we can answer this question only in part. For a large portion of SIs the political action at a *national* level is extremely limited; 52 per cent of SIs are local, merely correcting errors or changing ecclesiastical law. A further 1 per cent of SIs are consolidation SIs. These are the only categories of SI which we can with some confidence suggest are likely to contain very few measures touching major national issues of political significance.

For the remainder we can only give a less direct answer the question of political significance. Political importance, we argued at the outset of the chapter, is

---

[7] Although the mass release by animal rights activists in 1998 of mink from a Dorset farm threatened to make this a candidate for political controversy.

a function of the significance of the issue and the degree of discretion in the policy process surrounding the SI. The latter condition is important since, for example, the commencement orders for the legislation setting up the Welsh Assembly involved relatively little political action as the main controversies and choices were made long before the implementing legislation.

How important are the issues set out in SIs? One difficulty in assessing significance derives from the fact that understanding the wider significance of an SI in the context of a particular policy area requires a very high degree of knowledge and understanding of the issues involved. Such knowledge across the whole range of government activity is simply unavailable to any single observer. For example, one has to be on intimate terms with the development of education and social security policy to understand the significance of the commencement order which set a single school leaving date for 16-year-olds. Even those who own small workboats are unaware of precisely how they will be affected by new workboat and load-line regulations, according to one official who helped draft them (see Chapter 5).

Nevertheless, on *a priori* grounds, and with the caveat that more detailed knowledge may reveal the apparently important to be insignificant and the routine to be a matter of vital principle, SIs appear to touch on public policy issues which are of general significance for citizens as well as for specialised constituencies. Of our 100 detailed in Appendix 2, we find many affecting larger constituencies such as the definition of hazardous substances, the specification of protected tenancies, mortgage eligibility under right to buy legislation, maintenance payments for absent parents, air passenger tax, definitions of homelessness, who hears tax or immigration appeals, who has to be consulted when Anglia Water wants to extract from the Norfolk Broads, who is a member of a health or police authority, how children are to be represented in complaints over fostering and council care, what appears on the list of prescription-only drugs, air safety regulations, which government departments get responsibility for energy or which give MAFF the power to inspect and destroy animals suspected of being treated with banned hormones. Others, such as those excluding landowners in Northern Ireland from liability for rock climbers injured on their land or prohibiting fishing for anglerfish, appear far more limited.

The conclusion that we can draw for this survey of SIs is that a very large portion of them appear, on *a priori* grounds, to be of relatively little political importance. Here the analysis of what is measurable about SIs takes us only so far, so let me conclude provisionally with a rather less scientific appraisal of the political significance of SIs which mixes measured facts and hunch. If you pick an SI at random there is at least a 50 per cent chance that you will find something that is completely uninteresting in terms of national significance because it is something to do with a trunk road, a local issue, it makes a minor correction or deals with Church law.

Discard these 50 per cent and pull out at random another ten from the remainder. The chances are that you will find nine that are, at first glance, incomprehensible.

Look closely at their explanatory notes, which will get you at least a little further in understanding what they are about. Go and have a look at the primary legislation too, and of the ten you may find four that look so innocuous and routine that, while you cannot be sure, you would dismiss them as politically uninteresting. Of the remaining six, you may have heard of one beforehand. Yes, you remember reading about new regulations protecting hedgerows; these must be the ones. And yes, they were pretty important even if some of the environment groups claimed they did not go far enough. The remaining five you cannot be sure about. Are anglerfish very important? Somebody must want to fish for them as it is unlikely that someone would want to ban angler fish for the hell of it. These new regulations on miners' safety lamps look impressive, but were they hammered out over protracted negotiations with the miners' unions and employers or were they innocuous changes to long-standing practice?

What might you conclude from sampling in this way? Probably that well over half of all SIs are politically uninteresting. That some SIs involve major political controversies, but relatively few do. A larger number (than those touching major political controversies) appear at first glance to raise what might be termed narrow gauge political issues, although you must remain uncertain about two key issues which we defined as central to our understanding of the nature of political action involved in SIs: how sensitive such issues were to those concerned and how far these issues were really things that were under debate while the SI was being drafted, rather than issues decided in advance well before work on the SI was started. So while we have begun to see the stuff of politics in perspective, cutting back the mass of undergrowth which obscures the more exotic and interesting plants, we need more detail on what SIs actually do and what was involved in drafting them. Since you may conclude from your sampling exercise that you cannot reasonably tell from reading the SI and other published material how much political action was involved, it would be sensible to go and ask those involved what it was about. The next chapter sets out their answers.

4

The origins of regulations

How much of political importance is involved in delegated legislation? Examining the text of an SI and any published material about it will, as Chapter 3 has shown, get you only part of the way in understanding the process of everyday government. In order to understand the central question of what sort of political issues are at stake in the process, and how the process is conducted, one has to talk to the people who are actually involved in it. This chapter is based on an examination of 46 individual SIs issued between 1997 and 1999 by 13 government departments. Talking to those who were involved in creating SIs allows one to offer specific answers to key questions about the nature of the everyday political process. This chapter is concerned with the character and origins of delegated legislation—what sort of issue is at stake in the SI and how do SIs originate? The nature of the SI gets us somewhat further in setting out the question of how much political action is involved in SIs. The amount of discretion that those drawing up the SI believe they have is related to the broad context in which the legislation is introduced. This is discussed in the first part of this chapter. The second part of this chapter goes on to explore the precise source of the legislation: where did the idea come from to legislate?

The 46 SIs which form the basis of this and the following chapters were not randomly selected SIs, so the sample cannot claim to represent the totality of SIs. In consequence no tabular presentations are offered of quantities of SIs falling into different categories, since to do so would imply a degree of confidence in the estimates which could be justified only if the sample were random and larger. Moreover, the numbers that are presented against different categories of SI in this chapter must further be regarded as indicative, since it is in the nature of many SIs that they have more than one purpose, so many SIs could be placed in more than one category. Here I have assigned them to what I believe to be the most appropriate one. The mode of selection of the 46 SIs is discussed in Appendix D, but in a nutshell they were SIs which were not obviously humdrum (as defined in the previous chapter), which reflected different aspects of a government department's work and which were close enough to the intended time of interviewing to make it likely that the people responsible for the SI would still be in post and would remember it.

The potential for diversity in reporting conversations with over 150 respondents about 46 items of delegated legislation is huge. Interviews covered issues from major changes in social security legislation to the use of additives in flour. However, it soon became apparent that, while the precise detailed issues surrounding any particular SI are unique, SIs tended to fall into categories. The categories are inductive and based on common sense rather than deductive theory. These categories, or some very similar, are routinely used by officials to make distinctions between different types of delegated legislation. The precise terminology used by officials is not standardised, although, of the categories used below, 'European', 'consequential' and 'implementing primary legislation' came up frequently in interviews. The other two, 'shaggy dogs' and 'making discrete changes', are my own categories that reflect my interpretation of officials' conception of the sort of matter they were dealing with. These different kinds of SIs tend to differ substantially in terms of how much political action is involved in their development—how much was actually decided in the process of developing the SI (as opposed to how much was decided long before the SI was drafted), and how significant the SI is.

Discrete changes (26 cases)

A majority of the SIs examined were more or less free-standing changes in policy, practices or procedures. They brought about changes in the law which were not simply directly implementing European law or domestic primary legislation and did not simply result as an automatic consequence of other laws. This is where the discretion of those involved in drawing up the legislation—politicians and civil servants—was greatest. Some of the discrete changes introduced through SIs were central planks of government policy. *The Social Security (Welfare to Work) Regulations 1998*, as the title suggests, were part of the 'welfare to work' initiative. This SI sought to encourage more people on incapacity-related benefits to enter the labour market by lowering some of the disincentives to come off benefits and try out a job. People coming off incapacity-related benefits could lose their earlier benefit entitlement if they tried working and found they could not continue. They would have to be reassessed and face the uncertainty of a different assessment giving them a different, possibly lower, benefit entitlement. *The Social Security (Welfare to Work) Regulations 1998* extended from eight weeks to one year the period within which the ex-recipient can give up his or her job and return to the same benefits without the need for a reassessment.

Other free-standing SIs reflected major issues within their own particular fields. While to the casual observer *The Fire Services (Appointments and*

Promotion) (Amendment) Regulations 1997 look relatively anodyne, they covered one of the most important controversies in the fire service of recent decades. The SI removed the maximum age requirement as well as eyesight and height requirements for firefighters. The height of firefighters has crucial implications for sex equality in recruitment of personnel. The issue had been of great importance not only to those interested in promoting sex equality, but also to fire brigades, such as those in London and the South East, which wanted to expand their pools of potential recruits. It was also highly controversial and, as we shall see below, was introduced in the teeth of strong opposition from some influential groups, with which ministers sided until opposition became untenable.

In the 1990 Broadcasting Act which restructured the financial arrangements for Channel 4, the funding formula created a safety net which meant that if it was a commercial flop, the ITV companies would support it (see Dell 1998).[1] Since Channel 4 was a great success, the funding formula worked in reverse—as a levy paid to ITV companies. *The Channel 4 (Application of Excess Revenues) Order 1997* meant that Channel 4 was no longer saddled with the huge burden of paying nearly £90 million (and rising) to the ITV companies each year. As will be discussed in detail below, this was a controversial issue made more controversial by the character of Channel 4 programmes. Channel 4 was in the vanguard of broadcasting the sort of sexually explicit material that has since become more widespread. This led Paul Johnson, a right-wing journalist writing in the *Daily Mail,* to give the Channel 4 chief executive at the time, Michael Grade, the title of 'pornographer-in-chief'—a 'grotesque distortion' that 'stuck . . . like glue' especially among Conservative MPs (Grade 1999: 357).

Other SIs effecting discrete changes were less controversial. *The Misuse of Drugs (Supply to Addicts) Regulations 1997* abolished the system of notifying heroin addicts to the Home Office that had existed since 1968.[2] *The Grants for Improvements in School Education (Scotland) Regulations 1998* were introduced to set out the formal arrangements for distributing £15 million extra spending on education yielded by the Comprehensive Spending Review. The money was to go to schools with 'a focused and radical Education Action Plan' (Scottish Office News Release 2724/98, 29 December 1998). Equivalent SIs were developed separately for England and Wales.[3] *The Pensions Appeal Tribunals (England and Wales) (Amendment) Rules 1998* made a series of minor changes to procedures of the Tribunal including changing the forms for giving notice of appeal and the ability to summon medical and other expert opinion.

---

[1] According to the formula, if Channel 4 received less in advertising income than 14 per cent of the total for all terrestrial companies, it would receive money from the other ITV companies. If it received more than 14 per cent, half of the 'excess' would be given to the ITV companies, a quarter would go to Channel 4 as revenue and a further quarter to a Channel 4 Reserve Fund.

[2] Although this was controversial among those, including those researching drugs policy and the history of health policy, who pointed to the disruption of long time-series data.

[3] *The Education (Education Standards Grants) (Wales) Regulations 1999* and *The Education (Education Standards Etc. Grants) (England) Regulations 1999.*

These SIs, which actually make changes to particular policy areas, tend to give substantial discretion to those involved in making them. This does not mean that the discretion always falls to the civil servants drafting them, or necessarily involves substantial scope for negotiation with interest groups. For example, the decision to save money by shortening the length of time for which people can claim benefits in *The Jobseeker's Allowance (Amendment) Regulations 1998* was a decision taken at Cabinet level. It appeared to be non-negotiable (until it was repealed) and the actual process of drafting the SI was quite straightforward and involved few significant subsequent policy choices. Moreover an exception to the argument that discrete changes involve the exercise of choice can be found in SIs which implement or apply a pre-agreed formula such as *The Statutory Maternity Pay (Compensation of Employers) Amendment Regulations 1998*. This SI upgrades the amount of money payable to small employers under the provisions for statutory maternity pay. The formula according to which the upgrading takes place is complex and technical. The result of its application is a percentage figure which refers to the additional percentage of maternity pay to be paid to small employers.

The majority of SIs, 26 of the 46 (57 per cent), fell into this category of SIs seeking to make a discrete change in existing arrangements. However, because this is not a sample taken at random, it would be mistaken to conclude that the majority of SIs are of this type. First, the sample is small. To illustrate the impact of the small size of the sample, according to standard significance tests we would expect an estimate of 57 per cent to be accurate within plus or minus 15 per cent (i.e. we can be 95 per cent confident that the 'true' figure is somewhere between 42 per cent and 72 per cent). Secondly, the sample is not random, so even significance tests cannot be validly used. The sample of 46 SIs examined in greater depth in this and the next chapter excluded local SIs, and no attempt was made to select at random or using any statistically valid sampling technique (see Appendix D). However, despite these reservations, it is possible to state that one does not have to search very hard among the complete corpus of delegated legislation to find relatively large numbers of such instruments which make discrete changes.

'We were implementing primary legislation' (nine cases)

All SIs result from primary legislation and in this sense can be said to implement it. However, the relationship between primary and secondary legislation can be more direct. Secondary legislation is often needed to determine details as well as the timing of the bringing into force of provisions of the legislation.

As will be discussed below, this is not necessarily a straightforward matter. Why do governments not implement the provisions of primary legislation directly, without delegated legislation? In some cases the government is not sure that it wants to bring into effect all the measures it has introduced. Maybe it does not have the political will or the money to introduce them. In other cases the flexibility of secondary legislation allows government to make use of powers which government believed it should grant itself without knowing whether or how it would like to exercise them.[4] In yet other cases the logistics of effecting change require the close co-ordination of different items of primary and secondary legislation. A further reason for using delegated legislation is that it offers greater scope to consult with affected interests on a matter of detail without holding up the passage of the primary legislation.

In some cases the primary legislation, or the debates surrounding it, set out in some detail how the legislation is to be implemented. For example, *The Bank of England (Information Powers) Order 1998* gave the Bank of England, with its enhanced powers in monetary policy given under the 1998 Bank of England Act, legal power to collect information from banks and building societies on, among other things, their assets, liabilities and transactions. This was a new statutory power for the Bank, but not a new activity. The Bank had been collecting the information on a voluntary basis before this, and the statutory power itself did not require any significant expansion of the information to be provided. It was envisaged in debates about the primary legislation that this power would be given to the Bank straight away.

However, in many others *what is decided in drafting the SI can be at least as important, if not more so, than what is decided in the primary legislation.* A clear example of this is in *The Crime Sentences Act 1997 (Commencement No. 2 and Transitional Provisions) Order 1997* under which the new Labour administration brought into force some of the outgoing Conservative government's policies on criminal sentencing. The primary legislation was passed under the Conservative government, specifically under Michael Howard, who as Home Secretary sought to highlight his toughness on law and order. The provisions in the Act included the removal of the discretion of the Home Secretary in determining lengths of life sentences and raising minimum sentences for some sexual offences. Since the 1997 Act contained a wide range of possible fundamental amendments to sentencing policy, the choice facing a Labour administration of which ones actually to bring into effect was a highly political one. The choice was shaped by the perceived costs in terms of prison space and the broader penal policy preferences of the new Labour administration. Among the more radical portions of the Act not brought into effect were provisions on 'honest sentencing'. These were intended to mean that nominal prison sentences, which had little relationship to the actual time a convicted criminal served in jail, would be replaced by fixed sentences which criminals would actually serve in full. They were not implemented by Labour. The costs of these measures would probably have been just as prohibitive had the Conservatives stayed in power.

---

[4] The Cabinet Office's (1997) brief report on bringing into effect primary legislation lists 69 pieces of recent primary legislation with significant portions which have not been commenced, although in many of these it is only one or two sections which remain to be brought into effect.

Moreover, just because a controversial issue was settled by primary legislation does not necessarily mean that the secondary legislation will be uncontroversial. *The Education (School Leaving Date) Order 1997* brought into effect a single school leaving date (i.e. school leavers left on this one date rather than after whenever their 16th birthdays happened to fall) first set out in primary legislation in 1993. However, it raised controversy within government as well as between government and trade unions because of the extra resources it committed (described in more detail in Chapter 6).

Another example is the introduction of conditional fees (no-win-no-fee arrangements for engaging legal representation). This arrangement was established under the Legal Services Act 1990. The issue aroused such controversy that the relevant provision of the Act was not brought into operation until *The Conditional Fee Agreements Order 1995*. The 1995 Order itself was quite modest (i.e. it allowed only limited types of cases to be handled by conditional fees) a result of the opposition from the legal profession faced by the Conservative Lord Chancellor, Lord MacKay of Clashfern. As one official involved pointed out, the 1995 Order was designed to test the water for a more extensive conditional fee scheme planned for two years later. It eventually emerged as *The Conditional Fee Agreements Order 1998*. The Welsh Office found itself highly constricted by the primary legislation when it came to *The Education (School Performance Targets) (Wales) Regulations 1998* which implement the provisions of the 1997 Education Act. The Act obliged the governing bodies of all schools to set targets for the attainment levels of their pupils. As appears to be common in the Welsh Office (see below) a drafting lawyer took the initiative:

> We knew the targets were to be coming in on September 1st. I wrote to the administrators asking for instructions on May 1st. The administrators responded by saying they would write them as soon as they could.

Many of the arrangements for Wales were similar to the English. The administrators eventually issued instructions to the drafting solicitor and:

> they helpfully sent a copy of the instructions sent by DfEE administrators to their lawyers . . . 'here are the English instructions and this is what we want different for Wales'.

The administrator had marked some paragraphs of this draft 'same for Wales', others 'different targets', and still others 'what does this mean?'. The education minister in Wales indicated that he wanted targets on absences and truancy, and this (among other features specific to Wales) would have made the Welsh legislation substantially different from the English. In fact, proposals to this effect were contained in a consultation document. However, the powers to include such targets were simply not there in the 1997 legislation. To get round this problem the lawyer arranged to have a section placed in the 1998 School Standards and Framework Act to allow the Welsh Office to bring in the targets that it wanted. While the relevant provision was included in the Act, somewhere along the line something had gone wrong. The provision was not brought into effect on the date the Bill received the Royal Assent in July, but over three months later—too late for the planned Welsh regulations. As an official put it:

> We got to the final draft and I got a proof copy of the Act as soon as it had been signed, and I looked for our section AND THE POWERS WERE NOT THERE! So we had to drop it [the part on unauthorised absences] and cut it all out at the last minute.

Without the appropriate powers in place, the Welsh Office was unable at the time to introduce the targets to which it had more or less committed itself. Instead it had to be dealt with in subsequent regulations (*The Education (School Performance and Unauthorised Absence Targets) (Wales) Regulations 1999*) requiring that attendance and truancy be covered in local education authority strategic plans.

SIs which implement primary legislation are a very mixed bunch. Some can be a straightforward matter of formally bringing into effect a provision already decided before. Others involve substantial decisions over policy, as we have seen. And even where major policy decisions are not at stake, the timing and sequencing of implementation can be very important. *The Government of Wales Act 1998 (Commencement No. 2) Order 1998* was an implementation of parts of the Government of Wales Act 1998 which brought a devolved assembly to Wales. Parts of the 1998 Act which allowed an election of the Assembly to take place had to be brought in at the end of 1998. For other parts of the 1998 Act commenced by this Order it was a matter of bringing into effect what could be brought into effect while leaving out the specific transfers of functional responsibilities (such as for school inspections and Forestry Commissioners) for later commencement.

'This was European legislation' (six cases)

Around 15 per cent of national delegated legislation is related to European legislation (Page 1998). Not all of this legislation will be directly 'implementing' or 'transposing'.[5] 'Implementing' EU legislation is commonly associated with *transposition* of EU directives. Three of the 46 SIs were transposing European legislation in this way. *The Telecommunications (Interconnection) Regulations 1997* implemented Directive 97/33/EC—the 'Interconnection Directive'. *The Environmental Protection (Prescribed Processes and Substances) (Amendment)*

---

[5] Some SIs may be essentially domestic in origin and have provisions in them designed to make sure the legislation is consistent with broad EU provisions, such as the free movement of goods provision in Article 30 (now Article 28) of the Treaty of European Union which shaped the need for *The Wireless Telegraphy (Control of Interference from Videosenders) Order 1998*; the Technical Standards Directive and similar provisions of European legislation also mean that some essentially domestic regulations have to be approved by the Commission and Member States. See for example *The Merchant Shipping (Small Workboats and Pilot Boats) Regulations 1998* and *The Bread and Flour Regulations 1998*. These have not been included as European legislation.

(Hazardous Waste Incineration) Regulations 1998 implemented Council Directive 94/67 and *The Action Programme for Nitrate Vulnerable Zones (Scotland) Regulations 1998* implemented Council Directive 91/676.[6] A fourth, *The Apple and Pear Orchard Grubbing Up Regulations 1998*, created the administrative arrangements (including inspection, enforcement and fines) for a European regulation governing a scheme to improve EU fruit production by taking apple and pear orchards meeting certain criteria out of production.

Implementation can also take a different form, not directly linked to an individual law. Where the Member State is putting into effect a bundle of different European rules and regulations which go to make up a broad set of conditions for administering an EU scheme, we may term this *developing* or *maintaining* an administrative régime based on European legislation. *The Cod (Specified Sea Areas) (Prohibition of Fishing) Order 1998* prohibits cod fishing by small vessels in specified areas as part of the system of fish quota management and is a direct consequence of fishing quotas agreed between Member States.

Typically, officials feel they have very little discretion in the broad outlines of legislation which directly implements EU directives. While the sample covered two SIs which were so delayed that the Commission started infraction proceedings against the British government, eventually European legislation has to be implemented. It is not always fear of the Commission taking action that gives officials the impression that their discretion is relatively limited. One official suggested that the formal system of reporting to the Commission was not the main incentive to stick closely to the European directive when drafting implementing legislation:

> We would never send [the Commission] implementation tables [papers setting out exactly how each section of European legislation was implemented in the UK legislation]. We would send the SI and explain vaguely how it works. If you ever hear from the Commission, it's years down the line . . .

Rather any deviance from the directive, if it involved significant costs or benefits for major interests, would be challenged in the courts. The prospect of judicial challenge remained in the minds of those drafting transposing legislation.

This is not to suggest that EU legislation involves no negotiation between government and interests about how to implement EU legislation, but rather that such discussions are highly constrained by what are believed to be the imperatives of the European legislation. Officials are aware that there are often several ways of implementing complex directives. However they generally view this as a puzzle rather than an opportunity to offer their own interpretation of European legislation—the puzzle of what the directive means and what is technically the best way of bringing it into effect in a manner which cannot be legally

---

[6] Portions of one SI implemented a non-EU international obligation: *The Crime Sentences Act 1997 (Commencement No.2 and Transitional Provisions) Order 1997* contains provisions on life sentences which the Home Office felt bound to introduce in order to comply with a judgment in the European Court of Human Rights.

challenged, while at the same time minimising dissatisfaction among domestic interests.

'This was pretty much consequential' (three cases)

The term 'consequential' suggests that the change in the law made by the SI was an almost automatic change made necessary by some event or some other change in the law. 'Pretty much' or 'more or less' consequential were the words used to describe three of the 48 SIs I looked at since there was no pure piece of consequential legislation in my selection.[7] *The Education (Amount to Follow Permanently Excluded Pupils) Regulations 1997* were drawn up to amend the 1994 regulations of the same name, parts of which were rendered problematic by local government reorganization in the 1990s. There needed to be a change to the regulations to calculate the amount of money that was to be paid, and to whom, in the case of pupils excluded from secondary schools in local education authorities that had been reorganised.

With this and the other two[8] 'pretty much' consequential SIs there was a feeling among those interviewed that there was virtually no choice in passing this legislation: 'we are not allowed not to do it', said one. The changes were at best highly formal: '[i]f I had failed to do the SI there would have been no adverse consequences. I doubt if anyone would notice or even care'. In one case an official said he 'resented doing this SI' and added that 'a more skilled lawyer could have drafted the [primary] legislation so that the whole thing could be handled without an SI'. Here there is very little at stake. While one of these SIs dealt with payment to optometrists for sight tests, and might be expected to arouse substantial controversy between government and optometrists, the level of payments was set much earlier, outside the SI process. The SI itself was necessary only for rather technical administrative reasons (related to the particular legal requirements of a voucher scheme to reimburse a relatively small group of claimants for sight tests).

---

[7] *The Environment Act 1995 (Consequential Amendments) Regulations 1996* is an example of a pure consequential SI. It is a 'Henry VIII' law which amends a body of primary legislation. Henry VIII legislation was the focus of much criticism of the process of delegated legislation since it appeared not merely to bypass Parliament, but also to negate its legislative power by delegating to ministers the authority to amend parliamentary legislation (Hewart 1929). Like most pieces of Henry VIII legislation I came across, however, it appears entirely unremarkable in the way in which it, as mere delegated legislation, changes legislation which reflects the decisions of Parliament. It makes any references in relevant primary legislation to a 'National Rivers Authority' refer instead to the Environment Agency that replaced it in 1996.

[8] *The National Health Service (Optical Charges and Payments) Amendment Regulations 1997* and *The Dual-Use and Related Goods (Export Control) (Amendment) Regulations 1998*.

Shaggy dogs (two cases)

With many SIs it is impossible to understand the measure without understanding a much longer story. Of course in some senses all SIs are part of something bigger. They are legitimised by something bigger: primary legislation.
Moreover, in most cases, as will be discussed below in Chapter 9, an SI is generally a phase in a long-unfolding story. However the term 'shaggy dog' is used
to highlight a specific type of SI. A shaggy dog story is a long, involved story
without any obvious end. Two of the 46 SIs selected for examination can only
be understood as a by-product of what appears at first sight to be rather unrelated processes. One of these SIs concerned aircraft operators' tax and the other
the payment of duties on warehoused cider and perry. Nobody started out
directly seeking to change arrangements in either of these two fields. Changes
were made as a result of bigger changes elsewhere.

   Unlike consequential legislation, these two SIs do not simply tidy up the law.
They make changes but as part of (rather than a necessary consequence of) a
series of related changes. The only way one can make sense of their origins is to
see them as part of a broader legislative sweep. The tell-tale signs of a shaggy
dog story come when officials start off discussing something that happened
many years ago and not obviously related to the SI in hand. In one way or
another the body of legislation for a particular area would look odd or unusual,
or raise obvious charges of unfairness, if changes in one area were not introduced in another. While this is a relatively small category, it is worth elaborating on it a little because many other SIs examined had features of shaggy dog
legislation, even though they could ultimately be classified as belonging to a different category.

   When in 1992 the government raised excise duty on tobacco, the tobacco
companies sought, and achieved, a change in the law to allow them to save
money by 'electronic removal'. Big money is at stake here. Normally, duty on
warehoused tobacco goods was paid at the point when the goods physically left
the warehouse. Since warehouses full of tobacco cannot be cleared overnight so
that the duty can be paid at the old (i.e. lower) rate, the tobacco companies are
allowed (following *The Tobacco Products (Amendment) Regulations 1993*) to
pay the duty *before* the goods are physically removed from the warehouse. The
goods are simply deemed to have been removed through an entry in their electronic stock control records—hence 'electronic removal'. Duty can then and in
future be paid at short notice before the budget increases in duty take effect. The
beer brewers asked for a similar arrangement (under the name of 'constructive
removal'), which produced an SI making equivalent changes for beer (*The Beer
(Amendment) Regulations 1995*). *The Wine and Made Wine (Amendment)
Regulations 1996* extended this to some other domestic producers of alcoholic
drinks. *The Cider and Perry (Amendment) Regulations 1996* sought to make the
same concession for cider and perry producers. So where does the SI selected for

this study (*The Cider and Perry (Amendment) Regulations 1997*) fit in? A solicitor at Customs and Excise noticed that the 1996 Cider and Perry Regulations were technically flawed and the 1997 regulations remedied the flaw. As one official explained, cider and perry contribute very small amounts of revenue, 'we only tax cider and perry because we are obliged to do so. The duties are peanuts and the new regs. only have effect when there is advance notice of an increase in duty'. So these regulations were a result of a wider set of changes on tobacco and alcohol duties.

There was a similar case which carried the implications of changes in VAT regulations through to the (related) aircraft operators tax. The degree of discretion involved in drawing up such regulations, and the consequent scope for political activity, is of necessity limited. In these two cases, the SI 'was close to the end of the chain in this story—the finishing off of a large job'. There was relatively little discretion and few choices to be made in the delegated legislative process. In the case of aircraft operators tax, those involved did not expect the story to end there as they anticipated challenges to the legislation through the courts or new European legislation which would blow open the question once again.

The shaggy dog is, however, more important than its modest numbers actually suggest. Although only two SIs were classified as 'shaggy dog' SIs, a much larger number had strong shaggy dog components even though they were classified in different terms. That is to say, while they cannot be classed as the simple by-product of a longer, apparently unrelated, process, SIs with strong shaggy dog components are significant episodes in a longer story with a variety of twists and turns.

Let us take *The Local Authorities (Transport Charges) Regulations 1998*. These regulations allowed local authorities to charge individuals, groups and firms for services such as licences for placing skips on public highways or signposting special events. 'The whole thing started in 1993', an official began laconically, 'the Local Government Finance section of DoE, as it was then, was doing a periodic review and looking for ways of reducing central government support of local government'. The issue was taken forward by officials who spoke to the local authority associations and came up with broadly agreed lists of what local authorities should be allowed to charge for. In 1996 the draft SI was sent out for consultation. Several months later, in 1997, the results of the consultation were reported to the junior minister who, according to one interest group representative, 'looked at it and took some persuading that he should do it. Although it had Cabinet clearance, the junior minister did not see it that way'. He authorised a further round of consultations, but it was by then too late to do much about this issue since the regulations required affirmative resolutions of the House and 'it was by then, in any event, probably too late to get . . . [them] approved by both Houses and made before the election'.

Shortly after Labour came to power in the 1997 election the proposals were re-activated, primarily by the London local authorities. 'But then we came up against a hitch', an official commented. It was a minor detail, trivial even, but had some bearing on the timing of the legislation. Back in 1989 the Automobile Association (AA) had:

> engineered a Lords amendment to make sure they were not to be charged to put up temporary direction signs for them. But we discovered that no order had been made to designate the bodies that were not to be charged.

Unless the Department did something about this, such bodies were going to face hefty bills for council services, even though nobody involved intended that they should be charged. How did this omission come to light?

> I think it came up over the transfer of powers to Wales under devolution. There was a question of whether this Act [the 1989 Local Government and Housing Act] should be transferred, and we realised when we looked at it that no order had been made under it.

Before anything could be done to allow local authorities to charge for these services, an exemption had to be put in place for organisations such as the AA. The parliamentary basis for regulations making any such exemption (i.e. negative resolution) was different from that of regulations needed for the main transport charges regulations (i.e. affirmative resolution), so the easy way out of including an exemption in the planned regulations was not open to the DETR. The Department had to pass *The Temporary Traffic Signs (Prescribed Bodies) (England and Wales) Regulations 1998* before it could go ahead on the main change in regulations. The SI was consulted on, laid before Parliament, objected to by the opposition and debated.

This is a long and somewhat convoluted story and stories of similar complexity, with twists and turns coming from unexpected sources, could be told in at least 12 more of the SIs examined in this chapter. Unlike pure shaggy dog SIs, however, there was a substantial degree of discretion involved in the content of these regulations.

WHERE DO THE INITIATIVES COME FROM?

To ask the origins of a decision is to raise complex and ultimately insoluble questions of causation which potentially degenerate to infinite regress. For example, an SI which merely acknowledges that there is a new form of local authority, a 'unitary authority', to be added to the class of authorities eligible for a certain type of government grant might be 'caused' by the official who noticed that this potential lacuna needed to be avoided, the commission that recommended the creation of unitary authorities, the government that decided to create them, the appointment of Michael Heseltine as Secretary of State for the Environment who was keen on the creation of unitary authorities, the Heath government of 1970 which created a system of local government that needed reform only 20 years later and so on.

Asking people who thought of a particular initiative is likely to yield an answer, but it is in the nature of ideas that they do not always emerge fully formed in one individual's head. An official illustrated this precisely when asked how a particular omission from a set of regulations had been picked up just in the nick of time. He replied in all seriousness and honesty:

> I'm not sure. It could have been someone working out the operational guidance we were going to send out to the field, or in the legal service, or it could have come up in relation to something else. It could really have come from anybody. It could have been mentioned in a phone call and passed on to someone else. It could even have been me when I was looking at something completely different . . . When you get wind of things like that you go to other people who help you and put it right in the final draft.

Descriptions of causes and origins of decisions can never be complete, precise, accurate or fully documented. They can, however, be adequate. The aim here is not to give an exhaustive analysis of the causes of SIs, but to render intelligible the emergence of legislation at a particular time. Such explanations are of necessity diverse in their timescales and the factors they take into account.

On the question of where the idea for the legislation came from, we may divide the sources of the 46 SIs examined in detail into five broad groupings. *Internal sources* are those within national government: the ministers and civil servants of national ministries, the agencies which are part of them and the non-departmental public bodies which are attached to them. *External sources* are individuals, groups and bodies, including local authorities and NHS institutions outside the central civil service. *Programmed in primary legislation* refers to SIs which are the direct and effectively automatic consequence of primary legislation. *European sources* are European laws and decisions which produce domestic SIs implementing them or otherwise bringing them into effect. *Committee-led* regulations are those which result from formally constituted committees and advisory bodies which include members who would otherwise be included as 'external' sources of legislation.

Doubtless the fact that this study examines only 46 SIs avoids confronting complex problems of definition that arise whenever one seeks to categorise the status of public organisations and in particular which organisations are part of or not part of a ministry would make it hard to distinguish between external and internal origins of SIs (see Hood, Dunsire and Thompson 1978). However, none of the SIs examined in this chapter actually raises such problems. Yet the 46 do offer a broad range of possible ways in which SIs can start life.

Internal sources (25 cases)

The immediate stimulus to legislation is often internal—coming from within the ministry or the agencies attached to it. Within the ministry, civil servants are important initiators of regulations. Some SIs are part of a set of administrative routines which result in the production of SIs at more or less regular intervals. In the MAFF building near Trafalgar Square a Higher Executive Officer monitors on a spreadsheet the nationwide fishing returns sent in by different local offices. He has to look at the returns sent in by different sizes of fleet, as large boats come under different administrative arrangements from small boats. When the small boat fleet (those boats under ten metres long) looks as if it may overfish one area, he tries to swap quotas—arrange for the small boats to borrow the quota from another fleet. If he cannot arrange a swap he will 'pull' fishing certain types of stocks by the small fleet in that area. *The Cod (Specified Sea Areas) (Prohibition of Fishing) Order 1998* is one product of this process. This particular SI pulls cod, in this case in a set of sea areas in the English Channel and Western Approaches. Three months later the ban was lifted by the same routine which imposed it in *The Cod (Specified Sea Areas) (Prohibition of Fishing) (Revocation) Order 1998*. Similarly, *The Statutory Maternity Pay (Compensation of Employers) Amendment Regulations 1998* are part of a process of upgrading conducted by economists in the DSS based on benefit levels, fertility rates and earnings distribution data, among other variables, triggered off by the announcement of the Retail Price Index in September of each year.

Civil servants can also initiate one-off changes in legislation. The Veterinary Adviser in MAFF has extensive contact with the veterinary profession, directly through his contact with government veterinary laboratories such as the Central Veterinary Laboratory, and indirectly through the wider contacts government veterinary laboratories have with professionals outside government. Through these contacts he became aware that changes in technology meant that new types of pathogens—infectious agents such as that causing foot and mouth disease—could now be created. Small portions of the genetic material of the pathogen were enough to be able to transfer an infection. Consequently, the old law on pathogens was becoming out of date. The Veterinary Adviser put up a report to a Grade 5 vet who minuted an SEO in the Animal Health (Disease Control Division) to 'get the SAPO amended'. *The Specified Animal Pathogens Order 1998* (the 1998 'SAPO') was the eventual result.

With *The Pensions Appeal Tribunals (England and Wales) (Amendment) Rules 1998*, making a series of minor changes to procedures in the Tribunal, ideas for change had been 'floating around' for many years (the original regulations were made in 1980 and not changed since) and from several sources including the War Pensions Agency, the Tribunal itself and the Lord Chancellor's Department. When the LCD felt there were enough changes to warrant a regulation and set up a meeting with government organisations involved, including the Department of Social Security, the clear signal that the LCD intended to conduct a review of the regulations prompted even more suggestions for change right up to the time the new regulations were made. 'While you are at it, how about changing this?' was how one official described this aspect of the process.

In the case of the Scottish and Welsh Offices, London-based departments can be the stimulus for Scottish legislation. As one Scottish Office lawyer described it:

> The first thing I heard about [these regulations] was a copy my administrator sent me from [the London-based ministry]. We wanted to get our regulations out before England did theirs. This is unusual because we normally come later. We had a rough few paragraphs on what was intended. The administrators got the papers from their opposite numbers [in England] and they passed them on to me.

Moreover, with a Scottish Office SI implementing a European directive, an official explained:

> What happens with these European regulations is that we are notified for the Scottish interest. It does not happen a lot that it is different, but when the differences are important, someone from the Scottish Office will be involved.

He continued with a smile 'that's the theory anyway'. In fact the 'original impetus comes from Westminster'. The timing of the implementation of some directives also betrays the Whitehall role in stimulating legislation in Scotland. *The Action Programme for Nitrate Vulnerable Zones (Scotland) Regulations 1998* implemented a 1991 Council Directive (E91/676). Implementation was very tardy—in fact the British government faced infraction proceedings over this legislation. The Scottish legislation was made seven years after the EC Directive on 25 November 1998. The virtually identical English SI, *The Action Programme for Nitrate Vulnerable Zones (England and Wales) Regulations 1998*, was made on 7 May 1998. Both English and Scottish SIs came into effect on 19 December 1998.

In both Scotland and Wales, especially Wales, the shortage of 'policy people'—civil servants who specialise in particular policy areas (also termed 'administrators')—is the first feature to strike an outside observer. A Scottish Office lawyer pointed out when talking about a particular SI that 'the person up the road [i.e. the administrator at St Andrew's House] is clueless . . . nobody knew much about this up there'. A lawyer in the Welsh Office was just as blunt, except he was referring to the whole Welsh Office not just parts of it: '[n]ot a lot of policy goes on around here'. In consequence lawyers in the old territorial offices, especially in the Welsh Office, were more likely to play a role in initiating the SI.

Where the policy impetus was Britain-wide, lawyers in the Welsh Office would know that their colleagues in Whitehall-based departments were working on their regulations and could nudge their administrators into action. A Welsh Office legal adviser, who on his own decided that a particular piece of delegated legislation had to be drafted, went on to draft it almost entirely without involving an administrator. He described the process in the Welsh Office more generally:

> We go [to the administrators] and say 'I think you want this', we present them with something as clients. I was working this [particular SI] out myself, not on the basis of

an instruction. They do all the clearing with the Secretary of State. Look at this other one I'm doing now. I'll send it to the people over there [the administrators] and say 'this is what you need', and I'll suggest that it has to be copied to all departments—in Whitehall too, because it has implications for outside Wales.

An administrator in the Welsh Office reinforced this point when he stated 'we tend not to look at what [our counterpart English ministry] is doing, I rely on the lawyers to do all that'. He went on to say that his lawyer suggested (effectively) mirroring the English regulations, and he went along with that. At one stage he complained that there is one lawyer who 'pesters me every week to follow up on one thing or another and get regs. in place before the [Welsh] Assembly comes along'.

Political initiatives play an important role in the emergence of legislation. Some initiatives clearly come from ministerial level. The Treasury's concern with public spending commitments was a major source of the initiative in several cases. *The Jobseeker's Allowance (Amendment) Regulations 1998* was perhaps the most controversial of all SIs in the sample selected for this and the following chapters. It sought to cut the length of time for which people are paid this benefit by increasing the days they must wait before first receiving it. According to one official it:

> started with a proposal from the Treasury [under the preceding Conservative government]. It was part of the Public Expenditure round. I think arrangements with the Treasury have changed since the election. I never actually got involved in that side. It was handled by the people in the Finance Division . . . It was a Treasury proposal, of course it was not announced as a Treasury proposal. It gets announced as a DSS proposal even if we fought it tooth and nail. That's where the balance of power lies.

Along with changes in benefits to single parents, also inherited from the previous Conservative government, these proved among the most controversial of measures of the early months of the Labour administration and produced protest from backbench Labour MPs. Eventually, in response to the controversy, the SI was revoked before it took effect.[9] As one group member interviewed commented, 'they panicked and withdrew them', reportedly on the personal insistence of Prime Minister Blair.

Occasionally a minister takes a direct role in initiating the legislation. For example, another deregulation initiative reaching the statute books under Labour as *The Merchant Shipping (Small Workboats and Pilot Boats) Regulations 1998* was developed to give legal support to a new regulatory system for workboats based on a code of practice. One observer from one of the groups affected identified this as the initiative of a specific Conservative Cabinet minister. The minister sought to increase overall numbers of regulations formally revoked as part of a deregulatory thrust. This did not happen in quite the way intended as the Department took a longer and more serious look at the area

---

[9] By the *The Social Security (Miscellaneous Amendments) (No. 4) Regulations 1998* which took effect in May 1998.

than the minister's original suggestions implied, and the Department produced an elaborate new code of practice to replace the old regulations. The SI brought the code of practice regime into effect.

Some SIs are part of general thrusts in government policy of deregulation; charging and contracting out and are the fruit of internal processes begun under the Conservatives and continued under Labour after 1997. While the role of ministers in delegated legislation will be discussed in more detail in the next chapter, *ministerial initiation of delegated legislation generally does not involve a vision or specific set of objectives for the particular policy area for which they are responsible, but the application of broad principles*, such as deregulation, being tough on crime or fraud or cutting waste. Generally, however, politicians do not have to intervene directly to achieve political objectives. With many of the deregulation-inspired regulations, ministerial involvement was indirect. Civil servants understand the broad objectives of government policy and do not need to be directly told to legislate. 'We work within the framework of the disposition of the ministers at the time', as one official put it. He went on to argue:

> Not only is it difficult to say what is the prime cause, it is almost as if there is no prime cause. We saw the government's policy prescriptions—removing red tape—and there were a number of potentialities. They were all mentioned, not directly intended to trigger action. This may stimulate someone else to comment. It may be serendipity—the idea gestates. Nobody has a specific objective that other people then pick up. [It is the combined] effort of a lot of people working and responding.

With *The Restrictive Trade Practices (Non-notifiable Agreements) (Turnover Threshold) Amendment Order 1997*, which lifts the burden of officially notifying the now no longer existing Director General of Fair Trading of agreements between firms:

> the new government came in committed to getting rid of red tape. One could be thinking about what this meant, what tools were available, one was able to think along the same lines and think of the possibilities in the same way as the government. We put it forward to ministers—we had been thinking about what policies were to be implemented before May 1st [when New Labour took office].

Civil servants developed ideas aimed at pursuing the goal of deregulation without specific instructions to do so in the area of casinos (*The Gaming Duty Regulations 1997*) and labelling (parts of the 1995 regulations that were re-enacted in *The Bread and Flour Regulations 1998*). The origins of such legislation tended to be described in terms such as responding to a general climate of reducing or simplifying regulatory burdens rather than specific 'pressure from above'—from ministers.

Similarly, the impetus to contract out National Savings functions arose not directly from ministerial instruction but from the appointment of a new Director of National Savings. National Savings is a departmental agency attached to the Treasury. Part of the logic of agency structures was to bring desirable private sector practices into the management of ministerial functions.

Peter Bareau, appointed from Lloyds Bank in 1996, was the initiator of the contracting-out process of which *The Contracting Out (Functions Relating to National Savings) Order 1998* was one result. His personal involvement was emphasised by one official: 'there was no indication that we were going along this route with the previous Director'. Neither did he have to send out instructions to develop the contracting-out policy. There was no memorandum or other edict ordering the whole process. Once it was made clear that this is how Bareau wanted to develop the agency, his colleagues developed the specific measures required. 'Mr Bareau got the idea and the general idea ripples down. People in different parts have to look at how it would work for their patch . . .'.

A further example of the initiation of SIs as an official response to a green light given by government comes from the area of social security fraud. *The Social Security Administration (Fraud) Act 1997 (Commencement No. 6) Order 1998* brings into effect the obligation of postal services not to forward Housing Benefit cheques as the forwarding service had been widely used illegally to claim benefit. 'The whole thing started life five years before' one official explained. Local authorities were aware of the problem and had tried to get a voluntary agreement with Royal Mail to prevent envelopes containing benefits from being forwarded. Officials realised they would need primary legislation, but also believed they were unlikely to have a Bill of their own in the near future.

> But when the last Conservative government, towards the end of its time, said it was going to introduce a new Fraud Act, we saw an opportunity. The Minister's private office sends out a minute canvassing different policy branches to put forward ideas for inclusion in the Bill. This was all done extremely quickly—in days—there was not much time. We asked for redirecting to be brought into it.

The plans for a ban on redirection were already a significant priority within the branch, and were brought out when it was clear that the government intended to legislate. The SI was a (rather complex, in the event) commencement of the primary legislation—see Chapter 6.

Courts are a significant impetus to legislation. SIs produced following the actual loss of a court case, or in the wake of directly threatened or initiated legal action cannot be classed as 'internal' in origin (see 'external sources' below). However *perceptions* of the possibility of losing in court were also an important stimulus. The pamphlet 'Judge Over your Shoulder', published by the Cabinet Office although prepared by the Treasury Solicitor's Department, appeared in 1987 and again in a revised form in 1995. It aimed to 'give administrators at all levels an introduction to the basic principles of law and judicial review' (Cabinet Office 1995: inside back cover). In particular, it sought to make officials sensitive to the legal dimension of their activities, and to the increasing likelihood that departments will have to 'defend their decisions in the Courts' (Cabinet Office 1995: 3). Few civil servants interviewed for this research were familiar with the pamphlet. However, in developing SIs civil servants frequently sought to act as if the judge were there by their side, even in initiating legislation. For instance, when, according to one official, the law relating to VAT 'was challenged in the EC, and the court was coming out in favour of saying that long-established VAT law was deficient. There was a danger you would have claims going back to 1973' and that could cost lots of money. This prompted a change in VAT law and, given that it was a shaggy dog story, eventually produced changes in the law governing aircraft operators tax in *The Aircraft Operators (Accounts and Records) (Amendment) Regulations 1998*.

External sources (eight cases)

An external impetus is one that comes from outside a civil service department or an agency and is not directly related to a change in European law. The sources can be many and varied. German customs authorities were the immediate impetus behind *The Excise Duty Point (External and Internal Community Transit Procedure) (Amendment) Regulations 1998* since they had started legal proceedings against an alleged fraudulent use of the Community Transit Scheme. After the German authorities had highlighted an apparent loophole in the law, DTI officials involved, according to one of them:

> drew it to the attention of the National Audit Office . . . They had already looked at this and given it a clean bill of health. When they came to visit us here I told them all about it . . . that we had not adequately implemented the directive.

The external impetus might be direct loss of a court case or the initiation of proceedings against the government. The workboats SI is classed as of internal origin, but it arose in part because, as one official put it:

> we lost a legal case, because the international . . . convention says that the vessels we exempted [under domestic legislation passed in 1968] were not exempted in the international convention. This found a loophole in the law, so we looked for a new code of practice.

Chance also played a part in the inclusion of one particular clause of *The Dual-Use and Related Goods (Export Control) (Amendment) Regulations 1998* since it remedied a very minor drafting error in an earlier regulation. As an official explained:

> We put out point 4 of the regulations as a consequence of a mistake. When we made the previous amendment, we had a late insertion [which referred to a provision that had already been revoked] . . . Butterworths law publishers pointed it out to me—it would have been something that made absolutely no difference. It would have caused puzzlement, that's all. After Butterworths phoned, I told [the administrator] that in the next amendments I would put things right. It was of no interest to anyone.

Contact with the sharp end of service provision is another source of legislation. With *The Mental Health Act (Hospital Guardianship and Consent to*

Treatment) Amendment Regulations 1997 a whole series of forms was issued under the primary legislation but:

> we missed one . . . we only discovered relatively late that the form was missing. X [in the Department of Health] phoned and told me the form was lacking—I looked and found that it was *missing*! There were a number of calls to the Department about this: 'I have someone who has returned from going AWOL. What do I do?' . . . When I looked at the Act I saw there was supposed to be a prescribed form, and when we looked further we found there was no such form.

In addition the professional administrators' organisation also got in touch. 'We heard from the Association of Mental Health Act Administrators . . . They also said there were general problems with the [39 forms we had already issued]'. Similarly, the original impetus behind *The Education (Amount to Follow Permanently Excluded Pupil) Regulations 1997* was a telephone query to the DfEE asking for guidance on interpretation of the 1994 regulations.

The original *The Wireless Telegraphy (Control of Interference from Video-senders) Order 1997* came in part in response to outside pressures. Videosenders (devices which are designed to allow televisions in one room to receive without wires images transmitted by a video player in another) were causing problems mainly by interfering with other frequencies, notably police radio frequencies:

> It was not that there was a huge pressure for prohibition. There were complaints to local offices, the odd letter sent to us here [in London], maybe a letter sent to an MP. The real driver here was people viewing TV. But we only needed one police officer to be put in trouble by failing to get a message through and we would have had to say why we did not use our powers to ban them.

The fact that the 1997 Order might not conform to European law—the point corrected in the 1998 Order—came from the parliamentary Joint Committee on Statutory Instruments (JCSI); Speaker's Counsel advising the JCSI picked the point up and this was reported to both Houses of Parliament by the Joint Committee (JCSI 1997: para. 6 and Appendix V). As a civil servant involved put it, '[w]e made a mistake here, but rectified it quickly. There was six months when there was not good law. But the likelihood of anyone being affected was very low.'

In one case (*The Local Authorities (Transport Charges) Regulations 1998*) local authority association pressure revived the process of reviewing the areas for which local authorities were allowed to make charges for services, although this SI was not unambiguously a local authority association initiative as it started life under the Conservatives as a way of increasing local revenue other than through taxation. However, in two of the 46 cases the SIs resulted from the direct approach by an outside group.

Perhaps the clearest and most important case of outside group impetus came with the Channel 4 Order. The case shows the difficulty for non-government bodies getting significant items on the political agenda, even a body led by someone as politically connected and skilled as Michael Grade, then Chief Executive of Channel 4, and is worth developing in some detail here.

The central question in this order was the levy that Channel 4 paid to the ITV companies (see p. 57 above). According to the 'safety net' provisions set up under the 1990 Broadcasting Act, the independent television companies would support Channel 4 if its advertising revenues were small (i.e. below 14 per cent of the total for terrestrial television). The same formula gave the independent television companies a share of Channel 4 profits if it was successful. Channel 4 was far more successful than had been predicted and was paying large sums of money—£88 million in 1997—to the independent television companies. As Michael Grade saw it:

> You had a public service broadcaster giving vast chunks of its revenue to fat cat ITV companies. Only the crackpots in the Home Office could have thought of something like that . . . The ITV companies' lobby machine was very strong . . . We knew when we heard Douglas Hurd's announcement of the formula in June 1989 that we had to do something. There was no consultation with us. It was an IBA stitch up with the Home Office and the Treasury . . . They got the formula wrong. The downside for them [ITV companies] was capped, but not the upside. We failed to get on the inside track on this one. Probably they knew they were stitching us up, that's why we were kept out of the loop.

Grade had been arguing against the formula all along; as he wrote in his autobiography, 'getting rid of this funding formula and staving off further attempts to privatize Channel 4 were to occupy me until I left the television industry' (Grade 1999: 313). In 1993 he started a 'relentless and aggressive campaign' which consisted largely of using every possible opportunity to air Channel 4's grievance at every meeting with government ministers and with every appearance on television.

The campaign start in 1993 was deliberate. Grade knew that to abolish the levy would probably require primary legislation, and knew further that he was unlikely to get a parliamentary bill just for the purpose. It was widely anticipated that the government would put forward a new Broadcasting Bill in 1994 to regulate for new broadcasting technologies, above all digital transmission. He saw his chance to get the Channel 4 levy dealt with in this legislation, but it was delayed and the campaign was 'left dangling in the wind'. Grade sought to keep the momentum going which he describes as:

> hard. You could not list a set of downsides if the government did not give us what we wanted. I have learned that politicians need a downside—people dying on trolleys in hospital—to get them to change anything. You need a downside or there is no change. Somehow I managed to keep it going. Every lunch, every meeting I addressed I'd make the point that money was being taken out of programming and shoved into the pockets of the ITV shareholders.

The campaign reached a low point in 1995 when Stephen Dorrell, the Conservative Heritage Secretary, said that the government would not table any legislation ending the formula and that it would be 'wrong' to do so ('Channel 4 loses battle on funding formula', the *Financial Times*, 19 January 1995). The campaign gained support through 1995, including the support of the parliamentary National Heritage Committee and the Independent Television Commission.

Although the campaign had gained support within the Conservative government by the time the delayed Broadcasting Bill came along in 1996 (notably Virginia Bottomley, the Heritage Secretary, was now in favour of diminishing the levy), the government had not made a clear commitment to remove the levy, but announced that it was planning to review it. To this effect the Conservative government included a clause in the Bill (which became the 1996 Broadcasting Act) to allow the size of the levy to be reduced by Statutory Instrument. In debate in the Lords the Lord Inglewood, speaking for the government, indicated that the levy would be reduced in 1998 and set at zero in 1999 (see also *Financial Times*, 3 March 1996).

There was a curious twist in the plot here. An invitation to the Labour Party Conference in 1995 was another breakthrough in the Channel 4 campaign. Grade and the Channel 4 delegation were given assurances that Labour would support Channel 4 in a vote on the issue in the upcoming Broadcasting Bill. But a change in the Labour opposition team meant that, surprisingly, Labour made the issue a free vote in the Lords where the Bill was introduced, as Michael Grade put it:

> to our horror. We thought we would win in the Lords, we lost the vote. Labour went back on its promise to support us. Virginia [Bottomley, the Conservative Heritage Secretary] was concerned about losing, and we lost the vote on the amendment. Virginia was worried as she was in the MPs Gallery in the Lords. We were shattered that it was a free vote.

The apparent shift in Labour's position was expressed when Jack Cunningham, the Party's Heritage spokesman, argued in the House of Commons that 'the formula should not just be ended, giving a blank cheque . . . to Channel 4' (HC Debates, 16 April 1996, vol 275, col 558). The *debacle* reached the senior levels of the Labour Party who were most apologetic and promised to set things right, and changed their stance when the relevant clause was restored in the legislation in the Commons.

The setting right extended through to the 1997 election campaign, when the Labour Party made some strong noises that it would end the levy. After the election, as a civil servant put it, 'in true civil service fashion we prepared briefs and the brief on Channel 4 was "how do you want to play this?". Chris Smith, the Culture Secretary, started the process of ending the levy on 30 May in a letter to the Channel Three companies telling them the formula was no longer sustainable. All that needed to be decided was how the levy was to be phased out. *The Channel 4 (Application of Excess Revenues) Order 1997* was the first order reducing the levy which was phased out entirely by *The Channel 4 (Application of Excess Revenues) Order 1998*, and the final payment of £66 million was paid in 1999 (see the *Daily Telegraph*, 12 February 1999).

Reflecting on the success of the campaign resulting in the orders, Michael Grade acknowledges his own strong position:

> For something like this you have to be on the inside track. I had lots of experience. I cut my teeth opposing the privatization of Channel 4. Once under Thatcher and twice under Major . . . I was in a prominent position and had wonderful access.

However, the task was difficult in part because the target of the campaign was the 'Heritage Department and ultimately the Treasury', and because 'ITV had powerful friends in both parties'. In addition, the nature of the issue created further difficulties. As Grade said, it was 'a dry old formula and you have to do a lot to get people interested in the case'. To overcome the problems, Grade owned up to having 'a loud mouth and I know how to run a campaign'. In the end he put its ultimate success down to the fact that 'we shamed them into it. The robber barons at the ITV were taking our money.'

This is the only external SI, indeed the only one of the 46 in the sample, where an outside interest has had to lobby hard to get an SI, admittedly made more complicated by the fact that the primary legislation had to be created as well. The combination of skill, access and tactical vision needed to bring the Channel 4 Order into being makes it clear why this is the only one in the sample, as few other individuals and organisations would possess them.

There is a second case of outside group suggestion which was less spectacular in its effects: *The Enforcement of Road Traffic Debts (Certificated Bailiffs) (Amendment) Regulations 1998.* Here the group had less success and its lobbying role did not extend beyond raising the initial suggestion that its grievance needed to be looked at. Nevertheless, it underlines the difficulty of groups placing items on the delegated legislative agenda and how, like the Channel 4 Order, once it is there, the outcome is not a foregone conclusion. On the face of it the regulations look quite straightforward. They simply increase four sets of fees that certificated bailiffs may charge to recover debts incurred through fines for road traffic offences: the SI consists of four lines ('for £20.00 substitute £25.00; for 20% substitute 25%; for £4.50 substitute £5.00; and for 45p substitute 50p'). It originated in a letter from the Association of Civil Enforcement Agencies (ACEA) to the new Lord Chancellor, Lord Irvine of Lairg, shortly after the General Election in 1997. ACEA wanted to raise the fee its members could charge for sending an initial letter to the debtor from £10 to £25 to cover the administrative costs incurred if the debt was not paid off in response to the letter. The Lord Chancellor passed it on to the County Court Policy Branch and asked if this could be looked into. At first the Branch replied why this had not been done in the past—ACEA had asked for the rise under the last Conservative government. The reason the Branch gave for not taking any action remained that it could not because it could not spare the time or the personnel to look into it. The Lord Chancellor wrote to ACEA to this effect. ACEA persisted, the Lord Chancellor asked again, and County Court Policy Branch eventually found a space.

At this stage what the officials were being asked to do by the Lord Chancellor was to look into whether there was any reason for the Department to raise these charges. They looked at equivalent charges (including those made under DETR legislation in the same area) and broadly concluded that the specific charge ACEA wanted raising for sending out a letter was unjustified. The reasoning was that the letter was specified as a legal requirement for this particular debt enforcement and its fee was not an administration charge. Raising the charge along the lines suggested by ACEA would make the letter fee a general administration charge, and those who paid up promptly on receipt of the letter would be subsidising the tardy, since all the administrative costs ACEA had put forward as evidence were incurred after the letter was sent out. Moreover, since many certificated bailiffs were working under contract schemes, there was some suspicion that the letter fee increase was intended to ease the financial squeeze that some bailiffs had put themselves in through their competitive pricing strategies. However, the officials recommended that some of the other charges could reasonably be raised. The Department put this in a very brief consultation document which was sent out to 1,500 recipients. 'Under 20' replies came back, and the resulting SI gave the bailiffs an increase in charges, but not an increase in the specific charge they wanted in the first place.

Programmed in primary legislation (five cases)

Some clauses of primary legislation are never implemented, some are implemented years after they are passed, but the category of regulations 'programmed' in secondary legislation covers SIs that directly follow from the primary legislation. Indeed, the secondary legislation can in a sense come before the primary legislation. *The Broadcasting (Percentage of National Radio Multiplex Revenue) Order 1998* brought into effect the arrangements for licensing digital radio stations already set out in the 1996 Broadcasting Act. The details of this SI, setting the percentage of radio station turnover to be paid to the Treasury at zero per cent, had already been worked out before the 1996 Act was passed and the timing of this SI was determined by the timetable for licensing by the Radio Authority set in train by the 1996 Act. Other secondary legislation programmed in primary legislation can, however, involve somewhat greater scope for discretion (see, for example, the discussion of *The Crime (Sentences) Act 1997 (Commencement No. 2 and Transitional Provisions) Order 1997)*.

For major items of legislation it is common for the officials responsible for the primary legislation to take responsibility for the implementing secondary legislation. This can be handled in different ways, depending upon the breadth and complexity of the primary legislation. One official I interviewed had a corner of his white board in his office filled with a list of all the secondary legislation, some of it crossed off, required to give effect to one piece of legislation and dates by when it had to be prepared. He pointed to it and said:

> Around the time of the 1995 Act I put up a list of all SIs that would be needed. There are lots of sections of the Act where you need commencement legislation. There are also orders we have to do, but these are not SIs.

Another official interviewed kept the tally on a written list in his drawer. In another case, where it was unclear which of the provisions of the parent legislation would be brought into effect, especially after the Conservative administration that had passed it fell from office, the timetable for implementation had to be devised afresh. After the election an administrative official had to start the ball rolling again; 'I wrote a note to the Home Secretary on 30 May 1997 saying that he needed to decide which bits of the Act are to be brought into force and when'.

Bill teams—groups of officials responsible for handling primary legislation—also frequently handle subsequent delegated legislation. In the Home Office a project team was responsible for implementing the 1997 Police Act; the team working on the primary legislation, the Police Bill Unit, became the team responsible for implementing it as the National Crime Services Unit. The team was responsible for the secondary legislation, including *The National Crime Squad Service Authority (Levying) Order 1997*. This particular order set out the arrangements for local police forces' contribution to the finances of the National Crime Squad—essentially through the same levy arrangements that had been used to finance the Regional Crime Squads. The implementation arrangements for this Act were quite elaborate, including a steering group with representatives from police forces on it.

Teams can make sure that different parts of the legislation can be implemented in the correct order or at the right time. The Treasury team handling the Bank of England Bill 1998 (consisting of four officials plus a team leader at grade 7) recognised that the SI requiring banks and building societies to supply the Bank with the information it needed to carry out its monetary policy responsibilities (*The Bank of England (Information Powers) Order 1998*) had to come into force at the same time as the Bank of England Act since 'the Bill contained the need to provide information. We had to be thinking about the SI at the same time as the Bill . . . the SI was always understood as part of the Bill process'.

Europe (four cases)

Membership of the European Union can become an impetus to legislation through a variety of channels. In some cases the legislation arises from obligations from EU membership, but the stimulus is not directly European. For example, we have already observed that *The Cod (Specified Sea Areas) (Prohibition of Fishing) Order 1998* was not stimulated by a specific EU action but from the routine domestic implementation of an EU-related regime. Europe is here classed as a direct stimulus to legislate only where there is a direct causal relationship between a specific EU law and an SI.[10]

In the formal implementation or putting into effect of European legislation, departments are generally primed for issuing regulations while the European legislation is being considered in Brussels. With *The Telecommunications (Interconnection) Regulations 1997* domestic consultation with the industry started as soon as the DTI received the Commission proposals in late 1995. The same official involved in negotiating the EU directive was also involved in the domestic implementation, although another official from the same department took the lead in handling the SI—giving instructions and setting the domestic consultations in train. This appears to be common practice when it is a matter of direct implementation of EU directives or regulations. With *The Apple and Pear Orchard Grubbing Up Regulations 1998* the administrator concerned with the regulations dealt with the issue as part of a wider programme of reform. He:

> went to Brussels for the Council regulations. The negotiations were fairly tough as part of the whole régime—not only apple and pear orchard grubbing up, but the whole fruit and vegetable bit of the Common Agricultural Policy was being renegotiated. So this was part of a total deal.

The immediate impetus to change domestic legislation came, in this case and in others, from the officials involved in the European and international negotiations.

One exception to this principle of the officials responsible for implementing the legislation also negotiating it in Brussels was *The Environmental Protection (Prescribed Processes and Substances) (Amendment) (Hazardous Waste Incineration) Regulations 1998*. Here there was no involvement of the implementing team in the directive. The directive was not implemented immediately. As one official, asked to explain the timing of the SI, put it:

> The whole thing was sitting on my desk and I was getting more and more anxious about it. There were pressures within the Department to avoid infraction procedures and to be green . . . After the election—oh, hang on, we *did* get the start of some infraction procedure. That must have been the impetus.

In this case Europe was an impetus to legislate, but it was an impending court case rather than the arrival of the European directive alone that produced movement. *The Action Programme for Nitrate Vulnerable Zones (Scotland) Regulations 1998* were similarly nudged into existence through the initiation of infraction proceedings.

---

[10] While 6 of the 46 SIs were earlier classed as originating in Europe (see p. 61 above), only 4 were stimulated directly by European legislation. *The Cod (Specified Sea Areas) (Prohibition of Fishing) Order 1998* resulted indirectly from EU legislation—the immediate impetus to legislate was the process of monitoring fish catches, classified as an 'internal' impetus. *The Excise Duty Point (External and Internal Community Transit Procedure) (Amendment) Regulations 1998* resulted from the discovery by an external source of a loophole in existing provisions in UK law implementing EU legislation.

Committees as originators (four cases)

Consultative committees originated four of the SIs examined in detail here. In some cases these were regular updatings of financial and administrative arrangements. The regular review of the levy on employers in construction determined by the Industrial Training Levy Board produced *The Industrial Training Levy (Construction Board) Order 1997*. The United Kingdom Central Council for Nursing, Midwifery and Health Visiting (UKCC) was the source of *The Nurses, Midwives and Health Visitors (Supervisors of Midwives) Amendment Rules Approval Order 1997* which sets out the qualifications required by supervisors of midwives—with specified qualifications and experience. *The National Health Service (Optical Charges and Payments) Amendment Regulations 1997*, while not the product of a formal committee, are a result of a set of negotiations between opticians optometrists and the Department of Health handled as one official put it, 'in the same way that we negotiate other items for service . . . a bit like a pay negotiation, but they are private practitioners'.

Not all committee initiatives are as routine as these cases. *The Fire Services (Appointments and Promotion) (Amendment) Regulations 1997* were a formal recommendation of the Central Fire Brigades Advisory Council on height and eyesight requirements for firefighters. Yet more accurately they developed from a protracted debate within the fire service and between the fire service and the Home Office, in which Home Office officials, the Fire Brigades Union and some fire brigades took a leading role in pushing forward proposals to allow more women to enter the fire service. Those supporting the change, including the Fire Brigades Union and Home Office officials, used a variety of tactics to persuade a very reluctant Central Fire Brigades Advisory Council to accept change. The opposition to scrapping the height requirements, according to one participant, was led by the Chief and Assistant Chief Fire Officers Association (and the Home Office Minister, according to one observer, 'stood by them' until this position became untenable). Eventually (see Chapter 5) those in favour of change outflanked those opposed to change. Central in undermining opposition was a programme of Home Office research into the impact of physical characteristics (eyesight and height among others) on the aptitude and effectiveness of firefighters. This research found that height had no effect on firefighting ability and exposed the maintenance of height requirements, the most controversial of the SI's measures, as serving no other purpose than maintaining sex discrimination.

CONCLUSIONS

Has this examination of the character of SIs got us any further than the enumeration of a few examples to show that 'some' are politically significant? After all, we have not as yet solved the problem of how one measures political significance, still less offered any categorisation of the political importance of the 46

SIs looked at in detail—even on an impressionistic basis. The chapter has, however, outlined the types of activity handled by Statutory Instrument and set out the issues involved in greater detail and relief than is possible by poring over law books and press cuttings. No attempt was made in selecting the 46 to identify topical or otherwise meaty legislation. If anything, the selection criteria had the reverse effect. Statutory Instruments which were obviously sensitive or controversial were avoided on the ground that it would be unreasonable to expect civil servants to talk openly about them. Thus while they are not a random sample of all SIs, not least because local and roads SIs were excluded, they offer as good an impression as one is likely to get of the actual political issues involved in delegated legislation.

A large number of SIs are carrying through decisions taken elsewhere. In this chapter we have seen examples of SIs implementing primary legislation without much discretion, bringing the logical consequences of changes in one policy area to bear on another, or tidying up UK law to get rid of features made clumsy by changes in European law. However, a large proportion of the SIs involve significant discretion in important areas: freeing Channel 4 from a huge financial burden, cutting social security benefit entitlements, introducing no-win-no-fee financing of civil litigation. What is possible under an SI is defined most of all by what the parent primary legislation allows, and primary legislation can allow broad latitude to politicians and administrators on key policy issues. The degree of latitude or the importance of the issue cannot be assessed by looking at the legislation alone.

The source of delegated legislation is primarily internal. While the stimulus may come from people in the field, from Europe, from perusal of court cases or interpretations of ministers' views and objectives, civil service perception that something needs to be done is a *sine qua non* of most delegated legislation. In the two cases where the legislation was proposed by external interests, the process of producing legislation was circuitous and difficult when viewed from the perspective of those outside interests proposing the legislation. What is the role of the minister in all this? This chapter has already established that ministers play a significant role in the initiation of delegated legislation since officials tend to anticipate their reactions and may propose legislation they feel furthers the minister's policy aims. However, the role of the minister in the delegated legislative process is not limited to initiation. The next chapter will show that ministers play an important part in the development of legislation.

5

Ministers on Top

Whatever the type of SI, and whatever its origins, it has to be approved by a minister. Powers to make regulations by SI are generally powers vested in a minister. At a minimum the minister has to sign most regulations. In cases where they are not signatories (as in the Customs and Excise regulations in our sample of 46), ministers are consulted as if they were. In most cases ministers will have been contacted in some form about the regulation long before it arrives for signature along with an explanatory submission outlining the background, history and content of the proposed regulation. Ideas for SIs cannot be generally worked up into fully fledged proposals on which the department can consult with outside interests if a minister does not support it. Once an idea for an SI has emerged within the Department, a minister is consulted, usually by memorandum, setting out the intention to legislate in the area as well as the range of issues on which consultation is likely to take place.

The purpose of this chapter is to outline the ministerial role in developing SIs. Regulations are issued in the minister's name, but what influence do ministers *really* have? Do they automatically sign what they are passed by their officials or do they actually shape what is done in their name? The first part of this chapter outlines the importance of referring proposals to ministers, and the second goes on to point out how, in the large majority of cases, approval is given by a minister outside the Cabinet (hereafter termed 'junior' ministers, although many may not consider themselves junior). The chapter then goes on to look at the nature of ministerial involvement in the process. Since ministers have some impact on the way in which SIs are developed, we may further expect at least some SIs to reflect party political preferences of the governing administration. The degree to which party policies shape delegated legislation and the way in which parties influence the apparently technical world of regulation are then explored.

WHAT GETS REFERRED TO MINISTERS AND WHEN

Once it has been established that any proposed change in the law through secondary legislation is going to be required, political approval for legislation may be sought. Wherever there is doubt that secondary legislation is needed, the matter may be settled following consultation with departmental lawyers and, in rare complex cases, further legal advice from Parliamentary Counsel. In part officials understand the need for political approval as a matter of maintaining the coherence of government. If preparations are being made to change the law, the minister responsible should know about it. This becomes even more pressing if the matter is likely to involve substantial consultation with outside interests, increasing the chances that the minister will be approached about the issue, especially if it is likely to raise controversy. As a Home Office civil servant put it, 'the worst thing that can happen for a minister is to hear questions about something being consulted on and about which he knows nothing. It looks very bad for us too'. It is possible to consult on the principle of the legislation *within* government (and that includes advisory committees and other bodies which do not publicise their discussions) before going to a minister, but the convention is, with some exceptions, that ministers are informed before the SI is developed.

Proposals for SIs need not necessarily be shown to ministers where the matter they deal with is routine or where the principle underlying the legislation has already been approved. The Department of Health (1995: 8) advises its officials drawing up delegated legislation:

> If no extension of policy is involved, a minister need not normally be consulted at this [initial] stage unless there is to be a formal consultation process, but ministerial approval will be needed later to the making of the instrument.

In eight of the 46 cases, officials interviewed reported that no early ministerial approval was sought to develop the SI.[1] In the case of *The Contracting Out (Functions Relating to National Savings) Order 1998*, the principle of contracting out National Savings services, to which the SI gives effect, was established through informal meetings between the Director of National Savings and the Treasury ministerial team. However, specific approval for the SI was not sought in the early stages of its development:

> The minister was not contacted on [what precisely was to be contracted out] until much further down the line. Peter Bareau [the Director] floated the idea soon after he was appointed and it is at this level that it would have been put to the Minister. He meets the Minister rather a lot. By the time we got to the question of which functions to keep and which to let go, it was all pretty much settled.

Similarly, SIs which have been effectively heralded in primary legislation also may not need approval. One official in Customs and Excise stated 'no permission was sought' for *The Aircraft Operators (Accounts and Records) (Amendment) Regulations 1998* since 'the primary legislation provides the approval. They lay it all out and the regulations do the fine details'.

On European legislation, officials are likely to see ministerial approval as something of a formality:

> We get a decision from ministers *eventually*. This government is all very keen on management, but it is no good at it. [Sending it for approval] is very much notification—

---

[1] It is quite possible that this is an underestimate of the number for which no early ministerial approval was sought.

they won't read the whole thing. The reality in this case was the fact that this was a [European] Community obligation, so even if the minister was unhappy it would have gone through.

In the case of limited technical changes brought about by European legislation, the minister may not even see anything to do with the SI before it is ready for signature. And in one case where an issue (not European) was so well known, the official felt initial ministerial approval unnecessary:

> X would have been aware this was coming up—she was opposition shadow minister at the time the primary legislation was being passed and I am sure she would have been familiar with what it is about.

One of the three Scottish Office SIs was not seen by the relevant minister because Scotland was implementing a UK-wide policy with no specific policy input from the Scottish Office:

> We did not have any ministerial clearance to do this. The first thing he would have known about it is when he gets a copy with the PS minute [i.e. when it is ready for signing]. Generally it is taken as a given. It is assumed that he has given consent to a whole package of mechanisms [developed on a UK wide basis].

In this case the different statutory frameworks in Scotland and England meant that the Scottish legislation was somewhat simpler and could be brought into effect rapidly—before the English legislation.[2]

At the other extreme, some SIs involve such sensitive issues that political approval has to be sought at a higher level than the relevant minister. *The Crime (Sentences) Act 1997 (Commencement No. 2 and Transitional Provisions) Order 1997* required highest level political clearance as it dealt with (among other things) issues of sentencing which were politically sensitive and which also had important resource implications through its potential substantially to increase the prison population. For the sensitive portions:

> the Home Secretary had to get collective agreement . . . In order to bring them into force you need agreement from the relevant Cabinet Committee. The Home Secretary set out what he planned to do and when—this must have been a month or so after the May 1997 election—and it was all fine. This took a week or so to gel.[3]

Some SIs originate in decisions taken at senior ministerial level, such as at the level of the Prime Minister and the Chancellor of the Exchequer, and thus political approval is granted in advance. When the DSS sought to make changes to Jobseeker's Allowance under *The Jobseeker's Allowance (Amendment) Regulations 1998*, it did so because 'the Treasury was holding departments to

---

[2] Although writing the Scottish SI before the English can be risky. One official remembered '[t]his is not the first time we have done the regulations before the English, and once or twice the English minister has not signed it, and we looked pretty silly'.

[3] One of the controversial features of the 1997 Act, which the then Labour opposition argued against, was the proposal for a mandatory minimum of three years in jail for a third burglary offence. This part also was likely to produce a large increase in the prison population.

stick to the targets' on spending inherited by the new Labour government. Their revocation required prime ministerial approval.

How do officials know that an issue requires political approval, and at what level? While this may appear a difficult question, in practice none of the officials I spoke to had any problem in identifying which SIs, or which parts of SIs, needed to be put before a minister. Neither was there any doubt about the type of issue that needed to be raised at Cabinet minister rather than junior minister level. When asked about whom one contacted, a Home Office official replied:

> It depends on the SI. There was never any doubt that this one [on the sensitive issue of sentencing] was for the Home Secretary. But you would not want to bother the Home Secretary about an SI which designates the responsible officer for [this or that] in different towns in England and Wales. Somewhere there might be guidelines about what goes to the Home Secretary, but usually it is pretty obvious.

In one case political responsibility shifted between Cabinet and junior minister as the first approval was made by the Cabinet minister who subsequently appointed a minister of state who was then assigned responsibility for relevant area. When the minister of state was replaced by a parliamentary secretary, responsibility reverted once again to the Cabinet minister, who eventually signed the SI.

Where it happens, initial contact with a minister is usually relatively informal. In contrast to a formal submission to a minister for signing, initial contact is simply a matter of informing; 'approval' at an early stage may be fairly cursory. With *The Broadcasting (Percentage of National Radio Multiplex Revenue) Order 1998* an administrator explained, when asked if ministerial approval had been sought at an early stage:

> I can't remember. I don't think I sought permission to get it drafted. [*Respondent thinks.*] I must have asked if he was happy for the level to be set at 0%. I'll go and get the file. [*He leafs in file.*] It was such a minor SI that I bunged all the material on this in with another one. We put a lot of things in one shopping list submission. This was sent to the Secretary of State on August 19 in a submission on Digital Audio Broadcasting telling him all the powers he had in terms of granting and modifying licenses. This particular order was dealt with in two small paragraphs on this submission. We said 'you may specify the turnover payments at 0%. This was the stated policy of the last government. We seek your permission to draft an order.'

Similarly with a largely consequential regulation needed to tidy up the law following an EU regulation on dual-use goods:

> There was a very short submission to the minister which was little more than 'here is the latest batch of amendments'. Because the minister was . . . a lawyer and former commissioner, he needed no explanation. He knew right away what this was about.

While the evidence for changing patterns of ministerial involvement over time is sparse, two respondents volunteered the suggestion that civil servants were increasingly likely to consult ministers. For example, one from Customs and Excise argued that:

until ten years ago we exercised the powers and told the ministers afterwards. If the matter was controversial we'd tell them before. Now the Commissioners [of Customs and Excise] do not exercise power without, in effect, getting ministerial approval.

Another official saw an increasing politicisation of the delegated legislative process in a different way. According to her, officials were becoming increasingly likely to take the political perspective of ministers into account in the process of delegated legislation:

The officials will not have gone to ministers, especially not under the Labour government, without intelligence about what the world is likely to think. Presentational issues have to be put up front along with financial and other issues. Nowadays officials do not wander into things naively thinking 'this will be alright . . .'.

These comments tended to suggest that any greater political involvement was not simply a feature of the new Labour government, but a longer-term trend.

DELEGATED LEGISLATION: THE DOMAIN OF THE JUNIOR MINISTER

For most purposes ministerial approval is generally sought not from the Cabinet minister responsible for the ministry, but from a junior minister. Junior ministers feel themselves to be in charge of SIs, where the Cabinet minister concerned has delegated responsibility among his or her team. One former junior minister argued, 'I got absolutely free rein in my area to deal with SIs'. To illustrate the importance of the junior minister in the delegated legislative process, Table 5.1 presents data from the year from May 1997 to May 1998 on SIs signed by Cabinet ministers and junior ministers. Signing is a formal recognition that the delegated legislation is being passed in the name of the relevant Secretary of State. Table 5.1 does not include the many SIs not signed by any kind of minister, such as many of the roads SIs and those from Customs and Excise.

One junior minister interviewed said that he was 'the Department's signer'. He went on to dismiss as:

a myth the idea that the Secretary of State is responsible for all that goes through the Department. There is a wide-ranging set of decisions delegated to the minister of state.

Table 5.1 reinforces this argument by showing that Cabinet ministers are far less likely to sign SIs than junior ministers. In only five departments do Cabinet ministers sign more SIs than junior ministers. For two of them (International Development and the Office of the Chancellor of the Duchy of Lancaster) there were hardly any SIs at all (three and one respectively). The Northern Ireland Office SIs are exceptional since under the constitutional practice of direct rule since 1972, Statutory Instruments are *primary* legislation (drafted, usually, in the Home Office). Northern Ireland has its own separate series of secondary legislation, Statutory Rules and Orders, which is not included in this analysis. This leaves only the Department of Culture, Media and Sport where four-fifths of the

Table 5.1 Signatories to delegated legislation: May 1997 to May 1998

Department	Cabinet Ministers	Junior Ministers	% Cabinet Ministers
International Development	3	0	100
Chancellor Duchy of Lancaster	1	0	100
Lord Chancellor's Department	42	1	98
Culture, Media and Sport	19	5	79
Northern Ireland	26	9	74
Health	38	137	22
Home Office	22	104	18
Foreign and Commonwealth Office	1	5	17
Defence	1	6	14
Welsh Office	10	189	5
Scottish Office	9	198	4
Agriculture	5	115	4
Environment	5	260	2
Education and Employment	1	68	1
Trade and Industry	1	86	1
Social Security	0	63	0
Treasury	0	322	0
Total	184	1568	11

Source: JUSTIS CD Rom May 1998

handful of SIs were signed by Chris Smith, the Secretary of State, and the Lord Chancellor's Department where it is the practice of the Lord Chancellor himself to sign most SIs. Outside these exceptions, delegated legislation is predominantly the sphere of the junior minister.[4]

Cabinet ministers are not, however, bypassed in this process. They are generally 'copied in' to (i.e. a recipient of) correspondence between civil servants and junior ministers. One official showed me the submission to the junior minister asking whether he should develop his SI, pointing out:

> This regulation was copied in to all sorts of people—the whole ministerial team, the Permanent Secretary, special advisers and other senior officials. If the minister felt it was important, it could go to the Secretary of State. You can get a call at any time from the Secretary of State's Office [for you] to give information.

---

[4] It must be added that the degree to which a Cabinet minister becomes involved in delegated legislation is also likely to be a matter of personality. Examination of the incidence of Cabinet ministers signing delegated legislation in the early years of the preceding Major government suggests that some ministers, such as Michael Heseltine at Environment and Kenneth Baker at the Home Office, took responsibility for a much larger proportion of SIs than many of their colleagues, predecessors and successors. The variation in Cabinet ministers' involvement in delegated legislation is an open empirical question which cannot, unfortunately, be resolved here. Nevertheless, the general tendency for delegated legislation to be predominantly the preserve of the junior minister remains.

However, it is unusual for a junior minister to discuss an SI with a Secretary of State. One said:

> I would only discuss SIs with the Secretary of State in unusual circumstances—the scale of the Beef Bones Regulations.[5] In the normal run of things you don't discuss it . . . I have no recollection of any particular SI I discussed with the Secretary of State.

For the most part there is an extensive delegation which puts junior ministers in effective charge of the delegated legislative process in the large majority of cases.

An interesting illustration of the importance of a junior minister comes in a letter received from a former Cabinet minister under the Conservative government in response to a question about his role in shaping SIs. He wrote, comparing his experiences as a Secretary of State for one of the non-English departments with his tenure as a junior minister in major Whitehall departments:

> Whilst it was possible to remove items of secondary legislation or to reduce their incidence *when I was in direct control of the policy as a minister of state* in a large English regulatory department . . ., it was much more difficult trying to do it as a Cabinet member representing [a non-English part of the UK] (emphasis added).

Here he is pointing out that it is possible for a junior minister in a Whitehall department to have greater influence and discretion in shaping policy through the delegated legislative process than a Cabinet minister responsible for a non-English part of the UK.

THE NATURE OF MINISTERIAL INVOLVEMENT

What do ministers do in the delegated legislative process? One can expect that ministers, as politicians seeking publicity and approval for their policies and leadership skills, may find delegated legislation an unpromising area in which to develop a career. However, there is substantial evidence of clear ministerial involvement. Of course, the research design of this project does not allow one to assess the role of ministers fully. It is quite possible for ministers to kill a proposal for a Statutory Instrument at this early stage by indicating that they will not support it. Some officials interviewed referred to some episodes along these lines in rather vague terms. However, that ministers can effectively block SIs can be shown by the histories of two SIs that were held up by junior ministers but eventually reached the statute book.

The first SI in our sample blocked by a junior minister was *The Wireless Telegraphy (Control of Interference from Videosenders) Order 1998* which addressed the problem posed by videosenders interfering with broadcasting frequencies. These devices were used to beam pictures from a video player in one part of the house to a television in another, although there were other uses. The

---

[5] Referring to *The Beef Bone Regulations 1997*. See p. 149 below.

videosenders on the market were generally poorly constructed and scattered interference in a rather unpredictable way. There were numerous complaints to the Radiocommunications Agency. One episode, notorious within the DTI and the Agency, involved interference, some of it several streets away, from the house of a videosender owner using his machine to beam hardcore pornography to his bedroom on a Sunday night during a popular religious broadcast, *Songs of Praise*. For many people in the neighbourhood, the signal from the videosender carrying pornography drowned out the religious worship. Another notorious case involved a caravan park owner in a seaside holiday resort who tied his videosender to the top of a 30 foot pole to transmit his security camera pictures to his home. Helped by the location, the atmospheric conditions and the height of the transmitter, interference was scattered over a wide area and was picked up by the radio receivers of emergency services a long distance away.

Use of videosenders played havoc with the police broadcasting frequencies, adjacent to those used by videosenders, and police complaints led the DTI and the Radiocommunications Agency to think about restrictions on them. However, as a group representative pointed out, the proposal was not developed initially due to the opposition of a Conservative junior minister who did not want to impose new regulations and restrictions upon industry. After this minister had moved on, however, another Conservative junior minister indicated that he was in favour of legislation and allowed his officials to develop the regulations. The regulations were not finally passed until after the Labour election victory of 1997, but the work had started on them under the preceding Conservative administration.

A second case of junior ministerial reluctance to legislate came with *The Fire Services (Appointments and Promotion) (Amendment) Regulations 1997*. This was less a matter of a junior minister opposing legislation than aligning with those who opposed change. There had been pressure from the Equal Opportunities Commission, the Fire Brigade Union, some fire brigades as well as the Equal Opportunities Joint Committee of the Central Fire Brigades Advisory Council to remove the height and age limits on recruitment to the fire services (the SI also relaxed eyesight requirements, but these were less controversial) (see Howell 1994). A programme of research into the effects of height and age on firefighting ability, of which perhaps the most important for this SI was conducted at the Robens Institute, University of Surrey, concluded in 1994 that the limits in operation could be relaxed without any danger. Consequently, the issue was raised at the Fire Brigades Advisory Council, a statutory body which has to be consulted before changes in the regulations.

> The Fire Service saw themselves having 4ft 10in fragile women in their teams . . . You can see from the papers the sorts of thing the discussion covered. What you won't see, and you will have to read between the lines, that feelings ran *very* deep on this one

one observer from outside the Home Office commented. The most active opponents to change were, according to another participant, the Chief and Assistant

Chief Fire Officers Association. The junior minister, who chaired the Central Fire Brigades Advisory Council, sided with the Chief and Assistant Chief Fire Officers Association in supporting the *status quo.*

The circumstances under which the position of those lined up against change, including the junior minister, were forced to allow the legislation to be developed are themselves quite interesting. Gillian Maxwell, an unsuccessful woman applicant to the Northern Ireland Fire Service, who was below the 5ft 6in minimum height requirement, was beginning legal proceedings against the service on the grounds that the height requirement was discriminatory. The lawyers for the applicant wanted to use the Home Office research on height and firefighting for her case, and planned to call a Home Office official as an expert witness. The case did not come to an industrial tribunal as the Northern Ireland Brigade gave in. But the prospect of a Home Office official testifying that there was no factual basis for maintaining height requirements, that they were essentially discriminatory, as well as the recognition by the Northern Ireland Brigade that the limits were likely to be ruled unlawful, forced those who had wanted to retain the minimum height, including the junior minister, into accepting that the rules had to change. While the case was reported in Northern Ireland in the *Belfast Telegraph* (20 January 1997), it was given greatest prominence on the mainland by the *Daily Mail* (21 January 1997) under the headline 'The 5ft 3in mother who cut the fire services down to size'. Moreover the newspaper made clear the wider significance of the Gillian Maxwell case when it pointed out the implications of the case outside Northern Ireland: 'the Central Fire Brigades Advisory Council is expected to drop the height limits in England and Wales' (see also Home Office 1997). As one observer commented, 'once the Home Office legal people told them that you cannot win this under any circumstances' opposition to the changes disappeared and the regulation was drafted in February 1997.

Other episodes of ministerial reluctance related by officials interviewed referring to SIs not in the sample included one concerning a Secretary of State for Wales. Welsh Secretaries have to sign large numbers of SIs issued jointly with Whitehall departments (especially MAFF). These SIs are worked out in Whitehall (see Chapter 6), generally with no Welsh Office policy input. One Secretary of State had a reputation for making his own changes to the carefully-worded legal documents before he would sign them. This initially caused consternation as those around him struggled to determine the status and constitutional implications of what were regarded as rather homespun amendments, but after a while they were routinely ignored. Another revealing anecdote related to a minister who signed an EU-related regulation which required the regular inspection of electrical goods in the workplace. A few weeks later, when some electricians came to check his electric kettle, lamp and computer, it was the Eurosceptic pro-deregulation minister who blew a fuse, and told them to stop wasting time on petty makework tasks. When they told him there were European regulations requiring inspections, and his officials later reminded him that he had personally signed them, he was reputed to have 'got the hump and refused to sign anything for months after'. A third anecdote referred to a minister many years ago who refused to sign a set of regulations about mincemeat designed to oblige butchers to declare the contents of mincemeat. When the minister refused to sign it, the official explained, 'he said "this is what butchers do to get rid of their scraps. You can't do this, you will take away their livelihood. Anyway, mincemeat is for poor people, and they need it" '.

It is also possible, although exceptionally rare, to find ministers in conflict with each other about the desirability of a regulation. While not among the 46 in the sample, a good example of strong conflict between junior and senior ministers came in the dying months of the Conservative administration, in early 1997. A draft of *The Housing Benefit (General) Amendment Regulations 1997* was sent to the Social Security Advisory Committee in March 1996. It sought to reduce entitlements to Housing Benefit (by limiting rents subsidised for single people aged over 25 to those equivalent to the rent of a single room). This was vehemently opposed by benefit groups, and there was substantial opposition to it among junior ministers in the Department of the Environment as well as the Department of Social Security. One junior minister argued that he opposed it because:

> this was another department's war. It was a budgeting policy . . . something that we were pushed into. I could see it was dodgy. I could not see why we were doing it so close to the election, especially as it was unpopular and not going to come into effect until after the election and we could make the regulation in the event that we won, and if we lost, it would not be our problem . . . Another reason I dragged my feet was that I did not like Peter Lilley [Secretary of State for Social Security] very much . . . Social Security said we did not have a choice, they said we had to sign. The civil servants in DoE said that they did not like the SI either, but they said we had to sign too. I think they even enjoyed watching the whole thing as it unfolded—they were spectators. I realised I had no choice, but I made them fight for it by taking it up to the Prime Minister—and I thought we might even get away with it, as it was very close to the election. After all that, Labour came in and, although they opposed it at the time, continued with the same policy . . .

The SI was passed and was due to come into effect in October 1997, but revoked before it came into effect by the Labour government through *The Housing Benefit (General) Amendment (No. 3) Regulations 1997*.

Labour has reversed several of its own planned welfare savings—not only the famous cases of Lone Parent Benefit and Jobseeeker's Allowance but also planned savings on Council Tax Benefit and Housing Benefit. While backbench pressure was the most apparent cause of reversal in all these cases, one respondent from an interest group suggested that a junior minister who 'knew we were right and knew we were a solid organisation' helped by arguing against the changes from within. A different group actually 'blew the government out on this one, but not before we had got in there and opened things up' through the sympathetic minister.

While Cabinet ministers played a role in initiating several SIs, none of our 46 SIs started life directly as an initiative of a junior minister. As one representative from an interest group pointed out, this seems to suggest that:

> junior ministers are important because they can block things. In the DETR they are developing something now affecting small boat owners—a new code of practice. I hear that it went to [a junior minister who] blocked it because [of worries] about the impact it would have on jet-skiing.

She was here referring to a fear that jet skis would be caught up in some proposed regulations covering small workboats. Junior ministers can also make negative noises, but then stop short of blocking. An official involved in devising statutory forms for mental health workers pointed out how this reluctance to agree might be expressed:

> We had no trouble with this SI being signed off by the minister. With the other forms we had problems. He complained 'why do we need 39 forms?' There was pressure to reduce . . . red tape and all that. We had to explain to the minister that we were obliged by the legislation to produce the forms.

Or, in the case of an SI which was relaid to fulfil the requirements of European procedures:

> the . . . minister was not happy about it when he learned what was going on. He thought the whole thing about us having to re-lay the SI was senseless Euro-bureaucracy. But he approved it.

Whether approving or blocking, *civil servants* suggested that the junior minister's decision was final. If permission to develop an SI was refused, that was the end of the matter. You simply have to try persuasion or, if not, wait until a new junior minister comes along. To try to go over the head of a minister would be to create difficulties in the working relationship between the civil servants and the minister concerned. The *junior ministers* I spoke to suspected that the officials would take their complaints about 'awkward' junior ministers to the Cabinet minister via the Permanent Secretary as the most senior civil servant in the ministry. Both views can be squared to some extent by observing that while going over the head of a junior minister is possible, it is exceptionally rare. Morcover, on the few occasions it does happen it is likely to be done extremely discreetly by the civil servant concerned to avoid any unpleasantness. As one respondent said:

> When I was Permanent Secretary I sometimes had to tell a minister that a junior minister was getting out of line. It will be done just between the two of us. Nobody else in earshot, so nobody will know that this is how it has happened.

However, junior ministers are unlikely to let matters reach a head in this way. They are likely to know when they have to sign, even against their will. One former junior minister described three types of SI: the 'absolutely routine', those where they come to you for signature 'without you having played a part in the policy work' and those 'where you have lost the policy argument and you sign reluctantly'.

One official suggested that there was a trend for senior ministers to become more involved in the delegated legislative process under Labour:

> Junior ministers are very important. Now, under the new government there is a different dynamic. X [a recent Conservative junior minister] did things on his own. Now everything is copied to Prescott [the Labour Cabinet minister]. He has a voracious appetite for these things. There is an EU proposal on the crewing of ferries. The submissions were sent to the junior minister, who is not going to say 'no' to it. Everyone knows that it is Prescott's proposal, and that it is controversial, and even controversial within government. But he's the Deputy Prime Minister.

However, under the preceding Conservative government there is evidence of Cabinet ministerial involvement in details. In the early 1990s a Cabinet member proposed a wheeze to contribute towards the programme of deregulation by reducing the number of regulations in effect. According to one official this was a case of letting:

> numbers rule rather than common sense . . . [the Cabinet minister] wanted to get a number of deregulations in place. He suggested we deregulate and remake the regulations, revoke them and reintroduce them. We would set up a 'puppet' SI . . . and then remove it.

He continued:

> This was dropped because it was nonsense. [My superior] said he would not confront the minister and say it was nonsense. But it came back to us later on that they decided not to go through with it. The election was pressing then and the minister had other fish to fry.

Yet ministerial involvement, junior and senior, in the development of an SI is not invariably confined to initiating, approving or blocking. In part civil servants expect ministers to play a part in the parliamentary and public presentation of the legislation. Cabinet ministers can also shape the SI. For example, *The Road Vehicles (Construction and Use) (Amendment) (No. 2) Regulations* 1996 (not among the 46 in the sample), which made the fitting of seatbelts compulsory in coaches and minibuses carrying children after a 1993 coach crash in which 12 children lost their lives, were, according to one group representative involved, 'led by the politicians and not the administrators'.

Ministerial shaping is, in the 46 SIs in the sample, rather rare and limited to one or two decisive interventions in the development of the SI. A simple indication by the minister of particular things to be included in the legislation is usually enough to ensure that very serious attempts are made to include them. Civil servants who spoke of ministerial involvement in the development of an SI tended to view this as 'guidance'. *The Specified Animal Pathogens Order 1998* (SAPO) offers an illustration of how this happens.

SAPO changed the rules governing handling of animal pathogens (i.e. agents that cause diseases). One of the particular 'bugs', as an official put it, was how to treat Viral Haemorrhagic Disease of Rabbits (VHD). Because of an epidemic, VHD was going to be taken off the list setting out the list of diseases covered by the requirement that laboratories be licensed to hold infective material. As another civil servant involved explained, to include VHD as a pathogen for which one needed a licence was likely to make a mockery of the law. To include VHD as a specified pathogen means in principle that one is breaking the law by having on one's land without a licence a rabbit which has died of VHD. Such a law would be, he went on to point out, as absurd as *The Grey Squirrels (Prohibition of Importation and Keeping) Order 1937.*[6] This unenforceable and ridiculous SI, still in force, requires 'the occupier of any land, who knows that grey squirrels, not being grey squirrels kept by him under license, are to be found thereon shall forthwith give notice to the appropriate department', currently MAFF. 'You try phoning MAFF and saying you've just seen a grey squirrel on your land and see what reaction you get', the MAFF official added. However, conservationists wanted this pathogen controlled as they feared that it might be used by farmers to reduce the rabbit population—much like myxamotosis in the 1950s. In this case, ministerial pressure ensured that MAFF had to do something to include VHD, as ministers (of both parties) had promised conservation groups that VHD would be controlled. The minister made it clear that he wanted this pledge honoured in the revision of the SAPO and the officials worked hard to develop a satisfactory solution to the problem. They made the *spreading* of the disease an offence, although it was not an offence to have the pathogen itself, 'so if a rabbit dies of VHD on your land, you don't have to have a licence. But if you throw it over the fence and spread it, *that* is against the law'.

THE MUFFLED IMPACT OF PARTIES

Does 'party government' (Rose 1974) extend to the processes of everyday government? The role of ministers in the delegated legislative process suggests that political parties may be expected to shape public policy-making at this level. In the origins of legislation (see Chapter 4) ministers have an influence, apparently less by directly commanding and more by civil servants acting in anticipation of ministerial approval; they can block legislation coming up, and can offer guidance on specifics should they so wish. Nevertheless, party influence in shaping SIs is relatively weak. The change of government in 1997 came at a time when the ideological differences in many areas of policy between Labour and Conservative were small. To find a muffled impact of parties is possibly less surprising at this time than at any other. Many SIs drafted under the new Labour

---

[6] This Order applied to grey squirrels section 10 of the Destructive Imported Animals Act 1932 which had previously applied only to muskrats.

administration simply develop policy more or less in the same way as planned by the outgoing Conservative administration. Where Labour consciously deviates from Conservative practice, the differences turn out to be relatively small, and in many cases there is at least as much difference between ministers of the *same party* as there is between ministers of different parties.

Of the 46 SIs, eight were introduced and passed under the Conservative government. Of the remaining 38, 26 simply continued developing SIs started under the Conservatives. Of *the remaining 12, only four constituted clear party political initiatives*. Others, such as *The National Health Service (Pharmaceutical Services) (Scotland) Amendment Regulations 1998* (making prescription fraud more difficult), were similar to previous legislation developed under the Conservatives. The four truly partisan SIs were an SI effectively ending compulsory competitive tendering in local government (*The Local Government Act 1988 (Competition) (England) (No. 2) Regulations 1997*); an SI giving the newly 'independent' Bank of England statutory powers to collect information from banks and building societies (*The Bank of England (Information Powers) Order 1998*), although exactly the same information was previously collected by voluntary agreement; an SI arranging for the distribution of extra cash to education through the Comprehensive Spending Review (*The Grants for Improvements in School Education (Scotland) Regulations 1998*) and an order commencing some of the arrangements for Welsh devolution (*The Government of Wales Act 1998 (Commencement No. 2) Order 1998*).

There were two cases where the partisan character of the legislation is ambiguous. Under *The Crime (Sentences) Act 1997 (Commencement No. 2 and Transitional Provisions) Order 1997*, a Labour Home Secretary brought into effect only some of the previous Conservative administration's sentencing provisions. However, as observers interviewed pointed out, it is quite likely that resource constraints would have prevented many more of them being activated even if the Conservative Home Secretary remained in office. *The Social Security (Welfare to Work) Regulations 1998* allowed those on incapacity-related benefits to try and enter the labour market without losing benefit rights. They were a central plank of Labour's New Deal for the Disabled. There is some evidence from respondents in the DSS that the central point of this SI, extending the period that benefit recipients can work on a trial basis without loss of benefit status should they decide they cannot continue in work, was being discussed under the Conservatives, although it was not particularly far advanced by the time they left office in May 1997. As one official explained, 'some work had been done on this earlier . . . under the last government . . . we knew from some of the concerns raised earlier by voluntary organizations where some of the problems were'. Moreover, as she went on to point it out, 'one of the changes made in this SI was actually part of the *Conservative manifesto in 1997*—the change to the 16-hour limit to voluntary work' (Conservative Party 1997: section 3).

There are also SIs reflecting policies developed under the Conservatives that one might have expected Labour to have abandoned or softened under conditions of pure 'party government' (Rose 1974). There are SIs associated with Conservative priorities of deregulation: *The Merchant Shipping (Small Workboats and Pilot Boats) Regulations 1998*; *The Gaming Duty Regulations 1997*; *The Restrictive Trade Practices (Non-notifiable Agreements) (Turnover Threshold) Amendment Order 1997*). A number of officials interviewed pointed, for example, to the similarities between the 'Deregulation Unit' of the outgoing Conservative government and the 'Better Regulation Unit' (later 'Regulatory Impact Unit') of the Labour administration; a similarity which appeared to be confirmed by the fact (cheerfully pointed out by several civil servants) that for some months after Labour took office, the web page on the internet for the Better Regulation Unit was the old Conservative Deregulation Unit web page. A DTI official had difficulty in remembering who actually passed one of the deregulation initiative SIs in the sample ('[w]as it done under the old [Conservative] government or Labour?' he asked in interview) and a respondent from another department pointed out that one initiative concerning charging for public services was actively opposed by Labour until recently.

> There has been a lot of pressure on the current government to reverse this because they said they would in the 1992 manifesto—a lot of people have long memories, but so far they have shown no sign of moving. Brown and Blair are a different kettle of fish to Kinnock and Smith.

The difference under the Labour government was that when people wrote in to complain about the charges 'we used to be quite tough in our letters back to these people, telling them to "shop around"—the market offered the solution. We've toned that down recently.'

Policies associated with the Conservatives found among SIs passed under Labour in the sample also include SIs on contracting out (*The Contracting Out (Functions Relating to National Savings) Order 1998*) and substituting private sector finance for previously public subsidy (*The Local Authorities (Transport Charges) Regulations 1998*[7] and *The Conditional Fee Agreements Order 1998*). Among SIs reflecting other themes previously associated more strongly with the preceding Conservative administration, indeed many were set in motion under the Conservatives, were SIs restricting eligibility to social security benefits (*The Jobseeker's Allowance (Amendment) Regulations 1998*, although these were eventually reversed[8]), and SIs on the crackdown on fraud (*The National Health*

---

[7] In the case of the transport charges Labour councils were among those who actually wanted the Conservative government to introduce the legislation. But at the time the Government had little interest in developing it. After the 1997 election the New Labour government came under pressure to introduce it 'especially from London government, because they believed the new government to be more sympathetic'.

[8] *The Jobseeker's Allowance (Amendment) Regulations 1998* started as a Conservative proposal; they were developed at the end of the outgoing Conservative government, but could not be introduced partly because of the practical difficulties of implementing them (they would need to consult the Social Security Advisory Committee, which would in turn consult other groups, and the computer hardware and software facilities also had to be able to cope with the changes). Under the Conservatives, as one junior minister put it, 'the regs. were not going to take effect until April 1999,

Service (Pharmaceutical Services) (Scotland) Amendment Regulations 1998 and *The Social Security Administration (Fraud) Act 1997 (Commencement No. 6) Order 1998)*.

The continuation of Conservative policies by Labour has occasionally pushed the parties into clear reversals of positions on some occasions. *The Contracting Out (Functions Relating to National Savings) Order 1998* resulted from a process of contracting out which in general started under the Conservatives. It is therefore remarkable that the Conservatives in opposition should have argued against the measure. The objections to it, expressed in the Committee on Delegated Legislation by Michael Fallon, was that:

> This is an ill-founded project. Seventeen months ago the Labour Party called it a 'mortal body blow' to National Savings' 'loyal and hard-working staff'. I suggest that this measure is a U-turn. It is a back door privatization that abuses parliamentary procedure and fundamentally weakens the job prospects of those who for so long have worked loyally for National Savings (Standing Committee on Delegated Legislation, 6 March 1998).

As one official put it , it was curious to hear:

> the Conservatives concerned about the dire consequences of something that was really associated entirely with them. They saw it as 'privatization through the back door' and took the [trade] unions' line on it. Helen Liddell [who as Economic Secretary to the Treasury was the minister seeing the legislation through the House of Commons] was highly amused by it all.

With *The Conditional Fee Agreements Order 1998* developing the 'no-win-no-fee' principle of funding litigation, there was also a reversal of roles. The order was issued under primary legislation passed by the preceding Conservative administration, The Courts and Legal Services Act 1990,[9] and extended the possible use of no-win-no-fee arrangements beyond the modest range introduced by the Conservatives in *The Conditional Fees Order 1995* to include all civil proceedings. In the House of Lords debate on the 1998 Order, the Conservative Lord Ackner opposed the principle but sought to defeat the legislation on a technical point (the 'uplift cap' on the success fee). This was a similar objection to that raised back in 1995 in the debate on the first Conditional Fee Order, also by Lord Ackner, but at that time Ackner's arguments were supported by Lord Irvine—then Labour's Shadow Lord Chancellor. In 1998, as Lord Chancellor, Lord Irvine introduced the Order extending the

---

so if the [then] government lost the election it would not be their problem, if they won, it would not be difficult to get them through'. The incoming Labour administration made and laid the regulations as part of its pledge to keep to Conservative spending commitments.

[9] In the House of Lords debate on the Courts and Legal Services Bill Lord Irvine complained:

> All this free market hype pouring out of the Government's propaganda machine should not be allowed to conceal the basic truth, which is that they are unwilling to commit the resources *that only the state can provide* to secure equal access to justice for all its citizens [emphasis added] (House of Lords Debates, 19 December 1989 vol. 514, col. 241).

range of litigation coming under no-win-no-fee arrangements. The apparent change of heart by the Labour Lord Chancellor did not pass unnoticed by Lord Ackner who in 1998 referred to the 'important contribution . . . made by my noble and learned friend', Lord Irvine, to the debate on the Conservative conditional fees order back in 1995 when he was but 'a mere shadow of himself'. Moreover, in 1995 the then Lord Chancellor's (Lord Mackay) argument against Lord Ackner was very similar to that used by Lord Irvine against Lord Ackner three years later (see House of Lords Debates, 23 July 1998 vol 592, col. 1100; House of Lords Debates, 12 June 1995 vol 564, col 1544). Similarly, with *The Jobseeker's Allowance (Amendment) Regulations 1998*, which started life under the Conservatives as a means to reduce the welfare budget, one official commented, '[i]t was a source of some amusement to hear the Conservatives as the champion of the poor and the trade unions on this one'.

In one case the continuity between the Major and the Blair governments was strong but did not prevent the Labour government selling its initiative as a central plank of its own distinctive approach. *The Jobseeker's Allowance (Workskill Courses) Pilot (No. 2) Regulations 1997*, issued under Labour, were identical to *The Jobseeker's Allowance (Workskill Courses) Pilot (No. 1) Regulations 1997* issued under the Conservatives. These were regulations that allowed recipients of JSA benefit to go into full-time training courses. The No. 2 regulations applied the scheme to different areas. As with the previous Conservative regulations, an official explained that:

> the definite aim was to pilot . . . The pilots are, according to the [Jobseeker's Allowance] Act time limited to a year or so, so there is no danger of using them to bring about wider changes in the JSA regulations.

Nevertheless, the Labour government still presented the scheme as a central part of its 'Welfare to Work' strategy which had formed a central part of the successful campaign to defeat the Conservatives in the general election in May 1997. As one official put it, '[t]he idea behind the JSA changes has been incorporated into the New Deal' (another of Labour's labels for its new approach to welfare).

The notion that parties are the decisive feature in the political control of government departments and shape the direction of policy must further be qualified by the observation that in the one case where a minister managed to block earlier attempts to introduce an SI (in the videosenders order), it was the character and disposition of the minister that was decisive rather than party affiliation. An interest group official explained why the videosender SI took so long to develop:

> This had been in their [i.e. the Department's] minds for some time. The change of government might offer the opportunity to talk to new ministers . . . No, let me think, it was not the whole time of the last Tory government that it was blocked, but under one particular junior minister. When X came in [a Conservative junior minister] he started it moving . . . The old Tory minister did not want regulation. He thought this [principle] was more important than safety.

Similarly, while a particular Conservative junior minister was among those ranged against the legislation abolishing the height requirement for firefighters (eventually unsuccessfully), an interest group respondent suggested that the officials concerned knew that 'the Home Secretary would have agreed' with abolition. If correct, this implies that the character of individual junior ministers can be crucial and their approaches may differ significantly from those of their superiors were the same issues to be referred to them.

An additional feature of the role of the minister in the development of SIs is the effect of elections in the timing of an SI. It is well documented that during elections work on policy generally stops as civil servants do not want to develop initiatives which are likely to stall in the event of a change of government or change of minister. The 1997 election was cited as a major cause of delay for many SIs. An NHS regulation was:

> strangled off in the last days of the Parliament. There was a hiatus in April and May—we continued doing work on it. It was a phoney war period. We could not engage anyone about it, we could not consult people until it was clear that something could come of their comments.

A less well documented feature of elections is that it can give impetus to the development of a regulation through a change in the ministerial team. This can happen in cases where the proposed regulation is related neither to broad party ideologies nor to interest groups close to the new party in government. For example, with *The Education (School Leaving Date) Order 1997* one official pointed out:

> When the new government came in 1997 we set the issue in front of them without detail [i.e. we told them about the importance of the issue without going into the conflicts that it had engendered] and asked 'how strongly do you feel about it?' They said yes, they felt strongly about it and put it in their White Paper in June after only having been elected in May.

Also *The Enforcement of Road Traffic Debts (Certificated Bailiffs) (Amendment) Regulations 1998* arose from a proposal first made to a Conservative Lord Chancellor by the association representing certificated bailiffs. The fact that it was not developed until he had been replaced by a Labour Lord Chancellor had less to do with the views of either party on the matter than the fact that the election produced a 'clearing of the decks', as one official put it. 'Existing commitments were finished before the election, or shelved, and with a new administration it was easier to place things on the agenda.'

CONCLUSIONS

Leaving aside those items which they themselves have initiated (Chapter 4), most of the time ministers devote little attention to delegated legislation. 'They [SIs] come up to us as the flotsam and jetsam of political life', said one ex-minister. In most cases the development of the SI will be approved and its final version will be signed with no difficulty. There are a number of reasons for this, in addition to the generally technical nature of what comes across the minister's desk in this form as well as the sheer volume of SIs many departments produce. Civil servants know what ministers are likely to support, loathe and like, and will not usually propose SIs which they dislike if they can avoid it. 'Look', said another ex-junior minister, 'SIs are not dreamed up by officials who have nothing better to do. They are usually there for a reason.' Under the Conservative government there were some ministers generally hostile to the principle of regulation, but most ministers tend to accept that there is a good reason for the legislation and that the issue of consistency with general government priorities has already been discussed and settled, where, indeed, it occurs.

Ministers are politicians, and part of political skill is to make sure that the SI holds no embarrassment for the government—'trusting the political antennae', as one put it. Another part of political skill is to have an impact on government. The tools available to ministers, above all junior ministers, to react to their political antennae or to shape what is done in their name, is above all the ability to block delegated legislation. We only have one example of a minister actually managing to do this in our 46 SIs. However the research design is based on analysing SIs that have actually been passed rather than looking in addition at those ideas which never actually reach the statute book. The design used means that we could not reasonably expect to find any more than one or two such blocked instruments even if they were, say, twice or three times as common as such figures imply. But the available evidence—above all the comments of civil servants—suggests that blocking legislation is exceptionally rare. As has been mentioned above, ministers have been known to take umbrage over a variety of issues and refuse to sign, or refuse to sign speedily.

Yet the ability to block, constrained as it may be by the remote possibility that the Cabinet minister might become involved in sorting out the 'awkward' junior minister, is taken seriously by civil servants drafting regulations. This gives the minister a potential role in the development of Statutory Instruments that appears to be filled only occasionally in practice. A minister can suggest that alternative or additional provisions be included in a regulation. When we exclude the ministerial role in the initiation of regulations, there is only one clear case among the 46 in the sample of a minister insisting that something be included that would otherwise have been omitted—the inclusion of a reference to a rabbit disease in an order regulating animal pathogens. We only have firm evidence of ministers blocking one item from our 46 and trying to, unsuccessfully, on one other occasion (firefighters' height).

Securing ministers' approval is generally neither formality nor a battle. Where ministers want to get involved in the detailed development of an SI, they can. But there are very few cases when they are likely to want to. They are more likely to be interested in broad ideological or thematic issues—deregulation, welfare to work, combatting fraud—than the daily grind of administrative detail. Where such broad ideological or thematic issues are addressed, civil servants know what their ministers views are likely to be, and try to accommodate them.

6

Drafting SIs: the joint effort of administrators and lawyers

It can take a long time to develop even the most simple-looking regulations. In many interviews the suggestion that a short SI, only a few lines long, might have been quite straightforward to produce was greeted with a laugh followed by a look or expression that betrayed weariness or bemusement. Some SIs can be drawn up, written and put on the statute books very quickly. Most take at least a few months, and many much longer. The precise length of time an SI takes to be produced depends on when one defines the process as starting. Among the sample of 46 SIs *The Action Programme for Nitrate Vulnerable Zones (Scotland) Regulations 1998* implemented a 1991 EU directive, although the delay came less from any protracted debate about the regulation than from a reluctance (shared by many other EU Member States) to transpose this particular European law. The longest-running SI among the 46, in the sense that it was actively under consideration for a very long time, was *The Education (School Leaving Date) Order 1997*, first intended to come into operation shortly after its parent legislation in 1993. A variety of different reasons can make the process of producing an SI a long-drawn-out one. These include, among other things, the complexity of the matter in hand, opposition of a minister, the need to consult with the EU, especially on matters covered by the Technical Standards Directive, lack of time to get the *vires* in primary legislation, the relatively low priority attached to the issue under consideration or lack of money or general pressure of work elsewhere.

There are generally two types of officials involved in developing an SI: the administrator and the lawyer. The administrator is the civil servant within a specialised division of the ministry whose main function is to develop the specific objectives of the SI, including handling consultations. One of the administrator's main tasks is to produce the *instructions* to the lawyer working within the legal branch of the ministry (including a joint Department of Health and Social Security legal service as well as Treasury Solicitor which drafts for departments such as Culture, Media and Sport). The instructions are specifications which set out as fully and clearly as possible the provisions the new Statutory Instrument should contain. The seniority of the administrators working on SIs varies somewhat, although not necessarily by any measure of the 'importance' of the SI. The administrators interviewed were generally, in ascending order of rank, Higher Executive Officers (HEOs), Senior Executive

Officers (SEO) and officials at grade 7, with a handful of respondents at the higher level of grade 6 and above. Only one or two interviews involved officials in the top grades of the civil service, the old grades 1 to 5, now covered by the Senior Civil Service (SCS). In 1997 there were 3,700 officials in the SCS compared with 47,500 Higher Executive Officers, 22,660 SEOs, 14,940 grade 7s and 4,800 grade 6s.

The implications of the issue of the rank of those drafting SIs will be taken up in the conclusion. However, at the level at which SIs are developed, mobility is generally high as administrators and legal officials move frequently. One lawyer, when asked whether there was much mobility, answered 'higher grades tend to stay on longer than the junior levels. The idea is that we would tend to move every two to three years.' One interest group respondent, for example replied:

> Do I have constant contacts in DETR? They move people around a lot. We [i.e. the interest group] are an important source of continuity within the ministry. You see someone there and say 'I spoke to Fred about this in 1993' and they say 'Did you? Let's go and look at the files'. We are the conscience and memory of the department with the passage of time.

Nevertheless, some officials I came across have specialised and remained in a particular area for many years. The issue of mobility was not systematically raised during the interviews, so no precise estimates can be given here. However, some indication is given by the fact that most of the interviews for the 46 SIs were conducted within a few months of the SI being made and in ten cases at least one of the relevant officials (administrator or lawyer) had moved on since the date the SI was laid.

ADMINISTRATORS' ROLES

It is usual for a single administrator to be given the responsibility for developing an SI. Yet this is not to deny that the administrator's role, often described by administrators and lawyers alike as 'doing the policy work', is almost invariably as part of a policy team. With commencement orders which bring into effect recent primary legislation it is quite common for a more or less formally-constituted team to develop the secondary legislation; the same team that produced the Act. For example, *The National Crime Squad Service Authority (Levying) Order 1997* determined the way in which the National Crime Squad was to be funded. The National Crime Squad replaced the old Regional Crime Squads under the 1997 Police Act. A specialised unit, the Police Bill Unit was set up to develop and steer through the 1997 Act. When the Act was passed, the Unit became the National Crime Services Unit (NCSU) and given the task of implementing the 1997 Act, with largely the same people in it. After the implementing measures for the Act had been passed, it went back to being the Policing Organised Crime Unit. The NCSU had a project board as well as a set of steering groups. This particular SI was the product of the Financial Steering Group on which were represented the Association of Chief Police Officers and the Association of Police Authorities. Other SIs, which were developed shortly after the relevant primary legislation, were likewise team efforts.

In other cases administrators took the lead in arranging for the SI to be developed and drafted, but generally also relied on colleagues, superiors and subordinates to a varying degree. Even where, for example, an SI was concerned with changing a major area of social security linked to the new Labour government's 'welfare to work' initiative, and the changes were part of a team effort, responsibility for the regulations was allocated ultimately to a single HEO.

> We had to set up a new team for this . . . We now stand at 9 people here [in DSS] and 7 at DfEE. The project manager is a Grade 6. One of the principal concerns raised in the work of this team is that there are a number of barriers to prevent disabled people getting into work. I was given the benefits side of the job, along with a couple of other colleagues—to see if there were any ways of reversing or reducing these barriers.

Another relatively senior official pointed to the importance of the single official, again an HEO, who did the main work on the SI, although working within the context of a bigger team:

> My HEO at this time was extremely good, very competent. She would always do first drafts of all this. I would get involved as you need to get two people in on something like this [a potentially very sensitive political issue]. As section head this is important. I'd suggest changes, but she did all the work on what the regs should say and on dealing with the solicitors.

Yet another HEO described her relationship with her superior, a Grade 7, on one of the SIs:

> I liaise with my boss. Initially she was in on the meetings [which established the general need for the regulation]. I go away and do the work and the consultation, but I let her see the drafts.

In interview *the administrators often spoke in the first person plural, the lawyers in the first person singular*. Administrators involved in drawing up SIs are generally members of a team. The size and formality of the team, as well as the degree to which any one individual took a lead in it will vary. While lawyers almost invariably pass on drafts of SIs to colleagues and superiors, the activity of legal drafting itself generally involves less teamwork than the administrators' job of developing what should actually go in the regulation.

Settling the content of an SI in a form that can be sent to a lawyer as an instruction to draft can be extremely easy. In many cases the administrator's hard work, the 'policy work', is done in the very early development of an SI (see Chapter 4). For example, the Home Office officials involved in removing the height restrictions of firefighters (as a major step in removing sex discrimination in recruitment to the service), had to get the Central Fire Brigades Advisory Council to agree that this was a desirable course of action. This took years of grind for the administrators, including commissioning, digesting and disseminating several research projects. These projects looked in detail, among other things, at the impact of height on the functional effectiveness of firefighters. However, in this chapter the main concern is with the development of an SI once the need for legislation has been established and, where necessary, been agreed with the minister.

Moreover, in such cases, once the need to legislate has been established, there is little more for the administrator to do. For example, with the fish quotas SI, all the administrator's work went into establishing that fish stocks are running low in a particular area and that no alternative arrangements (through 'quota swapping') were available. The instructions are easy since, as one official pointed out, there may be several similar orders each year. For a standard SI of this type the instructions would simply take the form of a short minute to the lawyer setting out the species and the sea areas affected and asking for an SI to be prepared. Sometimes, with very simple SIs, the instruction can be given over the phone and followed up with a short commissioning minute. However, in many other cases the hard work for the administrator starts after the need for legislation has been established.

Consultation

Where the contents of the regulations are not a foregone conclusion, the 'policy work' involves consultation: internal consultation with colleagues in the same department and other departments as well as consultation with outside interests. While the next chapter will deal with questions of external consultation, this chapter outlines internal inter- and intra-departmental consultations.

Internal consultation can mean 'kicking around' ideas within the department. One SI that was produced entirely on the basis of internal consultation was *The Contracting Out (Functions Relating to National Savings) Order 1998*. The Director of National Savings wanted to contract out much of the work of National Savings. However he wished to retain some of the Director's functions. For example, decisions about secrecy and whether to reveal account details were sensitive issues which the government would have been reluctant to see handed over to a private company. The policy work in this case involved 'finding out what powers the director has at present' through examining all the primary and secondary legislation surrounding National Savings. 'Then we went through which ones we wanted to keep in', the official responsible continued. It was not hard to decide what should be kept and what should be given to the contractors. The administrators devised a set of criteria which allowed the contractors sufficient freedom so that they did not:

> keep coming back to us for permission [to do things] or . . . say that they can't do the job properly because they don't have the power . . . We can't cope with floods of questions or requests for permission coming from the contractors.

These criteria separated 'routine mechanical' tasks from tasks related to the public interest. When looking through the powers of the Director of National Savings the administrators found that he had many humdrum powers which he was unlikely ever to want to use. Formally:

> if someone loses a bank book, it is up to the discretion of the Director who may 'send the person' a bank book to replace it. . . . There were other things we needed to keep here, such as approved forms and deadlines. One major one was if someone has been naughty with a premium bond, we can keep their money. We didn't want that one with a private company.

In the event the administrator concerned argued that it was 'very straightforward' to come up with a list of tasks that the Director could let go of. The job of deciding which tasks to let go of was made easier by the knowledge that 'if we decided later that the Director really *did* need them we could always claw them back at any time'.

In the case of *The Pensions Appeal Tribunals (England and Wales) (Amendment) Rules 1998*, sufficient suggestions for reforming the regulations had accumulated since the last ones were made in 1980 for the Lord Chancellor's Department (LCD) to start consulting with, among others, the DSS, the War Pensions Agency, the Council on Tribunals, the Scottish Courts Administration and the Pensions Appeal Tribunal itself on changes. The most pressing change was the need for a new form for giving notice of appeal—the old form was set out in *The Pensions Appeal Tribunals (England and Wales) Rules 1980* and needed to be amended not least because it gave an out-of-date address for the Pensions Appeal Office. The process of consultation started with a meeting with interested parties within government, and at each draft people came up with new ideas about what should be included in an update of the regulations. As an official put it:

> just when you think you have got it right, someone comes along and says 'but have you thought of such-and-such?' So you go back to the lawyers and get the changes put in. Consultation can be smooth, or you can get spanners in the works for no real reason. This one got people to think of other things.

At around the fifth draft 'we were getting close to D-Day', an internally-set date by which the LCD wanted the new regulations to be made, they managed to come up with a set of reforms to the regulations with which 'everyone was happy'.

Consultations may take the form of securing agreement from different sections within the same department. An official within the Department of Social Security (DSS) involved in *The Social Security (Welfare to Work) Regulations 1998* which aimed to make it easier for disabled people to try out work without losing their benefits rights, had to get other sections of the DSS onside.

> The formal instructions were sent in December 1997. By then we'd have to have brought on side other policy sections. There was some resistance from other policy

sections that this was the thin end of the wedge. Disabled people had [this exemption], other people would want it too, and they would cost even more. The argument for disabled people was sound. Moreover few of them leave benefits for work. But others, they argued, such as lone parents, people on Jobseeker's Allowance or the long-term unemployed, for example, would be after it.

Her job of selling the new regulations to other DSS sections continued right up to the point of laying the SI and afterwards since other departments doubted that she had the legal powers, the *vires*, to pass the new regulations.

In the case of *The Crime (Sentences) Act 1997 (Commencement No. 2 and Transitional Provisions) Order 1997* which affected sentencing practices, the internal consultation involved gaining projections of the precise costs of commencing different parts of the 1997 Act:

> The new government thought it was a good idea, but the resource cost is big. You go to the people downstairs who do the modelling projections of the prison population and they tell you you need so and so many new prisons to bring that into force. Mandatory minimum sentences for burglary had a particularly heavy resource implication.

Consequently what could be implemented within existing resources was limited, and was reflected in the modest character of what precisely was commenced.

Some *inter*departmental consultations are made necessary by the character of the legislation. Anything related to extra public spending has to be cleared with the Treasury. With *The Social Security (Welfare to Work) Regulations 1998*:

> The Treasury will have been consulted. This is a benefit measure—any new funding and the Treasury is consulted. Our Planning and Finance Division will have been involved. Once we have a proposal and ministers are keen on it, our people approach the Treasury and say they want it, why they want it, and how they intend to pay for it. I think this was a case where they agreed to extra funding *without* the department having to make corresponding savings.

Another general rule is supposed to be that any penalties included in departmental legislation (i.e. where specific penalties or ranges of penalties for failure to comply with the law are set out in an SI) should be cleared with the Home Office, as is the creation of a new offence. The status, however, of such rules is unclear, as an exchange between two officials interviewed illustrates:

> *Fred*: We are supposed to check with the Home Office every time we create a new offence. Do *you* do that Charlie?
> *Charlie*: No, I can't say I do.
> *Fred*: I do, whenever I can. I did it last week.

There is another rule that SIs affecting the Channel Islands and the Isle of Man have to be cleared with the Home Office before being laid.

There are also rules specific to the particular legislation in hand about interdepartmental consultation. Where two or more departments share responsibilities in the same area there will be consultation. For example, Customs and Excise consults closely with the Treasury on VAT regulations or with MAFF for excise duties on agricultural products. Jobseeker's Allowance benefit is jointly run by the Department for Education and Employment and the Department of Social Security. As a DfEE official explained, 'we take the lead in the training side of the JSA'. In the case of *The Jobseeker's Allowance (Workskill Courses) Pilot (No. 2) Regulations 1997*, the DfEE took the lead but 'every single part went through with DSS approval'. Another JSA order, *The Jobseeker's Allowance (Amendment) Regulations 1998*, a controversial measure designed to reduce levels of payment to recipients, was handled entirely by DSS with no reported DfEE involvement. In the case of the joint responsibilities of the Home Office and the Department of Health for mental health legislation the delimitation involves some specific demarcations. As a Department of Health official explained:

> In the Home Office there is a Mental Health Unit. They are interested in patients before courts technically called MDOs ('mentally disordered offenders'). They can have a restriction order placed on them and they are 'restricted patients'. Any changes to legislation which has an impact on restricted patients and we have to consult the Home Office. We need to be sure that the changes we make will not impinge on them.

Similarly, as a further example, Home Office legislation on additions to the lists of drugs under the Misuse of Drugs Act involves consultation with Customs and Excise.

The territorial offices are consulted by the Whitehall-based departments. Generally consultation with the Welsh, Scottish and Northern Ireland Offices meant little more than 'copying in' these departments to major papers or drafts of the SI. In only one of the 40 Whitehall department SIs did the Scottish Office make a significant contribution, yet in the Whitehall-based departments several respondents suggested that the Scottish Office was the one territorial office most likely to make a substantive contribution. Such contributions were likely in areas where they had substantial expertise—fisheries and forestry, for example. In one case, where the England and Wales legislation was based entirely on consultations internal to government, Scotland was an influential consultee on the English and Welsh legislation because, as one official put it, 'they wanted their legislation exactly the same as ours, so [internal consultation] was not just for information'. In addition, some officials suggested that comments from the Scottish Office were along the lines of a useful 'long stop' or 'extra pair of eyes' for their proposals.

In general the Welsh Office was regarded as the least likely to make any positive contribution to developing an SI. After leafing through the files on a relatively straightforward SI, and mentioning a long cast of people who gave their comments, an official based in a Whitehall department added as an afterthought, and with an ironic smile: 'Oh, and we would obviously have consulted the Welsh Office. I forgot to mention that.'

The Northern Ireland Office (NIO) seems to have a special place in consultations, particularly within the DSS. In interviews, all DSS officials mentioned that suggestions for textual improvements were made by the NIO—one went as far as to describe the NIO as a 'checking service'. As this label suggests, respondents tended to associate this with a very close attention to fine detail. When an official was explaining how, at the last minute, an important omission from a DSS regulation was detected, I asked whether it could have been someone from the Northern Ireland Office who had found the mistake. He laughed and added:

> This is not the sort of thing they would have picked up. They are good at telling you whether you really should have put a full stop at that point, whether you use that wording and footnotes and if your indents are the right size.

More generally officials pointed to major differences in the policy-making environments to explain why the contribution of the territorial offices was relatively small. Mostly this was that 'the laws there are different', but also included reference to the fact that the scale of the problems or issues they had to face was smaller (for example, 'you don't need a big register for the number of registered drug addicts in Northern Ireland').

There was only one major example of strong disagreement between departments in the 46 SIs in the study—disagreement going beyond suggesting relatively minor amendments. *The Education (School Leaving Date) Order 1997* is a simple and very brief SI designating 'the school leaving date for 1998 and for successive years shall be the last Friday in June'. The commitment to this was made in the 1992 White Paper and in the 1993 Education Act (section 277(4)). As one official tells the story:

> Well, back in 1993 we put round a note starting off the whole consultation process and we got a letter from the DSS saying 'all very interesting, but you do realise that this will cost money in terms of extra Child Benefit, and where is the extra coming from? You did not clear this with us'.

Then the DSS said that the total cost of the proposal was six times higher than what DfEE argued it could possibly be. This started a lot of wrangling and the issue 'hit ministerial discussions and looked like it would get much higher'. The issue dragged on for four years. An official remembers:

> Typically the discussions about this happened in the last week of June. I remember it as being about the time of Wimbledon. In fact, I remember conducting a mobile phone conversation with the DSS while I was at Wimbledon and it was raining—Yes, I think it was the time when Cliff Richard was singing.[1]

The position was made more complicated by the fact that although one union, the ATL, was openly ambivalent about the new date, the other unions shared reservations despite being publicly in favour of it. The episode ended in a com-

---

[1] The popular singer Cliff Richard entertained the Wimbledon crowd when rain stopped play in July 1996.

promise made possible by a change in government. The compromise with the teachers was the provision of money for schools where there were larger num-bers of low-achievers. One official explained the deal between DfEE and DSS:

> We said to the DSS 'here's what we are offering, plus a part in a campaign against DSS fraud' (for example, people who drop out of FE colleges and the fact that they drop out only gets picked up the next time that they have to declare that they are or are not in college). We said we would draft a letter to heads of FE colleges to cooperate with us, and that should be some compensation. The ministerial letter came back giving us the go ahead. With a new minister it is always easier to get things moving.

The whole experience was parodied by an artistic member of a teachers' union who, in an idle few moments at a meeting on the subject, drew a series of cartoons and passed them on to one of the officials involved.[2] It starts with two Permanent Secretaries in a club coming up with the bright idea of making chil-dren stay at school longer to save money. The next picture shows one turning to a minion and ordering 'draft me an SI'. Another picture shows the DSS saying 'sorry you can't do this, it costs us too much'. Then the Permanent Secretary says 'give the schools some money, and say it is a "challenge" ', and goes on to give them a pilot scheme. Another picture shows two civil servants in a bar play-ing darts trying to decide the school leaving date, '1st dart for the month and the second for the day' is the caption. Another shows a man from the ministry ask-ing a headmistress 'how would you like £3,000?' 'Thank you very much' she says. 'Keep all the low achievers as far away from the school as you can, and far away from the high achievers and your league table performance will improve' is the advice from the man from the ministry. Another picture shows a civil ser-vant throwing money at failing schools.

Logistical work

In addition to consulting internally, administrators may also have to do some detailed work to cover the logistics of what they are seeking to legislate for. An official in the Home Office spoke of an earlier experience of visiting sites in northern England to look at holes in the ground so that the SI he was develop-ing got the correct definition to cover the particular sort of holes in question. Detail is often a matter of brainstorming along with the lawyers working on the SI (see below). However, administrators also do detailed preparation on their own. For example, *The Social Security Administration (Fraud) Act 1997 (Commencement No. 6) Order 1998* sought to combat social security fraud through the postal system. Once the 1997 Fraud Act had been passed, officials from the DSS started negotiating with Royal Mail. DSS wanted Royal Mail to separate out any letters from Housing Benefit authorities which were being forwarded to other addresses. At issue in the negotiations were questions of envelope design (finding an envelope that would pass through Royal Mail

---

[2] Permission to reproduce the cartoons was not available.

sorting systems and at the same time be easily recognisable) as well as of cost (DSS had agreed, in principle, to pay for the service). The HEO responsible had to negotiate envelope designs, to arrange for a four-week pilot of the service, partially commence the 1997 Act[3] (i.e. bring the postal provisions of the Act into force for the two areas, Hounslow and Richmond, where they were being piloted) and evaluate the results of the pilot.

The pilot indicated savings of £100,000 in the two authorities over the four-week period and showed Housing Benefit being redirected to addresses in far away places including France, Spain and Rio de Janeiro. After the trial the same official had to negotiate the scope of the service Royal Mail would offer (DSS wanted Royal Mail to include intercepting post redirected by hand from its delivery address); visit sorting offices 'many at 6 am' to examine Royal Mail claims of the difficulty and cost of the task it faced; talk down Royal Mail claims for compensation for the possible loss of business it alleged from people who perceived the integrity of its redirecting service being compromised; agree charges for the new service; and get funding for the programme from the Treasury (together with a representative from Finance Branch at the DSS). The detailed issues were in danger of getting so bogged down on minute issues (e.g. how long it took a person in the Royal Mail sorting office to walk to the 'do not redirect' sack) that the official decided to force the pace:

> To gee things up a bit we sent a submission to the new minister of state saying we would like to commence it. We would then get the negotiations moving or go ahead without their agreement. We did not want to do this, but their [Royal Mail's] lawyers knew that we could have required them to do it without their agreement.

The negotiation did not end there: after the SI and even after dealing with Royal Mail, the local authorities which deliver Housing Benefit had to be persuaded to sign up to the scheme. This included a launch of the scheme in February 1999, three months after it was commenced, and the invention of a system of service level agreements to which individual authorities sign up. In addition, there was the further matter of dealing with the Benefits Agency (BA) which had a whole range of different logistical problems to face. Not least among them was the fear that redirected BA mail would deluge the six *regional* centres responsible for sending out benefits and get back to the *local* offices only with great difficulty.

In all four of the DSS SIs, hardware and software capacity was crucial in shaping the timing of the legislation, and administrators had to deal with the constraints of information technology to a greater or lesser extent. As one official explained:

> It looks like we took a long time over the whole thing, but we had to wait for consultation and so on. Anyway, a year before we could not have done it. The Income Support computer did not have enough memory . . . In May 1998 they updated the

---

[3] This was done through *The Social Security Administration (Fraud) Act 1997 (Commencement No. 2) Order 1997.*

memory to keep cases for 18 months—without that the change could not have been operated effectively.

With the (eventually aborted) SI aimed at increasing the 'waiting period' for Jobseeker's Allowance, an official pointed out:

> Part of the reason for delaying the regulations was an IT/technical one. Waiting days are, so they tell me, put in the hard coding of the computer system. It was never going to be easy or quick to make these changes. IT changes have massive lead times.

And computer programming issues played a role in the timing of the SIs on maternity pay and postal fraud.

Getting to know the details of the activities you are regulating is crucial for the quality of the instructions to the lawyer and the resulting regulations. One common technical problem was how to develop regulations for the particular set of activities you wanted to cover and not affect activities you were keen to leave alone. For example, the small workboats regulations were difficult to develop precisely because small boats were used for different things:

> A big difficulty is that on Monday a boat might be used in one capacity and on Tuesday another. How do you legislate on this? On one day it is taking a dozen holi-daymakers around the bay and the next day it is loading steel pipes in Poole.

In consequence, administrators developing SIs may spend time in the field observing the people and activities affected by their regulations. Civil servants also have to conduct assessments of the costs of regulations under the Regulatory Impact Assessment system (replacing Regulatory Appraisal and Compliance Cost Assessment in 1998)—the amount of effort put into these assessments varied enormously with some officials using backs of envelopes and guesswork and others conducting relatively elaborate surveys.

Presentation

Civil servants also have to offer support to the minister in presenting the policy to the outside world. This can involve helping to prepare press releases, writing speeches and providing information and points to raise in Parliament, setting out potential points of criticism. One HEO described her role in this respect in answer to a question about a rather straightforward SI:

> There were no speeches to write on this one . . . [With others] you end up drafting speeches. Recently I did [a speech for regulations which were] an affirmative resolu-tion and had to be taken through both Houses. It might be taken by the Standing Committee in the Commons, but will be taken on the floor in the House of Lords and there will be a debate. You have to have a speech ready—what we are doing and why. And brief them on Q and A. And you have to attend in case we have to brief the min-ister should something come up.

The role of Parliament is considered in more detail in Chapter 8.

While it was rare to find clear examples of civil servants opposed to the policies they were implementing, on two occasions this was evident. The response of the civil servants involved offers an interesting perspective on the minister–civil servant relationship. Heclo and Wildavsky (1981) found that civil servants will, like Sir Humphrey from the television programme *Yes, Minister*, tip a nod and a wink that a policy proposal is nonsense but should be allowed through because the minister likes it. Yet the civil servants whom I spoke to about their experience in this respect pointed out that such an approach would generally be considered unprofessional. As one put it:

> Although it is not justified in policy terms, you do your best. Still, we cannot go along [to the Committee whose approval we needed] and say 'we think this is nasty too, but we can't do anything, so go on then [and approve it]'. We had to tell them it was a very good idea. We have to do our jobs properly. We have to prepare the minister for questions and give them material they can use to counter criticisms when they stand up and defend it. *That is what we do, it's our job.*

Later on, when this particular SI appeared to be doomed as support in Parliament had ebbed away and even the Government was not advancing arguments to support it, the same official added, '[i]f we needed to have done, we would have advised on the points to put forward in favour of the regs.'.

The administrators also draft the press releases. Not all SIs have press releases. Normally all SIs which are likely to raise interest from a wider public have press releases, as well as many which never get taken up by the daily press, such as *The Apple and Pear Orchard Grubbing Up Regulations 1998. The Social Security Administration (Fraud) Act 1997 (Commencement No. 2) Order 1997* had at least two press releases—one when the SI was actually made and one when there was an official launch of the scheme. Another important SI had no press release partly because, as one official explained, 'it was a bit sensitive'. The SI gave local authorities powers to charge for services, but they had been charging for these services for many years. Moreover, they continued to charge for some services for which they had no legal powers even with the new legislation. A press release, so it was argued, would draw attention to this and 'could have been embarrassing'.

LAWYERS' ROLES

Advising

For lawyers SIs are not always the most exciting form of work. As one lawyer put it, 'I thought doing law was going to be great: Perry Mason and all that. But here I am drafting SIs'. For most administrators and officials, SI work is like the proverbial 24 bus—one can go for a long time without seeing any, and then several come along all at once. Often this bunching is due to the introduction of a new piece of primary legislation which needs secondary legislation to bring it into effect and subsequent orders to be issued under it. Some public policy areas are more likely to involve SIs than others— for example, in the DfEE, teachers' pensions regulations are likely to involve an official in more SI work than most other areas of its work.

Lawyers working on SIs are usually described as 'legal advisers', and even those who write larger numbers of SIs, at least those interviewed in Whitehall-based departments, tended to spend between one-fifth and one-third of their time on SIs as opposed to more general advice and legal services. However, as one lawyer pointed out, advice might include how to avoid making an SI by, for example, using existing legislation. Nevertheless, while not the most glamorous part of legal work, SIs were still objects of professionalism and pride: delivering elegant solutions to difficult legal problems, the ability to deal with issues without major fuss, the capacity to identify and head off potential problems among other things were obvious sources of satisfaction.

Lawyers are usually assigned a range of responsibilities, although precise arrangements for this vary from department to department. The allocation of responsibilities generally matches the division of administrative responsibilities in the department as a whole. These responsibilities can be fairly specific, especially for law-intensive areas; there is a lawyer in MAFF who deals exclusively with animal welfare, and another who deals with meat hygiene. For less law-intensive areas, diverse responsibilities may be vested in a body of legal advisers; with Culture, Media and Sport a legal adviser in the branch of the Treasury Solicitor servicing the department may draft SIs on broadcasting, the designation of wrecks and football grounds. Moreover, in some legal departments there is occasional sharing of responsibilities, a legal adviser who started work on a set of regulations in some circumstances passes it on to another official.

Lawyers in the Scottish and Welsh Offices, before devolution, had unusually wide responsibilities. This was especially acute in the Scottish Office which produces more of its own legislation than the Welsh Office (the Welsh Office is more often a signatory to legislation developed exclusively in Whitehall than the Scottish Office, which has to draft more of its own legislation). In the Scottish Office it was common to find one lawyer responsible for drafting and advising in areas where there would be several in a Whitehall department. As one SI drafter put it, '80 per cent of my desk was being covered by 13 lawyers of my grade in Whitehall, and 1.5 grade 5s'. Another experienced Scottish Office lawyer said of SIs, 'I have to churn them out like sausages'.

In formal terms, legal advisers write SIs on the basis of instructions from administrators. On occasion this will be the first time that the lawyer has heard of the intention to legislate, but more often the lawyer will be aware the legislation is coming. Indeed, as legal advisers their opinion on, say, what is and what is not possible under existing legislation may lead to the discovery that new regulations are necessary, or that planned regulations are unnecessary. When a fraudulent use of the European Community transit scheme was brought to the attention of an administrator, he went to the lawyer who was:

certain that *somewhere* in current regulations we had the power [to deal with it], but I could not find it. Why [did the loophole exist]? Well, we are all fallible. We are very *communautaire* and all that, but nobody thought about this wrinkle.

The lawyer went on to devise a way of closing the loophole in the existing law. *The Pensions Appeal Tribunal (England and Wales) (Amendment) Regulations 1998* were another example of legislation which emerged following Lord Chancellor's Department administrators approaching lawyers for advice over several years over what was possible under existing legislation.

Even on relatively simple SIs an administrator will check with a lawyer that what is being sent up to the minister for approval in principle is legally possible. On complex or novel pieces of legislation, lawyers are often likely to be brought more actively into discussions about the SI long before it has reached the stage when formal instructions can be issued. In the case of *The Environmental Protection (Prescribed Processes and Substances) (Amendment) (Hazardous Waste Incineration) Regulations 1998*, the lawyer responsible for drafting had been advising DETR administrators on the meaning of the European directive the SI was to implementing (94/67) before a consultation paper was sent out. With *The Contracting Out (Functions Relating to National Savings) Order 1998*, the SI itself was quite simple, but the broader issue of contracting out National Savings functions and negotiating a commercial contract for the purpose was more complicated and involved the Treasury legal team as well as outside legal advisers well in advance of producing the SI.

Lawyers may also be aware in general terms that an SI is likely to be needed in the near future for an issue in their sphere of responsibility. For example, a lawyer involved in an SI implementing a second generation of European legislation in a particular area said:

> I knew about these regulations long before the latest EU regulations. I knew there had been difficulties and complexities and that the earlier job [i.e. the domestic implementing regulations of the first generation of EU law in the area] had gone badly wrong . . . In 1996 I was already . . . involved in trying to close loopholes in the previous regulations. As soon as the text of the 1997 [EU] regulations came out we had a first meeting.

For complex European legislation legal advisers are likely to advise those negotiating in Brussels, although none of the lawyers interviewed directly participated in European negotiations for their SI in the sample. One suggested that although she did not go to Brussels for her particular directive, 'of late things have been changing and we are getting more directly involved'.

Getting instructions

Instructions generally come in written form, although this is highly variable. In one department a legal adviser insisted that all instructions are written 'even in the simplest case' while another in the same department involved in the implementing regulations for an EU directive said that instructions:

> can take the form of 'here's the directive, please do all the implementing regulations'. Or they can be a 20-page note dissecting the policy issues covered in the directive and telling you what they want you to achieve. Instructions tend to be like the first type, not usually quite as bald as that. I have never seen a set of instructions like the second.

The fact that two lawyers interviewed appeared mildly apologetic that the instructions they received were not written suggests that there is a widely held belief that it is good practice to be given written instructions. However, the diverse means of communicating with lawyers was illustrated by a Customs and Excise official based in Salford whose lawyer was in London:

> By and large the instructions are written. Sometimes it is done on the telephone and copied in writing. There were no actual meetings—maybe there would have been if the administrators had been in London . . . we have a videoconferencing facility for bigger issues.

Electronic mail was also an important means of communication, especially for those based outside London (although there is no obvious reason why provincial or suburban centres should be more reliant on email as telecommunications and physical postal systems are not necessarily slower in the provinces than within London).

Some lawyers tend to insist on formal written instructions. With other lawyers, the instructions can be less formal. A DTI lawyer drafting one of the SIs in the sample remembered:

> I got no formal instruction here apart from a call telling me 'such-and-such is happening'. I did not have to think about it because I had done it before.

A Customs and Excise administrator worked out instructions for his SI interactively with his legal adviser. The lawyer 'had an idea about what he wanted the regulations to do, we spoke, I worked something out on the back of an envelope and he used it'.

Administrators and lawyers work together remarkably closely. The gap between administrators and lawyers only ever appeared as an issue in the Scottish and Welsh Offices, and this was largely related to the overworking (relative to Whitehall departments) of administrators and lawyers alike. In Scotland and Wales any one official was likely to be responsible for a much wider set of issues than any counterpart based in London. Otherwise, relationships between administrators and lawyers tended to range from the mutually respectful to the exceptionally warm, and there was little evidence of the different policy perspectives on framing regulations resulting from different professional backgrounds and perspectives noted by West (1988) in the USA. This close relationship between lawyers and administrators is crucial for developing SIs. As one lawyer put it:

If you know your instructions come from someone experienced at doing them you have the feeling of being more confident when it comes to drafting. When you get instructions from new people it may be that they have not absorbed the full horrors of what it is like to legislate in that particular field.

Administrators in London-based departments can develop an expertise in the legal provisions surrounding their patch. As one lawyer put it:

The administrators who work on the SIs are not lawyers, but they have a background in the area they are working on. There is no magic in this. Anyone can read an Act or an SI.

An administrator who knows the law can give better instructions. A Customs and Excise lawyer referred to his counterpart:

She knows how to give good instructions. She is rigorous in going through things. The last thing you want is an administrator who says your first draft is 'fine'. There is a zero per cent chance that your first draft is really 'fine'.

When a Home Office official drafting an SI on police finance found there was nobody within her own ministry or the DETR who knew enough about this issue to be of any help, it was a Home Office administrator who 'said to me, here's the local government levying regulations, we can base them on those, but we need to make one or two alterations here and there'.

The stronger lead taken by lawyers in the initiation of SIs in the Welsh and Scottish Offices was noted in Chapter 4. This carries on into the development of SIs. In the Welsh Office, administrators seemed often quite passive. One lawyer described what happens when you take a draft SI to an administrator: 'they say "oh, alright then" '. Lawyers in many areas of Welsh Office activity appear to get relatively little help from administrators. The role of lawyers in developing SIs was not quite as dominant in the Scottish Office, although in one of the three Scottish Office SIs the lawyer pointed out that after a first draft was sent to the administrator the SI 'died a death' as his office was overworked. Activity on it was not resumed until the lawyer spoke to a new administrator appointed to the relevant post. After a brief meeting when the lawyer pointed out the need to push on, the administrator 'phoned to say "fine, let's go ahead" '.

Developing regulations

Once the administrator has sent (or otherwise communicated) the instructions, subsequent action depends on the complexity of the SI, or the issues it raises. Many SIs are extremely simple to write, especially those which are virtually identical to SIs issued before. For one which simply changes a percentage in the rules governing the Industrial Training Levy for the Construction Board, the legal adviser responsible described his involvement:

I get a five line submission and I have to draft it up. In this case it is nothing very original. It used to be done as a scissors and paste job. You used to have to go through it and substitute '21st period' for '20th period' and the new sum for the old sum. Now on computers that is much easier.

Sometimes developing the legislation involves little more than getting the old text up on the word processor, checking that you have changed all that needs to be changed, and passing the SI on for checking by the administrator. Even if the SI is not largely based on an existing SI, the legislation can be extremely straightforward. For example, while *The Social Security Administration (Fraud) Act 1997 (Commencement No. 6) Order 1998* involved lots of work on logistics for the administrator, for the lawyer it was quite a straightforward matter:

> This was a routine SI. If it had been a bit more complicated I'd have given it to one of my lawyers. It only took about 15–20 minutes. The only slightly complicated bit was putting in the list of earlier commencement orders—but there I just copied the list from the No. 5 Order and added the No. 5 Order to it.

Approximately 15 of the 46 SIs could be classed as very easy to draft in this way.

What makes an SI difficult to draft? Lawyers gave a variety of answers here. Legislation that is complex and in need of consolidation (tidying up through a new law) is one source of difficulty. The length of the regulation can also make it difficult to write. While many SIs are very short, a few lines, some can be very long. *The Export of Goods (Control) Order 1994* is among the longest of the SIs written in the past 20 years. It contains around 64,000 words contained in 13,000 lines on 223 pages. Long regulations can not only be tedious but also present other problems:

> Here's one that is 59 pages long—lots of local government precedent, cross-referencing and technical stuff. You have to make sure you don't repeat yourself and so on.

Regulations which are in character 'closer to primary legislation', since the parent legislation allows great latitude for delegated legislation, were also cited as difficult since the policy often needs to be developed while the SI is being drafted. Transitional arrangements (i.e. arrangements written into the law to make sure that the transition from the old law to the new does not have consequences that one wants to avoid) can complicate regulation writing. Some areas of law are reputed to be particularly complex. Jobseeker's Allowance is an area of legislation so difficult and littered with mistakes and revoked orders that an official parodied the formal recommended style of giving names to regulations by describing a recent order he had been working on as 'the Jobseeker's Allowance open brackets Oh Dear close brackets, open new brackets, Let's Reverse Another Mistake, close new brackets, Regulations 1998'.

Imprecision and lack of clarity was mentioned frequently by lawyers implementing EU legislation. The view of one lawyer was put in different ways by many others:

> In UK law you have to be precise. European law is wiffly-waffly. You can't gloss directives. You are faced with sometimes contradictory vague clauses and you don't really know what they were trying to do.

All lawyers who were being asked to draft something new had as their first priority 'to make sure that I understood' what was being proposed here. European law can be 'mind-bogglingly difficult' in this respect. The lawyer trying to close the loophole in the Community Transit scheme, for example, said:

> One difficulty is that the European implementing regulation envisages a customs debt if an offence or an irregularity has been committed, but does not give a definition of what an offence or an irregularity is. In the Annex they use a different word. I had to define that. There are many other things I had to define . . . The Courts will use the Community wording of the legislation, but in Britain you have to be specific . . . or you can't enforce it. We require gold plating.

Another difficulty with European legislation is working out precisely which portions of a directive can be truly varied in individual member states. As one lawyer put it:

> There are bits in the EU legislation providing that 'it is for member states to decide how to provide for this or that . . .' *But the rats have got at that.* [What do I mean by that?] I mean *do it at your peril!* You may think you can, but there are all sorts of legal consequences if you try. You'll get taken to court and the European Court does not always like it.

Many officials interviewed suggested that the terminology of EU legislation often made it very difficult to understand and interpret for UK implementation.

It is not only in EU legislation that understanding what the proposed regulations are trying to achieve can be a major difficulty for a lawyer. For example, the lawyer drafting *The Specified Animal Pathogens Order 1998* was expected to draft a law covering issues that related to recent advances in gene technology:

> The difficulty in drafting was getting out of the vets exactly what a specified animal pathogen is. They know what it is and can't explain it or write it down. My difficulty is that I am scientifically illiterate. I was lucky because, quite fortuitously, the administrator on this has a degree in microbiology. The people we work with are the vets in Tolworth.[4] They think very differently from lawyers. If you are talking about a test, you get the vet to come in and do it—get a 10 cm bit of bone, put the gunge on it and put it in water—do it right there in front of you. Vets can't write it down. But you sit down with them and a cup of coffee and say 'I'm not going and you're not going until I understand this'.

A lawyer from another department was more blunt about her reliance on the expertise of her administrator to tell her 'when the [technical people] are talking crap'.

Similarly, with an NHS primary care regulation setting up pilot schemes, the administrators had to explain to the lawyers precisely what effect they wanted the regulations to have. This was a task made necessary by the fact that it was already known what schemes were likely to come forward and the regulations had to be drafted around them. Several solicitors interviewed recalled incidents

---

[4] MAFF moved out of its centre in Tolworth, Surrey, in early 1999.

when they had to involve themselves directly in the logistics of what their regulations were proposing. One official recalled travelling to Derbyshire to inspect the factories that his department wanted to pass regulations for, and another in a different department outlined a similar set of experiences with mines and quarry legislation adding 'how can you legislate sensibly if you have never been down a mine or quarry?'.

Once the lawyer has an idea of what the administrator wants to achieve and has started work on drafting, further contact may have to be taken up with the administrator to clarify what the legislation should be achieving or point to some of the limitations of the legislation. As one said, 'I set out [issues] in a paper to the administrator. Sometimes you deliberately overstate things to get their attention sufficiently on it'. Or the administrator may approach the lawyer to explore a change in approach:

> Implementing regulations like these is all about working out a reasonable way forward. One on which you are not going to be challenged legally and which is reasonable in policy terms. You work closely with the lawyers on this one. Maybe you get a comment from a respondent that looks attractive. You ask a lawyer to see if it can or cannot be done in the context of the Directive. You get them to look at the chances of it being successfully challenged in the courts.

Settling details with lawyers is not simply a matter of routine. Important issues can be at stake in the methods chosen to draw up the legislation. What appears to be a legal-technical or even semantic matter can be of major importance. For example, with *The Mental Health Act (Hospital Guardianship and Consent to Treatment) Amendment Regulations 1997*, which prescribed a form to be filled in in cases where a patient is to continue being detained in hospital after over 28 days' absence without leave, '[w]e . . . argued about the word "renewal"— whether the form was really about a "renewal". This was actually quite a major issue and it was passed on to a higher level to resolve the question.' One lawyer writing a regulation concerning a major industry termed such matters of apparent legal detail yet with important consequences:

> detailed policy issues . . . It was not a policy issue in ministers' terms, but it was one as far as the [people in the industry] were was concerned because it would have an enormous effect on them.

Apparently small details can have important consequences. Perhaps the clearest example of a 'detailed policy matter' comes from *The Social Security (Welfare to Work) Regulations 1998* which sought to make it more attractive for those on incapacity-related benefits to enter the labour market on a trial basis. It extended from two months to 12 the period within which the recipient can decide to leave work and go back on benefits without being reassessed and risking losing some level of entitlement. Originally the instructions to the solicitor envisaged achieving this by altering the 'linking period' provisions (section 30c) of the 1992 Contributions and Benefits Act 1992. However this provision only really covered Incapacity Benefit. This would affect primarily only one benefit.

Recipients of other benefits including Housing Benefit and Council Tax Benefit would be no better off. As one official put it:

> When I heard the government wanted to do this I thought 'how do we do it?' [Colleagues] seemed to think we had a simple power to extend the eight weeks to a year. I had to tell them it would not be as simple as that. I did draft something along the lines they suggested, but it would not have applied across the board.

Instead, the team responsible for the SI used the ingenious device of using powers connected with the *assessment* of incapacity which cut across a wide range of benefits—this cross-cutting role for the assessment of incapacity (section 171a of the 1992 Act) was created to avoid the need for multiple assessments for different benefits. As one official put it, 'incapacity is a linking thread through a lot of benefits'. Thus instead of a regulation covering two benefits, the SI covered the broad range of benefits and greatly expanded the scope of the regulations. The approach appeared to be controversial within the DSS as a number of officials warned that the Joint Committee would not agree that the Department had the legal powers to act in this way, but the Committee raised no problems. Thus a somewhat technical legal issue meant the difference between these welfare to work provisions affecting a narrow or a very much broader range of benefits.

The timing of legislation can also be a 'detailed policy issue'. In some SIs, for example, those affected by the legislation could be disadvantaged if arrangements for a transitional period were not set out. With legislation like *The Environmental Protection (Prescribed Processes and Substances) (Amendment) (Hazardous Waste Incineration) Regulations 1998*, one of the major difficulties in drafting was working out transitional arrangements.

> The difficulty is that you have to give time to allow for its application. If there are no transitional provisions, then you will stop someone carrying out their business. This was difficult to draft.

Similarly with *The Merchant Shipping (Small Workboats and Pilot Boats) Regulations 1998* one of the important features in developing the regulations was to take account of the 'interaction between these and other regulations'. The other regulations, in this case *The Merchant Shipping (Load Line) Regulations 1998*, removed an exemption that some had enjoyed for 20 years under *The Load Lines Exemption Order 1968*. They 'would now be expected to comply, hence the need to make provision for a phase-in period for vessels so affected'.

In Scotland lawyers have a role in developing regulations not found in England—applying legislation already made elsewhere. Many Statutory Instruments in Scotland put into a Scottish legal framework delegated legislation developed in Whitehall for England or England and Wales, often with marginal changes to the text. There appear to be two approaches to this task: one which looks at what is going on down south and develops its own legislation, and another which more or less takes the Welsh and/or English legislation and adds, subtracts or amends clauses from it. One lawyer described this as

'Scottifying' legislation. All three of the Scottish Office SIs examined had English equivalents—*The Action Programme for Nitrate Vulnerable Zones (Scotland) Regulations 1998*, implementing an EU directive on environmental protection; *The Grants for Improvements in School Education (Scotland) Regulations 1998*, setting out how extra money found in the Comprehensive Spending Review was to be spent on improving school performance; and *The National Health Service (Pharmaceutical Services) (Scotland) Amendment Regulations 1998*, taking steps against prescription fraud. In two cases the Scottish Office developed its own approach despite being aware of what was happening down south. The education regulation was developed without any significant influence from the DfEE. The pharmaceutical SI was entirely different from the equivalent English legislation despite the fact that the responsible administrator in the Scottish Office sent Department of Health papers to help the lawyer draft the Scottish regulations. The legal framework of the NHS in Scotland differs significantly from that in England and Wales. The description given by a MAFF lawyer in another context fits the relationship between Scottish and English departments quite well; 'Scotland had their own legislation on this. They were interested in who we consulted and what they said, but they did it all their way'.

The Scottish nitrate zones SI was largely identical to the equivalent legislation for England and Wales, *The Action Programme for Nitrate Vulnerable Zones (England and Wales) Regulations 1998*, on which it was based. In such SIs, where the legal framework is not traditionally different from that in England (outside education and other areas such as law and order where Scottish arrangements are most distinctive), much of the lawyers' work is 'Scottifying'. In this case it was described as 'developing Scottish tweaks' to the England and Wales legislation. More generally, the lawyer who outlined the term suggested that 'Scottifying accounts for about 70 per cent of my SIs, but they take a lot less time in terms of working hours. The other 30 per cent is much more work intensive.' Another Scottish Office lawyer agreed that:

> most of my SIs have no separate policy input. Since Mrs Thatcher, the whole idea that Scotland could have its own approach . . . seems to have been forgotten. it has changed a bit since the new government took over. But I still tend to have to keep Scotland in step. If I had to do them from scratch I would need at least two assistants to help me.

In Wales an equivalent process of 'Walesification' could be found with two of the three Welsh SIs examined, with the third Welsh SI (commencing the Government of Wales Act 1998) being distinctively Welsh. In most cases, however, the fact that the (pre-devolution) Welsh Office is a co-signatory with Whitehall departments to delegated legislation without any distinctive Welsh policy or legal input suggests a more limited role for the Welsh Office in relations to Whitehall departments than the Scottish Office.

Styles of working

Lawyers tended to work in slightly different ways. Some tended to try to use, wherever possible, existing models of legislation on which to base their SIs. 'Look', said one, 'this SI is about as simple as you can get. The administrator sent through a previous set of regs., quite helpfully. I checked out the footnotes.' But precedent can be limiting:

> I felt constrained by the 1990 regs. I would have used a simpler system. My style is to write shorter regulations. But the old formula worked and people knew and understood it, so it is best to leave it.

Another had 'thought of drafting it in a different way . . . but this had problems as to consequentials' (i.e. its relationship with existing legal provisions). For one official it was a matter of pride that the legislation on which his SI was based was passed over 90 years ago and had stood the test of time in the rapidly changing area of electronic communications. Others believed it was better to develop your own approach to the regulation. Several suggested that 'sometimes it is easier to draft something yourself from scratch' than try to develop what is being proposed within the confines of existing legislation. The approach of another lawyer to the question of precedent was altogether more radical:

> The old style of drafting has been discredited. When people have got used to the provisions of the old regulations is exactly the time you *should* change them. People *think* they know what the regulations mean, but they don't. You need to shake things up. When I was doing the Electricity Regulations people said 'why change them? They have been the same since 1908'. It made the work harder, but it needed to be done.

Another put it more self-assertively: 'you have to be a bit inventive. I'm a bit of a daredevil, I am.'

Lawyers generally try to keep the language of the regulations as simple as possible, but did not tend to agree on whether simple language was always achievable. In December 1997 the Plain English Campaign awarded the 'Golden Bull' award for gobbledegook to the Department of Trade and Industry for 'its ingenious 32-word description of a pram' (*Financial Times*, 11 December 1997). The description was set out in *The Wheeled Child Conveyances (Safety) Regulations 1997*:

> 'perambulator' means (subject to paragraph (2) below) a wheeled vehicle designed for the transport in a seated or recumbent position of one or two babies or infants who are placed inside a body of boat- or box-like shape, but does not include any carry-cot or transporter for any carry cot.

The SI goes on to define a 'pushchair' in a similar way. One official, not from the DTI, interviewed shortly after this award was announced said:

> I have real sympathy for the official who came up with the definition of the pram. It is all very well for people to point out the absurdity of some of the stuff we write. One

of mine reached the Times Diary with something like 'clause 1 refers to clause 1 and clause 2 refers to clause 2' and so on. It *does* look ludicrous. Yet it is the only way you can handle things in law. You ought to interview the person who thought up the pram one—though perhaps not, because they would think you were taking the piss. I'd give the plain English people a bunch of European directives and ask them what *they* can come up with in three days.

However a MAFF lawyer had little sympathy for this.

When I am drafting, I try to make things simple. I think of whether this judge in south west London, just off Lavender Hill, will be convinced by the legislation that the person in front of him has committed an offence. You have to keep it simple.

The Scottish Office has a legal official responsible for ensuring that the drafting of Statutory Instruments obeys commonly understood features of good style. The 'Stylist' in the Scottish Office is an institution which dates back to the early post-war years. The original idea was for the Stylist to concentrate on formal legal presentational points—whether parts of text should be capitalised, what size font they should be in and such like. The office developed to examine broader questions. The Stylist sees all legislation before it is signed and formally laid[5]. In addition to layout and presentational points, the Stylist looks at *vires* points as well as looking for other possible difficulties any SI may have with the Joint Committee on Statutory Instruments. The expansion of the role of the Stylist from presentational to more substantive questions was argued by one experienced lawyer to be inherent in the nature of the job. As a position concerned solely with presentation 'it must have been one of the most dull jobs going, so people started looking at the instrument to see if it could be improved'. Early signs are that the styling function has been retained and even expanded under the Scottish Parliament.

SIs are generally passed to senior lawyers within the division for comment and approval. In one department this was very elaborate:

I send it to a grade 5 lawyer—the manager here. There always has to be at least one other pair of eyes. No SI is printed before another lawyer has gone through it. So it goes to the grade 5 and then to the grade 3.

The input of other lawyers from the same department and seniors is made in a collegial rather than a supervisory manner. As one said, 'the senior people often suggest better ways of drafting an SI—they are not likely to find a problem with it'. Lawyers may also try out ideas on how to approach drafting in difficult cases with colleagues and superiors and appreciate whatever help they can get.

The lawyer's work does not always finish with the final draft of the SI. The Joint Committee on Statutory Instruments may find something it wishes to question on the SI as it goes through any parliamentary stages (see Chapter 8),

---

[5] The Scottish Office before devolution was also distinctive since it sent machine-readable copies of its SIs to the Stationery Office for publication on disk. Copies of the signed SIs were kept in the Scottish Office.

and this is primarily the responsibility of the lawyer drafting the regulation. Along with the administrator, the lawyer may have to appear in the House of Lords or the House of Commons if the SI is debated there (in the event that it raises some potential opposition in either House). Moreover some SIs are issued in conjunction with other documents—circulars, guidance notes, codes of practice—that have to be written either primarily by the lawyer or by the lawyer in conjunction with the administrator. Indeed some SIs make little sense without these documents. The small workboats regulations, for example, which change the regulatory regime from one based on statute to one based on a code of practice, could not take effect without the code of practice, a separate document. Similarly the NHS Primary Care regulations could not operate without the guidance notes.

In cases where the SI is implementing EU directives, the lawyer is usually responsible for drafting a document informing the Commission how EU law is being implemented, although actual notification is generally the responsibility of the administrator. In some cases this notification appears to be quite formal. 'Implementation tables' are sent to the Commission. One that I saw relating to a complicated directive was a single A4 sheet containing two columns. One column was a list of the number of articles (simply the words 'Article 1', 'Article 2' and so on up to 'Articles 24–25') and the opposite column had terse descriptions such as 'see regulations 6 and 7' or occasionally 'does not require specific implementation by Member States'. In another case the transposition table was sent before the SI was actually finalised:

> We consulted the Commission on draft regulations at the same time as we consulted other interests. We got comments back from them, not on legislative technique, but more by way of 'we could not find a bit that implements article X, paragraph Y' or 'this section does not look quite right since it does not quite address article Z, or have we missed something?'

In other cases the lawyers were less formal about notifying Brussels. One explained, 'we would never send implementation tables. We would send the SI and explain vaguely how it works. If you ever hear from the Commission, it's years down the line'.

CONCLUSIONS

By the time the administrator starts to develop the SI, it either has received approval from a minister or does not need specific approval. In consequence, the development of the SI generally falls to officials often at a relatively junior level in the civil service hierarchy, without much direct intervention from superiors— a point to which we will return in Chapter 9. Superiors are copied in to instructions and major drafts, but in only one case did they intervene directly in the process, and this intervention was by way of offering an interpretation of a particular word in a European directive in response to the lawyer and administrator working on the regulation. In the development of SIs the relationship between the administrator and the lawyer is generally crucial. In some of the repetitive SIs, such as the one putting a temporary ban on fishing in a set of sea areas in the English Channel and Western Approaches, this relationship matters less than at other times. *Yet for the most part the drafting of an SI involves two key individuals*—the member of the team responsible for the 'policy work' and the lawyer drafting it.

Often the lawyer's role is rather mechanical—doing a 'cut-and-paste' job on similar regulations drafted before, but substituting new dates or other amendments. However, it is not always mechanical. In the territorial offices the lawyers appeared, *at least before devolution*, to have a more central role in developing the SI than the administrators. Moreover, in many other SIs the lawyer's role was decisive in what actually was enacted. A good indicator of the importance of the lawyer in some circumstances for the shape of the regulation was the complaint by a lobbyist for a large pressure group that 'we don't get to the lawyers' in the course of consultations. The lawyers, he went on to claim, advise officials that something a group has recommended is legally impossible, 'but there is no mechanism for checking or countering this'.

If we consider that most SIs start life as initiatives from within government departments (Chapter 4) and add to this the fact that ministers rarely get actively involved in the development of the SI, and we also bear in mind the importance of internal processes of consultation with other divisions and/or ministries, we have a powerful potential for bias in the generation of secondary legislation. Viewed from this perspective, the delegated legislative process appears, if not entirely in the hands of civil servants, then certainly something dominated by concerns and issues internal to the executive. To what degree does this delegated legislative process allow for participation of groups outside the executive? One key argument against the suggestion that delegated legislation is a form of 'new despotism' exercised by the civil service is that the process allows, indeed encourages, groups affected by proposed regulations to play an active role in shaping such regulations.

7

Consulting outside interests

The process of *internal* consultation (i.e. within government) is a standard procedure used in almost every SI. To many civil servants the term 'consultation', unless prefixed by the term 'public', means consulting colleagues and superiors within the civil service, whether from the same or from a different department. When, for example, an official in the DSS stated that 'we consulted on this', he meant that he sought the views of officials in other divisions within DSS (see also Department of Health 1995: 8 for advice to civil servants on consultation of this type). This form of consultation was covered in Chapter 6. The concern of this chapter is with consultation with a wider public.

Public consultation can refer to three separate types of activity. In its first meaning consultation can refer to an *indirect* and often (though not necessarily) rather constrained process. Government consults committees and advisory bodies, such as the Advisory Council on the Misuse of Drugs or the Social Security Advisory Committee, which not only contain members from outside government but may themselves conduct an informal or formal consultation with outside groups. In its second meaning public consultation is a *staged exercise*. It involves writing a consultation paper explaining what the government is proposing to do, sending it out to virtually anyone the Department thinks might be interested in reading it, asking for comments to be submitted by a specified date and writing up a resumé of the responses to the exercise for the minister. Its third meaning is best described as *at large consultation*: officials and sometimes politicians floating ideas at different stages of their development to groups or individuals—sometimes by letter or by phone, sometimes at meetings arranged specifically for the purpose and sometimes during a meeting or in the course of correspondence which has nothing directly to do with the matter in hand.

In indirect, at large and staged consultations, the wider public in question is almost invariably a specialist audience; mainly interest groups, but also individuals with a declared interest in a particular subject including academics and professional practitioners such as lawyers and veterinary surgeons or chief executives of local authorities. Certainly the general public is not consciously excluded, at least from the staged exercise of consultation. In fact consultation documents can often be found on the internet.[1] This chapter addresses the

---

[1] The impact of internet consultations cannot be covered here. In none of the interviews with departmental officials was internet consultation highlighted as a feature of the consultation. One respondent, when prompted, argued that using the internet was something desirable for 'openness, transparency and democracy' but that it was 'too early to say' whether it makes a big difference to the process. She added that there were two observable effects so far: that the 'smaller groups with

question of how the process of consultation works on the basis of evidence in part gained from the analysis of the 46 Statutory Instruments examined in detail in the three preceding chapters, in part from talking to interest group representatives and in part from a survey conducted in spring 1998 of 400 interest groups (Appendix E).

The conduct of consultation is central to the questions posed at the start of this study. If the delegated legislative process is a private world, who is allowed into it? And is access to this world allowed to some and denied to others, and who does the allowing and denying? And does any of this matter? If those drafting the SIs have already made up their minds in the first place what they want, then is consultation only at best a device to legitimise decisions and at worst a smokescreen to hide executive dominance? This chapter addresses these three questions by looking, in section two, at what sorts of issue the ministries drafting SIs actually consult on. The third section asks who is invited to participate either in staged or at-large consultations and the fourth section looks at how the results of consultations are handled and whether the consultees' comments ever make any difference to what eventually emerges.

As far as it has been possible to tell, of the 46 SIs examined in this study, 11 involved no consultation during the preparation of the legislation, six involved indirect consultation, 12 were the subject of at-large consultation and 17 involved more elaborate staged consultations. The qualification 'as far as is possible to tell' is necessary because it is difficult to ascertain with any certainty that there was no consultation, or that the consultation was limited to those whose consultation was on the record or known to those closely involved in drawing up the regulations.[2] As a number of officials interviewed admitted freely, it is possible for ministers and others involved in drawing up regulations to meet informally with groups and these meetings may feed into the policy process. One official in the DSS illustrated this in the context of a welfare to work regulation of the new Labour administration:

> You also have to remember that government ministers had come from opposition where they had their own contacts with lobby groups and had seen the problems of the disabled and had their own ideas how to deal with them.

---

fewer resources' who had not been on mailing lists were being reached by the internet, and that the 'people who used to write to us using coloured biros', indicating writers of crank letters, now tend to use the internet.

  [2] A further qualification is that it is possible for an SI to be subject to different kinds of consultation, sometimes at different stages in its development or even at the same stage. The figures in brackets refer to the widest form of consultation to which the SI is subjected (from no consultation at one end through indirect and at-large to staged at the other end).

The design of the study unfortunately does not enable us to look at regulations that started life but never reached the statute book. Non-decisions are notoriously hard to analyse (see Polsby 1980). Yet we get hints that behind-the-scenes dealing—behind-the-scenes even to those closely involved—goes on. Two officials interviewed mentioned in passing particular proposed SIs that never saw the light of day because the minister had been 'got at' by powerful interests concerned—in both cases interests close to the ideological heartland of the respective governments concerned. One of these, for example, went on to say that:

> SIs cause a stink when powerful interests (e.g. the Treasury or [a major group]) are concerned. If it is prisoners or claimants being done down, there is nobody to speak for them, so it goes through.

Furthermore, an official in MAFF suggested that the Conservatives had a record of under-implementation of EU directives because of the closeness of the Conservatives to the National Farmers' Union, and a member of an environmental interest group claimed that legislation protecting hedgerows was diluted because, although a cross-section of groups were represented on a body convened by the Ministry to review the legislation, the locus of power appeared to lie elsewhere. 'The landowners are astute operators. They are all sweetness and light on the Review Group, but they have access to the corridors of power that we don't.' However, it must be added that respondents from interest groups tended to argue that contact with the minister was generally very rare. This was echoed by a junior minister who pointed out that groups 'get in touch with officials. Sometimes they might write letters to ministers—but the civil servants will handle these anyway'.

Nevertheless, consultation, or at least routes through which groups can let their feelings be known, can be diffuse and indirect. The Countryside March in 1997 had a powerful impact on the government, according to one observer of the hedgerows legislation, though it was more by way of making the government nervous about doing anything because 'it was not clear whether [the marchers were] in favour of hedgerows or of allowing farmers to rip them up'. In turn the environmental groups used diverse tactics to try to persuade the government to protect hedgerows. 'One or two story lines in *The Archers* have come out of this building', said the environmental group representative, referring to the long-running popular radio soap about everyday country folk.[3]

We can do little more than acknowledge that groups may have an unobservable but significant or even decisive impact on the shaping of an SI, and that where there is no apparent group contact, we may be missing a hidden contact. However, sticking to the observable contacts, what is the character of the regulations that were not subjected to consultations? It is not possible to divide SIs

---

[3] Attempts to shape story lines in *The Archers* appear to be commonplace. Vanessa Whitburn, editor of the show, claimed to be 'deluged with circulars from government departments and pressure groups seeking to suggest themes for the programme' (*The Times*, 2 June 2000).

up into clear types using categories set out in preceding chapters (e.g. whether they were implementing primary legislation, seeking to make discrete changes or 'shaggy dogs'), and explain the level or type of consultation for each category. For example, some SIs implementing EU legislation were consulted on in a staged consultation, others in at-large consultations and yet others not at all. Let us look in detail at four types of SI from the perspective of their type of consultation: those with no consultation during the preparation of the legislation, those with indirect consultation, with at-large consultation, and those with staged consultation. The following four subsections will largely describe the different types of procedures involved, and at the end of the section we will go on to look at the degree to which the delegated legislative process 'privatises' conflict—to what extent does government exclude some or all groups from the policy process by hiding issues from the process of consultation?

SIs with no consultation

The 11 SIs for which there was no external consultation at all include the politically important—such as the legislation setting out how the extra money found following the Comprehensive Spending Review would be channelled into education in Scotland, and the regulations determining which of the previous Conservative government's law and order provisions the new Labour administration was going to bring into force and which would remain unimplemented. There was no consultation on some routine technical matters such as the possibility of paying duty on cider and perry while it is still warehoused. The most important reason for not consulting appears to be that those involved did not see that there was much choice in drawing up the SI because a prior set of decisions limited or determined what would go in the delegated legislation.

The prior decision could be an international agreement. According to one official *The Dual-Use and Related Goods (Export Control) (Amendment) Regulations 1998* which tidies up UK law following an EU regulation:

> was not sent out to consultation. To some extent that depends on where it comes from. If it is agreed at the international level, then it is too late to go out to consultation. What might happen is that those people negotiating internationally will get in touch with the relevant sectors of industry to ask them what they think and feed it in that way.

An order limiting small boats fishing for cod in some parts of the English Channel and Western Approaches was not consulted on. Again, this was part of the management of fishing quotas, and a ban is imposed only after other avenues have been explored (mainly 'quota swapping': see Chapter 4). The order was perceived by those involved as inevitable in order to prevent or minimise overfishing, as required by the European fisheries regime. The regulations governing cider and perry duties were a technical change that applied to similar goods and consequently had to go ahead.

The prior decision which renders consultation inapplicable in the eyes of those drawing it up may be a political decision, such as over the timing of elections in 1999 for the Welsh Assembly or introducing a limited range of changes to the previous government's sentencing policy. The government did not consult over legislation that allowed the Scottish Office to distribute according to its own priorities extra money the Treasury gave it to spend on education or over legislation which enabled National Savings to contract out its services to private companies—these were non-negotiable policies and the legislation was more or less an automatic consequence of the initial decisions.

Indirect consultations

In some cases, where the legislation originated in a committee (see Chapter 4) consultation with advisory and other groups took place before the legislation was developed. The Fire Brigades Advisory Council, United Kingdom Central Council for Nursing, Midwifery and Health Visiting and the Industrial Training Levy Board were involved in generating three of our 46 SIs. Consultation with these bodies is a statutory obligation. The powers given to the Secretary of State to make delegated legislation are contingent on the ministry seeking the advice of particular bodies. In another case, *The National Health Service (Proposals for Pilot Schemes) and (Miscellaneous Amendments) Regulations 1997*, the Department of Health instituted a national consultative group to deal with the arrangements for the pilot schemes the SI set up, with 'representatives from the ministry and interested parties. All the usual suspects', as a department official put it.

In other cases the consultation comes after the ministry has decided to act. When the Home Office wanted to scrap the Home Office national register of drug addicts (primarily in order to save money), it had to consult the Advisory Council on the Misuse of Drugs (ACMD). An official argued that she:

> told it that this change was coming. As the proposal became firmer, we held a special meeting of the ACMD and it was formally consulted. We wrote a paper for them about the checking function. The Council was especially concerned about the problems that this would cause doctors who would not be able to check if addicts were registered at other doctors. We argued against this on two fronts. First, that any doctor worth his salt would undertake a proper examination . . . and be able to tell if he or she was being treated elsewhere. Also we pointed out that there is a new form of licensing in prospect for addicts . . . with new clinical guidelines covering the whole range of prescribing. We consulted groups only indirectly via the ACMD. This is unusual for drugs legislation since it was not done through the British Medical Association or other doctors' representatives.

With the legislation that set out the formula for levying police authorities to support the new National Crime Squad the consultation was with a Finance Working Group of a larger steering organisation set up to oversee implementation of the

Police Act 1997 on which was represented the Association of Chief Police Officers and the Association of Police Authorities. An official commented:

> The Finance Working Group agreed to stick with the historical contribution [i.e. the same used to fund the Regional Crime Squads which the new authority replaced] . . . The Steering Group was asked to endorse the policy . . . We went to ministers and said 'this is a solution they can all live with' and he gave it his consent.

An elaborate, broad and statutorily entrenched form of indirect consultation is found in the field of social security. According to the 1992 Social Security Act changes to secondary legislation in the field of social security (with some exceptions) must be submitted to the Social Security Advisory Committee (SSAC) (for a description of SSAC see Ogus 1998, Logie 1989). SSAC then decides whether it should ask the regulations to be actually 'referred' to it. In between asking for something to be referred to it and deciding this is not necessary, SSAC can ask the DSS to make amendments so that a formal referral can be avoided. SSAC can be approached before a department has finalised an SI to get its opinion before the SI is drafted. However this happens only rarely. The Committee is more frequently asked to use its 'general advice' remit to discuss broader policy issues in the context of a Green Paper or White Paper. However, when pieces of proposed delegated legislation are referred to it ('if it is referred then it is controversial', one DSS official explained), SSAC does its own consultation. As a member of the SSAC secretariat explained:

> We take the explanatory memorandum as the consultation document. We have a list of about 250 to 300 individuals and organizations to whom we write. The DSS issues a press release which goes to the specialist welfare magazines. The mass press never picks it up. We ask for comments back—we got only ten on one thing we did recently. 50 is about average. The record is 243, and still counting, on the issue of supported housing.

He went on to explain that SSAC had 'around 100 [people and organisations] who are interested in everything', and then there are different groups interested in specialist issues: Housing Benefit, student issues, disability questions. 'We judge who is likely to respond, and sometimes the Department [of Social Security] will suggest people'. In addition, since spring 1999 it has used the internet to post consultation documents, receive comments and publish reports.[4]

SSAC shows that indirect consultations are not necessarily limited affairs. SSAC enjoys a very close relationship with a wide range of groups with an interest in social security. Moreover, the existence of SSAC does not prevent the Department maintaining direct contacts with groups. As a group representative put it, when asked whether SSAC stood between his organisation and the government:

---

[4] See http://www.ssac.org.uk.

No. We hear things from civil servants before they go to SSAC. Also, SSAC does widen access to decision making to groups to whom the civil servants could not talk openly.

The closeness of the relationship was suggested when an official from the SSAC Secretariat argued that 'there are few cases where groups have come along afterwards and said "you really should have had this SI referred" '.

The notion that SSAC enjoys the confidence of groups and is not a rubber stamp for DSS proposals recurred in interviews with SSAC officials and group representatives. An interesting illustration of its independence comes from the appointment of the Chair of SSAC, Thomas Boyd-Carpenter, in August 1995. When the Social Security Secretary, Peter Lilley, announced the appointment it was widely assumed that Boyd-Carpenter was going to be a stooge of the then Conservative government. Under the headline 'General to command benefits body', David Brindle, a *Guardian* journalist, wrote, 'I do not know the gentleman, but he certainly does not appear to have the credentials for the job' (*Guardian*, 26 August 1995). Here Brindle was referring to Boyd-Carpenter's military background—he was a lieutenant-general and former Chief of Staff with the British Army on the Rhine—and the absence of any obvious qualification in the field of social security. Another journalist, Polly Toynbee, was even more strident in her criticisms of the appointment in her article, 'Eminently qualified—for some other job' (*Independent*, 30 August 1995): it was 'disgraceful'. In addition to the absence of any apparent experience in social security, she complained about the nepotism reflected in appointing a son of a former senior Conservative minister, Lord Boyd-Carpenter, and brother of Baroness Hogg, head of the Prime Minister's Policy Unit, as well as about the timing of the announcement just before the August Bank Holiday weekend, when it would attract less attention from journalists and opposition politicians. However, above all this appointment reflected the actions of a 'corrupt and decadent government' because it undermined the independence of SSAC. This independence, Toynbee argued, 'depends on the character of its members, especially on its chairman', and added 'Boyd-Carpenter may not turn out to be the man who will silence these troublesome people, but at least Peter Lilley must think he's on to a reasonable bet'.[5]

While Toynbee and others may have been right about Lilley's *intentions*, they could hardly have been more wrong about the *effect* of the appointment. It was not long before Boyd-Carpenter publicly criticised the government over controversial issues such as social security benefits for asylum seekers (see *Guardian*, 12 January 1996). A group representative commented:

Most of the SIs that we get go through SSAC. Peter Lilley appointed a three-star general who he thought would support everything the [Conservative] Government came up with. But he was quite critical of the government. Sometimes the [DSS] officials try to pull the wool over their eyes, but it does not often work

[5] This prompted the Permanent Secretary at the DSS, Sir Michael Partridge, to write to the *Independent* to deny the charges levelled by Toynbee. See *Independent*, 1 September 1995.

In fact, one official interviewed argued that Boyd-Carpenter's appointment coincided with SSAC finding a new voice to express opinions on the government's changes in social security which were sharper and more focussed in their criticisms than they had been in the past—a point endorsed by journalist David Walker, also in the *Independent*, on 28 July 1996 under the headline 'Bolshie Generals Shake Their Tory Masters'.[6] SSAC has certainly published many critical reports of government proposals since 1995. It has produced reports on issues which generate major controversy in social security legislation. Perhaps the most controversial of the 46 SIs in the sample—the regulation, revoked following substantial criticism from Labour backbenchers, limiting the time that Jobseeker's Allowance is paid (see p. 70 above)—was the subject of a critical SSAC report (see Department of Social Security 1998).

At-large consultations

At-large consultations can be conducted on their own or as well as other types of consultation. For instance, it is quite common for a department to consult with major affected interests before, during or after formal staged consultations. As one DETR official commented on the consultation on changes in small workboats regulations: 'The consultation on this was not lively. Most people with something to say were involved in drafting the code of practice [on which the SI is based].'

The problem with describing at-large consultation is that it is fairly ubiquitous and takes many different forms. The reaction of the official asked whether the new forms devised to handle a certain type of patient under the 1995 Mental Health Act was similar to that of many other officials who deal with relatively straightforward SIs:

> We might have mentioned it to AMHAA [the Association of Mental Health Act Administrators]. It was not a complete surprise to them. Most people will have had advance warning that the new form was coming.

Several respondents to the questionnaire sent to interest groups commented that consultation was not limited to the formal process. 'Pre-legislative consultation seems to work very well' was one such comment. Another argued that the technical issues they raised about a proposed SI were made in 'initial consultations'. A representative of a motor car-related group pointed out:

> We have close links with the Department. We meet quite often to review matters of common interest. One of our members belongs to the international parts manufacturers association COLEPA—means something in French, I'm not sure what. He goes to their meetings. They also discuss what is coming up in the next Geneva meeting

[6] This also refers to the appointment of Sir David Ramsbotham as HM Chief Inspector of Prisons. As with Boyd-Carpenter his military background led many to assume he would be a stooge, and he also proved to have few inhibitions against criticising government.

[where international regulations are developed]. Departments send representatives, sometimes someone from the Transport Research Laboratory. Nothing comes as a surprise. Other trade associations are also kept up to date all along the line.

In short, issues relating to SIs are raised in the dialogue between government and groups at different stages in the development of an SI.

In one form at-large consultations are a more limited version of the staged consultation, except that there is not usually a formal consultation document and the mailing list is more restricted. With the SI changing the Channel 4 levy (see Chapter 4), the Culture Secretary, Chris Smith, wrote to the ITV Association, GMTV, Channel 4 and the ITC—once on 30 May 1997 asking for views and again on 28 July 1997 setting out how the government intended to proceed. Similarly with the order designating rural areas in Wales for rate relief for post offices, the administrator in the Welsh Office contacted the Welsh local authorities.

Consultation can be limited to one or a few particular groups—the ministry gets in touch with them and has very informal discussions about the particular SI. With *The Gaming Duty Regulations 1998* which changed the regulatory regime for casinos, the British Casino Association was involved from the outset as well as sent a formal letter outlining the approach being taken by Customs and Excise:

> We worked closely with the industry all they way through—primary and secondary legislation. The industry may even have seen a draft of the relevant part of the Finance Bill [giving permission to change the regulatory régime by Statutory Instrument] before the Budget . . . They [the British Casino Association] did not say anything—they were very happy with the way we were going through [the regulations].

Or the contact can be somewhat opportunistic. When amending benefits for the disabled an official in the DSS realised:

> one big group we had not consulted . . . was employers . . . There is a panel of employers which meets twice a year at DSS to discuss National Insurance issues, but also considers other statutory measures which impact on it. One of our team went up to them and explained what we were planning with these measures. No problems. Overall we think, actually, they will produce a saving to employers.

With the SI banning the use of videosenders a civil servant pointed out:

> The trade was underground so they were not going to say anything. We got in touch with LACOTS [the Local Authority Council on Trading Standards] to see what they had to say. They were keen on it.

Staged consultations

Staged consultations are the most straightforward and uniform type of consultation. The department concerned will produce a consultation paper setting out the background to the proposed legislation as well as the precise proposals, along with any guidance on the type of issue on which it would especially welcome comments. Cabinet Office guidelines recommend eight weeks for comments on public consultations, but 'for consultations with clearly defined or specialist groups shorter consultation periods may suffice' (Lord Falconer of Thoroton, Written Answers, House of Lords, 25 March 1999). Departments allow usually around four weeks for comments to arrive when such groups are consulted. There was one case, *The Local Authorities (Transport Charges) Regulations 1998*, where one consultation was completed under the preceding Conservative administration which did not have time to complete the task so, as a DETR official stated, 'we added a couple of sections and consulted again'.

To be on the list for a consultation document is no rare privilege, granted only to the few. Civil servants will send such documents to anyone interested in receiving them. As an official put it, 'if people express an interest, they get sent the consultation package'. In one area of European legislation which has been changed so frequently, telecommunications, a civil service respondent spoke of 'consultation fatigue'—members of groups complaining that they have not got enough people to look at the implications of yet another set of proposals for their industry.

Merely expressing interest in studying SIs from an academic perspective landed me on several mailing lists for consultation documents. Clearly, the mailing lists can be very large. For instance, when the Lord Chancellor's Department consulted on changes to conditional fees (i.e. the extension of the principle of 'no win no fee' for lawyers) it sent out around 3,000 copies of the consultation paper—a figure inflated somewhat by the fact that each individual MP was sent a copy. Like many consultation documents, this one was posted on the internet.

Staged consultations often deal with issues related to, but not confined to, a single piece of delegated legislation. For example, with the no-win-no-fee SI consultation, the Lord Chancellor's Department was seeking views on wider questions of the reform of legal aid (Lord Chancellor's Department 1998). In fact, in this particular case, the government was initially planning to move ahead without consultation and develop an SI allowing the conditional fee system to apply to a wide range of litigation (since the principle, established under the previous Conservative government, had cross-party support and encountered no major opposition from the organisations representing the legal profession). However, conditional fees became linked with wider changes in legal aid under consideration by the Labour government (i.e. removing state assistance for certain types of legal cases which could be covered by conditional fees) and officials in the LCD decided that the general issue needed consultation, and delayed extending conditional fees until the whole area had been consulted on. The discussion of conditional fees and the issues it raised (e.g. the consultation document invited readers to tell the LCD if there were any types of litigation for which conditional fees were not appropriate) formed around one half of the document.

Response rates to staged consultations are highly variable. The words civil servants used to describe them are 'lively' (generally meaning more than 50

responses) or 'disappointing' (fewer than 20). A handful of replies 'at ministerial level'—i.e. responses sent direct to ministers by significant groups or individuals—are a further sign of 'liveliness'. However, an official in MAFF gives a
flavour of the sort of disappointment in the consultation process that tended to
predominate among the SIs in the 46 in the sample:

> I used to work on the meat side. Even on vital issues hardly anyone replies.
> Consultation is usually a damp squib. A thing we were just doing jointly with DETR
> on bromides, we sent out to 300 bodies and 65 replied, was a welcome change here.
> I'm used to sending out 600 and getting two back.

Another MAFF official dealing with a separate SI stated 'it was a waste of time.
There were hardly any replies. We found we were chasing up people to make
sure we got some'.

One official in Customs and Excise attributed the low response to consultation on new casino regulations to the fact that the SI was likely to give the casino
industry what it wanted:

> Prior to 1997 every casino had to render its own returns, so a big casino group would
> have to fill out a separate form for every one of its, say, 30, casinos. After 1997 it could
> fill out just one—obviously with breakdowns for individual casinos. This was some-
> thing that we suggested and they said 'yes, yes, the fewer forms the better'. The trade
> association did not say anything—they were very happy with the way we were going
> through them.

But there were also some very lively staged consultations. An SI which removed
the obligation for local authorities to put items out to tender 'had 300 responses.
Most of the comments were welcoming the change'. In the case of the SI extending the no-win-no-fee (conditional fees) principle there were 266 replies.

Occasionally, in staged consultations, departments will summarise and publish the responses to its consultation documents. With the conditional fees document, the Lord Chancellor's Department named the respondents (except
where they had asked to remain anonymous—'usually because they were complaining about their lawyers', as one official interviewed put it) and attempted
to set out the broad thrust of the responses. For example:

> There was general support for the availability of conditional fee agreements. Where
> concerns were expressed, they were mostly about the practicalities of conditional fee
> agreements being used in particular circumstances rather than reasons for prohibiting
> them in particular types of proceedings . . . Defamation is the one type of proceeding
> for which particular arguments have been put forward against conditional fee agree-
> ments being permitted . . . newspapers fear that conditional fee agreements would
> encourage people to litigate in the hope of a settlement . . . (Lord Chancellor's
> Department 1998: 2).

The summary of responses goes on to discuss the 'next steps', above all the decision to 'proceed as quickly as possible' in the light of the 'wide support to extend
conditional fees to all civil proceedings'.

IS CONSULTATION INCLUSIVE?

By all appearances, the consultation process seems to allow for the participation of a very wide range of groups in everyday government. One does not have to be especially prominent or even interested in the legislation to be on the list for a staged consultation. In at-large consultations officials interviewed seemed to be at pains to square things with groups and individuals with any interest in the matter in hand. However, whether the process of everyday government as portrayed through the development of SIs truly allows participation depends on at least two features of the process. Are any groups *excluded* from the process of consultation and do groups have any *influence* on the resulting SI?

To help answer these questions a survey was conducted of 382 interest groups (see Appendix E). To check that the central premise of the questionnaire, that SIs are a significant feature of government-group relations, the survey asked how important delegated legislation was in the range of contacts with government departments (Table 7.1). While the sample of groups surveyed, and even more so the respondents to the survey, cannot be assumed to be representative, the evidence suggests that *consultation over Statutory Instruments is an important part of government–group relations*. Only one-sixth (15 per cent) of respondents' contacts with government never involved SIs, while for just over one quarter (28 per cent) SIs were rarely involved. For one-half SIs (50 per cent) were involved some of the time, while for one-fifteenth (7 per cent) SIs were involved most of the time. SIs play a major, but not dominant, part in government–group relations.

Generally, the majority of groups responding to the survey feel that departments keep them informed about the government's plans fairly early on. On the question whether the government consults groups, only 12 per cent of groups feel that they are kept in the dark 'nearly always'. Under one-third said that it was 'frequently true' that they heard about SIs only when they were published, but well over half (57 per cent) felt that the department with which they had

Table 7.1 Importance of SIs in contacts with government

Statutory Instruments involved. . .

	N	%
Most of the time	26	7
Some of the time	184	50
Rarely	102	28
Never	54	15
Total	366	100

Source: see Appendix E.

most contact gave them advance warning that they were developing an SI (see Table 7.2).

Table 7.2 Are SIs published before groups get to hear about them?

	N	%
Nearly always true	40	12
Frequently true	109	31
Rarely true	174	50
Never true	25	7
Total	348	100

Source: see Appendix E.

Moreover, it is important to note that departments' failure to consult may be a result of oversight rather than exclusion. For example, an interest group representative in the field of pensions argued:

> We are consulted on most things by DSS, but where the legislation has a knock-on effect rather than a direct effect, things can get mixed up. In DTI employment legislation, armed forces and oddities like data protection legislation . . . some things slip through. You get that with primary legislation as well—sometimes consultation is too late. [Officials] have responsibility for a narrow area . . . They don't recognise knock-on effects. You get obscure unintended effects which create havoc. There are all sorts of exceptions and amendments that need to be taken into account.

This was echoed by a DSS official who had been working on some Jobseeker's Allowance regulations.

> Rather late on we realised an odd effect of the legislation for people not normally considered in our client group—people on retirement pensions . . . Retirement is not mainly our concern. Few would have thought of linking what we were doing in with retirement benefits. It shows how complex these things are and how careful you have to be.

The finding that the majority of groups feel they are consulted is confirmed by responses to the question posed of how often the departments consult on SIs affecting the group (Table 7.3). For 54 per cent this is most of the time and for a further 31 per cent it is some of the time. Only 15 per cent, fewer than one in six, feel that they are rarely or never consulted on relevant legislation. This perception that departments consult does not vary greatly by government departments, although somewhat larger than average portions or respondents felt that the Department of Health (26 per cent) and the Department of Social Security (33 per cent) rarely or never consulted them. However, it must be added that the small absolute numbers of respondents referring to these two departments (under 40 between them) means that no great emphasis can be placed on the figures.

Table 7.3 Does department consult you on SIs?

	N	%
Most of the time	172	54
Some of the time	99	31
Rarely	30	9
Never	18	6
Total	319	100

Source: see Appendix E.

The *process* of consultation does not generally appear to be a hurried one. Civil service respondents usually built time for consultation into their planning for delegated legislation, and this might be reflected in answers to a question about whether the Department left enough time for consultations (Table 7.4). 85 per cent of respondents believed the department allowed them long enough to consider the proposals 'most' or 'some' of the time. Fewer than one in six (15 per cent) believed that there was 'rarely' or 'never' enough time.

Table 7.4 Does department give enough time for you to consider SIs?

	N	%
Most of the time	134	44
Some of the time	125	41
Rarely	35	12
Never	9	3
Total	303	100

Source: see Appendix E

Overall, the evidence suggests that government departments generally make serious efforts to consult relevant groups. The notion that only 'insiders' are consulted, or that 'insiders' have any special privileges by being consulted earlier than others, is not apparent from talking to those involved in making SIs or through surveying a large number of groups involved in the policy process. Departments will generally consult anyone interested in the legislation.

RESPONDING TO CONSULTATIONS

The group perspective

It is easy enough to include a large number of groups in the process of delegated legislation by informing them of legislation on its way, and even asking for their views on the legislation. But do government departments listen and take on board their comments? On the face of it, groups appear overwhelmingly to believe that they can influence SIs through the consultation process. 49 per cent of groups responding reported raising objections to proposed SIs in half or more cases, 35 per cent in a minority of cases and only 13 per cent rarely or never. The response of those that make objections suggests that nearly three-quarters (71 per cent) believe the department with which they have most contact listens and 'usually' or 'sometimes' makes appropriate changes (see Table 7.5). An even larger portion (81 per cent) agreed that 'persistence in making known . . . objections to proposed Statutory Instruments . . . produces the desired result' 'most' or 'some of the time'. Only three per cent agreed that persistence never paid off, with 16 per cent saying it 'rarely' produced the desired result.

Table 7.5 The most common response of departments to objections to proposed SIs

Response	N	%
They tend to listen to us and usually make appropriate changes	15	5
They tend to listen to us and sometimes make appropriate changes	192	66
They tend to listen to us and rarely make appropriate changes	77	26
They don't listen to us	9	3
TOTAL	293	100

Source: See Appendix E.

Of course, perceptions of influence, let alone *stated* perceptions of influence, cannot be taken as entirely reliable indicators of actual influence. Interest group respondents may over-estimate their role. Indeed they may have an interest in overstating their influence since to admit little or no influence is to admit failure. This point was noted by Kerwin (1999: 200–1) in a similar study of delegated legislation ('administrative rulemaking') in the United States. The responses in Kerwin's study to somewhat different questions about interest group representative perceptions of their influence are broadly similar to those found in this survey.[7] Moreover while there may be equal bias against civil servants reporting they are influenced by groups, with the possibility that denying 'capture' by

---

[7] Kerwin (1999: 200) asked for the frequency of success in influencing rulemaking. 16 per cent replied 'one-quarter of the time', 41 per cent 'half the time', 42 per cent 'three-quarters of the time' and 1 per cent 'never'.

groups is more attractive than claiming their openness to the democratic virtues of group participation, Kerwin goes on to cite Furlong's (1997) survey of American bureaucrats, which largely supports the picture generated by the interest group survey of a civil service ready to listen to interest group representations. Kerwin (1999: 201) concludes:

> The case studies, information from the *Federal Register* and results of surveys confirm that the vast majority of interest groups are aware of the importance of rulemaking. They devote resources to it . . . They consider themselves quite successful in achieving their objectives. The rulemakers acknowledge their presence, listen attentively to what they have to say, and are convinced by their arguments with some degree of regularity.

Of course, the broad accuracy of the American survey does not prove the accuracy of the British one. Nevertheless, along with other evidence on Britain cited in this chapter, it supports the view that the perception by the majority of groups that they can influence government regulations is not a misrepresentation of their role in the delegated legislative process.

If groups are listened to to a degree approximating that claimed by the respondents to the survey, we may ask: why should government departments listen to groups? The process of delegated legislation is an obscure one. Let us assume that it is unlikely that a group is able to mobilise any significant political support for its position on an SI because the issues concerned tend to be, at least for the general public as well as politicians, highly technical, dull and specialised. Then we can ask: what is in it for the executive to pay any attention to what groups say? After all, Britain is supposed to have a political system dominated by the executive, and while consultation may be the preferred 'style' of government, the executive can and does ignore views of groups where it has clear political reasons to do so. This ability to disregard the views of groups was shown in the relationship between the Conservative government of 1979–97 and major interest groups such as teachers' and other public sector unions, the British Medical Association, the Law Society and the local authority associations, to name a few. It is worth examining this question in some detail since it may offer some clues, not only to why consultation appears to be so highly valued in Britain, but also concerning which types of group views are more likely to be listened to than others.

The drafters' perspective

While there are many officials who may believe that consultation is a good democratic thing, uppermost in their minds is the desire to avoid embarrassment, or, to use a popular phrase commonly used by interviewees, 'things going pear-shaped'. This motivation is highlighted by what they perceive to be the useful results of any consultations. In staged and indirect consultations, as well as in at-large consultations occurring after initial ministerial approval has been granted, *ascertaining views on the policy embodied in the SI is definitely not what officials are looking for* (for a discussion of at-large consultations with groups in the initial stages of delegated legislation see Chapter 4). A civil servant who handled consultation on a local government finance issue stated:

> When we had a draft ready we sent it to the Local Government Association and the Audit Commission for quick comment. We took the policy considerations as read— we were after the technical issues here.

Responses on policy questions tend to be, in the view of many officials inter-viewed, predictable and are discounted in advance. For example, when an offi-cial commented on the development of the SI which scrapped the old Home Office register of drug addicts. The BMA and other medical groups were not directly consulted (but were indirectly consulted via the Advisory Council on the Misuse of Drugs):

> partly because they could only complain about the principles of scrapping the register, and the Home Office took a view that the consultation was not needed. There is no consultation unless it is thought it is needed.

Another example of predictability came in the consultation on an SI relating to relaxing the requirements of the Conservative Compulsory Competitive Tendering (CCT) schemes in local government:

> The main players came back to us—the trades unions and local government. We had 300 responses. Most of the comments were welcoming the change. The views were split between the local authorities that thought the changes did not go far enough and the private sector saying that it goes too far. It was a typical thing that CCT would split along these lines.

No civil servants expressed surprise at any of the comments received from con-sultees—uncertainties over responses were admitted to by civil servants only in cases where the groups themselves were cross-pressured. For example, in the school leaving date extension any reservations that teaching unions had about the extra burdens this might place on teachers were countered by the need to support an apparent educational improvement.

The notion that policy is not generally at issue in staged, indirect or in the later stages of at-large consultations cannot be regarded as a clear guide to action since what is 'policy' and what is 'detail' is never neatly separated (see Chapter 6). Nevertheless, groups tend to recognise that *consultation on SIs is not the time to raise issues of principle* unless there is clear ambiguity in the gov-ernment's own position. One such case of ambiguity was found in one part of the regulations implementing the interconnection directive of the European Union:

> The main area brought out in the consultation was that of who has the right to inter-connect. Annex 4 is discretionary. We set out a policy approach to who should be in

> Annex 4. It was a change to existing policy we were consulting on . . . Lots of opera-
> tors were not happy . . . The operators said it was a significant change in policy, and
> for such a change in policy, they argued, they wanted longer.

The DTI decided to give them longer by not implementing Annex 4 before further consultations.

Where responses to consultation documents questioned the policy behind the
proposed regulation they tended to be ignored. One civil servant said of his SI:

> most comments were not actually relevant . . . there were general complaints about
> what we were doing. I think there was a deliberate misunderstanding of what we were
> trying to do in the SI.

But for the most part regular consultees know the score. One DTI official
pointed out that the industries he consulted made relatively minor suggestions,
even though they were not enthusiastic about the proposed SI because they
'knew what the ground rules were and that they were not going to get away with
anything more than they had already. But they were happy'. An interest group
representative in the automobile sector pointed out:

> 'construction and use' regulations *do* impose costs on manufacturers, but all manu-
> facturers are affected, and one firm is not penalised against its competitors. The indus-
> try as a whole might dislike it, but do not object as much as you might think . . . A lot
> of them now sell cars on safety factors.

Generally, by the time an issue goes out to consultation, the 'policy' has
already been settled. For example, while there was significant opposition within
the fire service to removing age and height restrictions on firefighter recruitment,
the battle for ending what was, in effect, a set of requirements discriminating
against women had already been won before the SI was drafted. The Home
Office research had been commissioned, proving that height made no difference
to the 'functional capacity' of a firefighter and there was a court case pending in
Northern Ireland that seemed likely to force the government to remove restrictions. As one official saw it, by the time the issue came to the Central Fire
Brigades Advisory Council:

> the majority of members of the Council were on board. Some saw the writing on the
> wall—the court case, the research, the move to end discrimination all converged to
> make them accept it. By the time we came to Council there was no argument against it.

If the issue the SI is dealing with is controversial in policy terms, it is almost certain to have been approved by a minister: a junior minister, if not a Cabinet minister. By this time it is generally too late to change the policy. At least, it is too
late to change the policy within the normal consultation process and without
seeking to mobilise broader political support, above all in Parliament (see
Chapters 8 and 9).

On the one hand this means that what gets listened to is not usually criticism
of the policy. But on the other this does not mean that the more detailed the

comments the more likely they are to be taken seriously. Rightly or wrongly, civil servants handling SIs, as well as the lawyers drafting them, generally feel that their own expertise and legal advice will overcome any problems of wording and very fine detail. The Department of Health's (1995: 8) advice to those involved in writing SIs is that consultation should not become concerned with 'the form of words' used to implement decisions. 'Great difficulty', it says, 'and embarrassment can be caused if agreement is on the basis of a form of words which at the drafting stage is found on legal advice not to produce the desired result.' More bluntly, a MAFF civil servant commented on a consultation paper she had sent out:

> Was the consultation lively? No! We sent out to hundreds, but noone was interested. This was very much a scientific thing. It was sent to the laboratories. Everyone who commented was a scientist. So we got lots and lots of pedantic quibbles.

Telling the department how to word its SI is not likely to carry much weight in the consultation process.

Swallowing the principle and arguing the detail is an important ground rule for groups participating in everyday politics. The group representatives interviewed tended to make this point. Moreover, it was written on the questionnaire by several respondents to the questionnaire. One occasional consequence of this ground rule is that a group may have to decide at some point whether the game is worth the candle—is the influence that they may expect to have in making proposed legislation less bad than it would otherwise be sufficient enticement to participation in an exercise that is fundamentally flawed by the policy thinking behind it? This was the choice, for example, facing the an environmental group involved in developing regulations ostensibly aimed at protecting hedgerows. Despite having lobbied long and hard for hedgerow protection, the group opposed them:

> The reason we opposed these regulations was that only one in five hedgerows were captured in it . . . they dealt mechanistically with length, age, number of woody plants and so on, but there is no taking account of the importance of the hedgerow to the landscape. And that judgemental part has always been how we have approached hedgerow protection. . . . Also, the regulations contained . . . exemptions that the landowners managed to put in. . . . It took us 30 years to get some sort of commitment to legislate on hedgerows . . . we had done all the lobbying and campaigning to get the legislation in the first place and we had to make a decision—do we want it? We decided we did not. This was because the next time we asked about hedgerows, the government could come along and say 'done that'. We made a formal response in consultation . . . [but] tried to get someone to pray against it [i.e. raise an objection to it in Parliament, see p. 27]. This is always a hard thing to do.

The group did not take an active part in drawing up the details of the regulations.

So if consultation is not about policy and not about 'pedantic quibbles', what is it about? Four main purposes are implied by the discussions with officials of the 46 SIs in the sample; *informing, making sure, fine tuning* and *getting guidance.*

Informing

One general expectation of consultation encountered in interviews with officials from government departments was of making sure that interested parties know there is likely to be a change in the law and checking that there are no mistakes or ill-conceived portions of the proposed legislation. An official drafting telecommunications regulations pointed out:

> We wrote it out in fairly rough form and we talked to the operators informally in the process. On a practical level, if you want useful comments on a detailed level, they need to see where the major policy options are taking you. Otherwise they would throw up their hands in horror when they see the draft. It is an educational process. It is beneficial to us. Also, if the whole thing is a non-starter you get to hear about it quickly.

Another official in Customs and Excise argued that it responded to the comments received in the public consultation and that most of Customs and Excise's replies 'were to explain what the intentions of the regulations were'.

Making sure

The function of informing is linked to that of making sure. From a civil servant's perspective, consultation is often about *making sure* that your proposals will do what you want them to do and will not have consequences you do not want them to have. If a new regulation comes as a surprise to, say, a sector of industry, they are likely to make a fuss about it in public. If the sector finds errors or unforeseen consequences in the regulation once it has been passed, it can mean being forced to make embarrassing changes. Moreover, as the Department of Health's (1995: 5) advice to its officials puts it:

> It is worth bearing in mind that even if the SI survives the Parliamentary process, there is always the risk of challenge in the courts. Interested persons or pressure groups can start proceedings in the courts to challenge an SI for lack of *vires* even when it has been passed by the JCSI [the Joint Committee on Statutory Instruments, the parliamentary body scrutinising most delegated legislation, see Chapter 6].

One official in the DTI commented 'if you make a mistake, someone will go to judicial review. That is why we need to go to [the industry] sooner [for its views]'. As such, consultation is one of many procedures that has to be observed to avoid 'difficulty and embarrassment'. This is a central feature of the group–government relationship as far as SIs are concerned. One representative of an interest group characterised the government's attitude:

> They say here's '*x* , *y* and *z*' or 'we are thinking of doing something like this' and we want your comments on its practical effects or on obscure repercussions we have not seen.

In abstract terms one might presume there is little a group can do to make its views prevail in the consultation process since the government has the ability to ignore any representations it chooses. The chances of the group mobilising significant political support, either through MPs or the media, in respect of a dry and technical SI are remote. Groups could be safely ignored, in principle. In practice, however, groups are a marvellous hedge against making mistakes.

One interesting illustration of this point comes from the Labour government's ill-fated *Beef Bones Regulations 1997* which banned the sale of beef on the bone following the BSE scare. The regulations attracted criticism because of the apparent imprecision of their key provision: '[n]o person shall use any bone-in beef in the preparation of any food or ingredient for sale direct to the ultimate consumer'. Whether 'gifts' of meat were included in the ban, and whether 'preparation' also included storage of meat to be sold on were two famous sources of imprecision. The government lost a court case (but later won on appeal) precisely because of 'procedural irregularities in the consultation exercise which preceded their making'.[8] The episode took on the characteristics of farce: the Bishop of Leicester urged the ban to be lifted as it pointed to a general lack of understanding by a metropolitan élite in government of rural life ('Bishop urges repeal of beef on bone law', *The Times*, 23 April 1998) and in March 1999 Prince Charles and the Secretary of State for Wales sampled some freshly-carved beef on the bone at an event designed to promote Welsh meat and declared it 'delicious'. Neither 'seemed to be perturbed by the apparent flouting of government guidelines which banned the sale of beef on the bone more than 12 months ago' ('Prince Charles chews over beef-on-bone row', *Independent*, 2 March 1999). One official from MAFF, not directly involved in drafting the regulations, pointed out:

> The big problem with the Beef Bones Regulations was that they used an old consultation list. The list was not that old, but it was not up-to-date. The problem was that they missed out the hoteliers. The legislation is going to go down on a consultation point. There was no time to consult properly. It was all done in a rush and they could have done with more time to consult. It was not the poor old administrator's fault.

At times this consultation may be simply confirmation of expectations. Where, for example, the officials believe that the SI is 'benign' (i.e. the people it is affecting will be better off because of it) they may expect consultation to confirm this. For example with the changes to casinos regulation, reducing the amount of form-filling for individual casinos, Customs and Excise officials anticipated and received no real comments from the casino owners other than that the changes were welcome. Where making sure is a major objective of consultation, no news is usually good news. Since there is no substantial feedback, there is little to change.

---

[8] *MacNeill v. Sutherland* 1998 S.C.C.R., 474.

Fine-tuning

Fine-tuning is a matter of finding the right formulation, or form of words, to put in a regulation. Since the consultation process is not generally about detailed wording, suggested amendments along these lines are usually a by-product rather than an intended consequence of consultation. For example, banks and banking organisations replied to the consultation document on the SI giving banks a statutory obligation to provide the Bank of England with an array of fiscal information. The main response was predictable:

> The consultation was not lively and most comments did not deal specifically with the subject matter of the order, not with the narrow set of issues it covered.

In fact there were only 13 replies. The officials concerned put this down to the relatively uncontroversial nature of the exercise, which put on a statutory basis that which had already been done on a voluntary basis:

> The banks were concerned about privacy. Their comments were similar to what had been said before about providing the information on a voluntary basis—privacy and the cost of providing the information, and we were already aware of these. Mostly they said 'this is fine', but some said it was arduous filling in the forms. We say they are 'forms' but they actually have to fill a great big thick manual. The other SI consultation that came under the Act—on cash ratio deposits—was much longer. Here we actually had to make a decision. What we were deciding was, in fact, close to a tax on banks. We asked them how much they thought they should pay towards running the Bank of England. We had lots of representation on that!

However one change actually accepted was the redefinition of a particular term ('charges per unit of service') since, as one official put it, 'the term the Bank gave us was unacceptably vague' in the initial formulation.

Getting guidance

Getting guidance is a purpose of consultation when the department faces a range of possible ways of framing its regulations, but seeks guidance from the industry or other groups affected about precisely which option should be taken. For example, *The Conditional Fee Agreements Order 1995* has been mentioned already (see p. 138 above). The consultation document on it asked which types of litigation should not be open to the no-win-no-fee financing arrangements. Another example is *The Local Authorities (Transport Charges) Regulations 1998* when the DETR wanted guidance on precisely which services local authorities should be allowed to charge for. One controversial issue in this was that:

> the London Authorities wanted to be able to charge for exemptions under lorry ban orders. But the bans were in the wider interests of the community, so it would not be reasonable for the charges to fall to the operator. This one dragged on for some time. Lorry bans and clearing up after road accidents—these were the controversial issues. Others were agreed by consensus from the outset. Skip licenses were uncontentious.

Similarly, this was true of *The Restrictive Trade Practices (Non-notifiable Agreements) (Turnover Threshold) Amendment Order 1997*. Here the DTI consulted on which of a range of possible limits should be used to determine the threshold for the value of agreements that had to be notified to the Office of Fair Trading. In this case, as in many others, civil servants discounted some of the comments since they appeared to be based on clear self-interest and were generally predictable—'most [firms] argued for the higher rather than the lower figure'.

Filtering effective influence

Effective influence is influence which directly addresses the objectives officials have when they seek outside views. Evidence put to an official that a proposal cannot work, or cannot work in the way intended, is likely to be listened to (informing and making sure). The research design on which this book is based means that none of the 46 was successfully opposed by groups which mentioned why the proposal was ill-conceived or had undesired and unintended consequences. However, one interest group representative described his role in the following way:

> After the Pensions Act there was a consultation document for each area covered—about 20 in all. They asked 'before we pass regulations please comment'. If we disagreed with them, they might ask for a meeting to discuss it. Nine out of ten officials would, anyway . . . When the policy intention is clear, even if we don't like it, we concentrate on pointing out that it won't achieve what they want it to. Most administrators we have a good relationship with. They try to take on board what we say, or justify why they are not going to. But one administrator handling one of the consultations just kept on saying 'but the minister has already decided' even though we pointed out problems. Some months later it dawned on him that what we said was right and he had to draw up amending regulations effectively undoing the[earlier] SI.

Showing up provisions as unworkable or having undesirable effects is not, of course, accepted uncritically by officials who tend to see in such responses ploys to block regulations opposed in principle. For such strategies to work, they have to overcome a strong belief on the part of officials that they know best. As one ex-official responsible for the bailiffs' fees regulations put it:

> I was in charge of the Branch advising the fee structure. We took the distressed rent fee structure as a model. This was a mistake. We should have looked at the fees of private bailiffs for the same work. But we were civil servants and thought we knew it all.

Or the department may feel that despite potential problems, the regulation should be carried through. With *The Social Security Administration (Fraud) Act 1997 (Commencement No. 6) Order 1998*:

> The Local Government Association (LGA) had mainly administrative concerns—some of them were things we too had been concerned about . . . There is no interface between the Housing Benefit computer [Housing Benefit is administered by local

authorities] and the disability computer. However the difficulties of administration were outweighed by the goals of the policy . . .

Occasionally civil servants think that the groups consulted did not actually understand the proposed regulation. In one case, *The Merchant Shipping (Small Workboats and Pilot Boats) Regulations 1998*, the difficulty of understanding a complex change in the regulatory regime for small workboats was compounded by the fact that the full implications of the SI could not be understood in isolation from other documents.

> Many owners of non-cargo carrying vessels did not understand the implications of these actions and that it was at the time only workboats which had been brought within the scope of the legislation.

This difficulty stemmed from the fact that 'the bits applying to non-cargo vessels were not apparent' since the regulations removed some exemptions for them, but retained them temporarily for sport or pleasure vessels until another code comes into force—the Nominated Departure Point (NDP) Code of Practice.

Not all requests for fine-tuning and getting guidance appear to be genuine. On some occasions, such as with the no-win-no-fee order, it struck one group member that the Lord Chancellor's Department had truly made up its mind that there were to be no civil law exemptions to conditional fee funding even though the consultation document was asking for suggestions concerning types of cases where conditional fees were inappropriate. There were reasoned objections from the newspaper industry that this might encourage speculative libel cases, but those who put them forward did not feel they had much chance of success.

Where departments were genuinely receptive to fine-tuning and getting guidance, the decision about which bits of fine-tuning or guidance could be accepted and which rejected tended to follow broad formulae which provided criteria according to which alternative suggestions could be evaluated. This was clearest in the question of which local transport services could be charged for in *The Local Authorities (Transport Charges) Regulations 1998*:

> The Local Government Association, as it wasn't then—it was all these local authority associations—was . . . looking at this area [of finding activities for which they could charge and raise revenue]. They sent a list of things for which they would like to charge. The DoE coordinated the response to the list. Some proposals were accepted—we approved about two-thirds of the list . . . The basic principle was that if there was a clear benefit to an individual or group that was clearly identifiable, we would approve charging. Where there was a benefit to the community or where the charge would not easily be recouped from the persons or groups benefiting, we did not allow it.

With *The Local Government Act 1988 (Competition) (England) (No. 2) Regulations 1997* (changing the compulsory competitive tendering regime for local government) it was similar:

The responses were analysed and weighted. We looked at whether they supported the thrust and what they had to say about the technical issues . . . We had representations about timetables, representations from unitary authorities who felt they needed more time because of the upheaval of reorganization. What you have to do is consider the comments. Weigh them in the round. The general yardstick is whether the proposals and suggestions go in the direction the government wants it to go.

In the case of *The Social Security (Welfare to Work) Regulations 1998*, the question was raised during consultation of how long people with previously certified incapacity to work should be allowed to spend in work before losing their eligibility for incapacity-related benefits if they cannot stay in work. 'Some people wanted a few months, others wanted a lifetime extension for certain conditions' an official explained. The eventual decision reflected a general principle of equity. 'There are policy reasons why someone who had been off work for ten years should not be better off than someone who has not'. Equity is a powerful norm used by civil servants to filter representations from interest groups. With *The Local Authorities (Transport Charges) Regulations 1998*, again, 'the accident débris parts got the interest of the insurance industry. The National Utilities Group warned of the costs to their members. They were already subject to charges, but we concluded there were no grounds for treating them differently.'

CONCLUSIONS

The empirical evidence in this chapter points in two apparently contradictory directions. On the one hand there is the evidence that the process of consultation, like that of initiation of SIs, is dominated by the executive. While the question who gets consulted is not always a matter for discretion by government departments, and while government departments seek to involve a wide range of interests in the consultative process, the terms of the consultation as well as the reception of comments, suggestions and objections are highly constrained by what those officials running the process want and expect from it. Comments are certainly not ignored; rather they are sifted through the largely preformed filter of what is useful and improves the proposed SI and what is off the mark or unacceptable. On the other hand, the evidence from the interest groups, above all the survey as well as speaking to interest group representatives suggests a much more open process of consultation—one where groups feel involved, believe they are being kept abreast of government department thinking and given time and opportunity to make a contribution to policy.

A sceptic might simply dismiss the survey evidence of interest groups as but another example of the principle, made famous by Mandy Rice-Davis during the Profumo scandal of the early 1960s, encapsulated in the phrase 'he would say that, wouldn't he?'. Interest group representatives are hardly going to admit, according to this argument, that they have little influence and are likely to talk up their impact in the process of consultation. It is true that the case studies of 46 SIs unearthed a number of rather limited examples of interest group influence, but no evidence of the kind of powerful role for interest groups associated with, for example, policy-making in the United States.

Nevertheless, the two directions in which the evidence appears to point— executive domination and interest-group participation—can be reconciled if one lowers one's expectations of what can be achieved through consultations on delegated legislation. Statutory Instruments are not exercises in communitarian participatory government, they are the means by which government exercises powers it has already given itself through Parliament in primary legislation. Interest-group representatives know and understand this. As one interest group representative put it succinctly:

> The [department] is very good. If you ask to meet them, they'll listen, but they will not negotiate. As civil servants they decide what they want to do and consult once they are clear. They change things only if there are very strong arguments to do so.

From this perspective, the opportunities offered by consultation processes give groups a chance to make their points, possibly early in the consideration of the SI rather than, or as well as, in the formal consultation. Influence is not guaranteed, but if their case can be made in a form that fits the conception of what government officials want to achieve with their proposed SIs, there is a chance that their views will be taken on board. This type of influence is clearly quite a step up for the groups from having no influence whatsoever, even if it falls far short of the model of group pluralism shaping policy outcomes. In an executive-dominated system with what Lijphart (1984) terms a 'majoritarian' approach to conflict management (i.e. where majorities feel no need to share power with or make concessions to minorities), it is not surprising that the opportunity to have an influence, limited though it may be, offers significant cause for satisfaction among those groups who do participate in this way.

Yet group participation is not limited to consulting on SIs in the manner and at the time determined by the government department. This chapter has concentrated on the role of groups in everyday politics. It is quite possible for groups to take issues *out* of the realms of everyday politics and move them into a much wider political arena. This and earlier chapters have already discussed some SIs that have become less obscure and caused political problems for the department and minister responsible for issuing them—the SIs dealing with Jobseeker's Allowance cuts and the Beef Bones Regulations. The ability to shift an issue out of one arena which is dominated by the executive into an other where majorities and political support matter is a major resource for interest groups in the delegated legislative process.

It is not always an easy task to make the subject of an SI the subject of substantial political controversy. We will come back to this point again in Chapter 9. However, the most important route through which issues can leave the world of everyday politics and enter the world of what will be later termed 'high politics' is through Parliament. It is tempting to believe, along with Walkland (1968), that Parliament's influence on the process of delegated legislation is limited. Such a view is mistaken. Parliament is crucial both in understanding the mechanics of the delegated legislative process and in understanding the limits of everyday politics, so it is to the parliamentary role in delegated legislation that we now turn.

8

The discreet impact of
parliamentary scrutiny

In an executive-dominated system the role of Parliament is limited. The whole point of delegated legislation is that Parliament does not *have to* look at it closely[1]. And Parliament does *not* look at it very closely. In 1993 Bob Cryer argued that the 'torrent of [delegated] legislation is turning Parliament into a sausage machine' (HC Debates, 17th Feb 1993, vol 219 col. 319). Although Parliament's precise involvement in any one piece of delegated legislation varies with the status of the individual legislation (see Chapter 2), parliamentary scrutiny broadly takes two major forms. The first—which the vast majority of SIs have to pass through—is scrutiny over *legality*. This form of scrutiny concerns above all the ability of the government to make the legislation, the *vires* question, the way in which these *vires* are exercised, and the internal consistency, coherence and clarity of the regulation. The second form is parliamentary scrutiny of *policy*—whether the regulation ought to be made in the first place and whether its substantive effects should be altered. As with all distinctions between 'policy' and 'administration' the dividing line between scrutiny of legality and policy is not always clearly identifiable. In the case of SIs, to judge whether a department is, for example, acting within its *vires* when it issues a regulation is not always a technical matter. It can involve an interpretation of what Parliament intended when it passed the parent legislation and thus scrutiny of legality can start to appear to define policy.

While such fuzziness must be acknowledged, it does not invalidate the fact that the distinction between the two types of parliamentary involvement usefully distinguishes between the different roles that Parliament performs in most cases. Central to the scrutiny of legality is the Joint Committee on Statutory Instruments (JCSI).[2] Scrutiny of policy is conducted in debates in the House of Lords and the House of Commons, both on the floor and in standing committees. A minority of SIs pass through any form of scrutiny of policy—the opportunity to provide such scrutiny is guaranteed only in the relatively few cases

[1] As a Welsh Office lawyer pointed out, devolution for Wales, based as it is upon the exercise of a range of delegated legislative functions by an elected body, may lose some of the advantages of delegated legislation of speed and flexibility.

[2] This chapter is concerned with the generality of delegated legislation and excludes the work of the Deregulation Committee, as well as the House of Lords Delegated Legislation Committee. The latter is not directly involved in delegated legislation since it examines the delegated legislative powers contained in primary legislation.

when the parent legislation requires it (above all in 'affirmative resolution' SIs), but others can become the subject of such scrutiny because they have been 'prayed against' and allocated time for debate. The formal procedures for scrutiny were outlined in Chapter 2. The purpose of this chapter is to show how these forms of scrutiny work in practice and, above all, to assess their impact upon the everyday process of delegated legislation.

THE JOINT COMMITTEE ON STATUTORY INSTRUMENTS

The work of the JCSI

All SIs, including those not subject to parliamentary procedures and those which are not required to be laid are examined by either the Commons-only Select Committee on Statutory Instruments (SCSI) or the JCSI. Where the parent legislation specifies the SI be laid before the House of Commons only, it is examined by the SCSI. Most SIs are considered by the JCSI—of the 11,003 SIs considered by both Committees between 1991/2 and 1997/8, all but 786 (7.1 per cent) were considered by the JCSI. The discussion of this form of parliamentary scrutiny therefore concentrates on the JCSI.

The JCSI has 14 members—seven from the Lords and seven from the Commons—and is chaired by an opposition member of the Commons. The seven Commons members form the SCSI. The JCSI was created in 1972 to replace the separate committees in the two Houses scrutinising delegated legislation. Under the present Commons Standing Order 151 (like its predecessor orders) the Committee is to have 'the assistance of the Counsel to the Speaker'. There are, besides the Speaker's Counsel himself, two Assistant Speaker's Counsel to assist him in the work of scrutiny and advice. The Joint Committee also is to have the assistance of Counsel to the Lord Chairman of Committees. The Standing Orders of the House of Lords require that the meetings of the JCSI take place on Tuesdays. They generally last an hour.

When the SI is laid, a procedure handled by the parliamentary branches of the main issuing departments, copies are sent to the Clerk of the Joint Committee from the parliamentary office of the department issuing the SI. The Clerk passes it on to the two Assistant Counsel, one of whom assigns it to a particular week's agenda. The scheduling of the instrument depends in part upon how pressing the SI is—a negative instrument needs time to be prayed against, for example—and in part on how heavy is the workload on any particular Tuesday. The assistants try to even out the amount of work over the weeks ahead. Each SI is assigned a letter (running from 'A' and 'B'—the affirmatives—through 'G' to 'M') defining its status and place on the agenda. For example 'G' refers to instruments subject to annulment, 'J' stands for instruments laid but not requiring any parliamentary process and 'M' refers to SIs subject to special procedures.

Affirmative resolution SIs are sent straight to the House of Lords, to the office of the Counsel to the Chairman of Committees.

Affirmative resolution SIs by convention are sent directly to the House of Lords because under its Standing Orders all affirmative SIs have to be considered by the Joint Committee before they can be considered by the House of Lords. In fact the Lords' consideration of affirmative resolution SIs offers them a form of influence not found with other sorts of SIs. Although Speaker's Counsel handles all the instruments (including those requiring affirmative resolution) within the jurisdiction of the SCSI, with affirmatives (and draft affirmatives) which are to come before the JCSI, Speaker's Counsel has no role. In such cases scrutiny and advice to the Committee are the function solely of Counsel to the Lord Chairman of Committees. He can directly contact the department concerned if he sees something in the SI he does not like. Since the affirmative resolution SIs are drafts, it is possible for the department responsible to be directly asked to change something in the SI, a possibility not available for most other SIs which a minister has already signed as law.

The bulk of the work of the Joint Committee is done by Speaker's Counsel, the assistants and, as regards affirmative instruments, the Counsel to the Lord Chairman of Committees. Both Speaker's Counsel and his assistants will go through each SI, along with the parent legislation and look for issues to report to the Committee. There are three broad stages in considering an SI. The first stage is deciding whether the Committee should write to a department asking a question about an SI. This is the only stage for a large majority of SIs since the JCSI asks further questions about very few. Of the 1,565 SIs considered by the Committee in 1998 no action was taken on 1,352 or 86 per cent. On the few that do attract its attention, the Committee decides to issue a question if the SI appears as though it may offend against any of the criteria by which it is asked to consider them. The position is summarised by Boulton (1989: 552):

> The Committee may draw the attention of Parliament to an instrument on any series of specified grounds, or on any other ground not impinging on the merits of or policy behind the instrument. The particular grounds on which the Committee may act are that an instrument imposes or prescribes a charge on the public revenues or requires payments to be made for any license or consent or other service from a public body; is made under an enactment excluding it from challenge in the courts; purports to have retrospective effect where the parent statute does not so provide; has been unjustifiably delayed in publication or being laid before Parliament; has not been notified in proper time to the Lord Chancellor and the Speaker where it comes into effect before being presented to Parliament; gives rise to doubts whether it is *intra vires*, or appears to make an unusual or unexpected use of the powers conferred by the parent statute; requires elucidation as to its form or purport; or is defective in drafting.

Such decisions are largely made on the advice of Speaker's Counsel rather than the members of the Committee. If a question is asked, the Department has 14 days to reply (the second stage). In the third stage, the SI comes before the Committee again with the reply from the department. Counsel will advise whether to accept the department's explanation. In 1997/8, the Committee took 213 SIs past the first stage, 59 gave satisfactory replies and 154 were reported.

The grounds for reporting are dominated by the criticism of 'defective drafting'. This covered over one half of all points raised against SIs between 1991/2 and 1998/9 (Table 8.1). Defective drafting can refer to a variety of largely technical errors. For example, in the 20th report of the session 1998/9 it reported *The Scottish Parliamentary Elections (Returning Officers' Charges) Order 1999* for defective drafting on the ground that 'reference in article 1(2) to section 8 of the Scotland Act 1998 should be to section 9'. SIs that are reported as requiring elucidation usually contain some imprecise or some apparently confusing provisions. For example in *The Secure Training Centre Rules 1998*:

> Rule 11(1)(b) entitles a trainee to receive a visit once a week. Rule 11(2) gives him an additional entitlement to 'receive visits'. The Committee asked the Department to explain the purpose of paragraph (1) (b), given the quoted words of paragraph (2). The Department explain that the entitlement in rule 11(1) (b) is an absolute entitlement, and that the entitlement to receive further visits under paragraph (2) is subject to the provisions of the Rules and therefore discretionary. The Committee reports rule 11 as requiring the elucidation provided by the Department [31st Report 1997/8].

The 'dubious use of *vires*' covers fewer than one in six of the grounds for reporting an SI. Criticism of an SI on the ground of the use of *vires* may be the simple claim that an SI may be *ultra vires*. *The Public Record Office (Fees) Regulations 1999* were criticised by the Committee on the ground that they did not specify the fees to be charged for the supply of documents, preferring to state that the fees would be 'supplied on request'. Section 2(5) of the Public Records Act 1958, under which the SI was made, requires that fees be specified. 'Unjustifiable delay' (1.6 per cent of grounds for reporting SIs) refers to delays between the making or laying of the instrument and it reaching the Joint Committee. The 'other' category in Table 8.1 includes a variety of reasons for reporting an SI including incomplete footnotes or the absence of an explanatory note.

Table 8.1 Reasons for Reporting SIs 1992–1999[†]

Grounds	%
Defective Drafting	53.9
Elucidation required	20.9
Vires in doubt	15.4
Delay	1.9
Other	7.9
TOTAL	100.0

N=1,764
[†] A single SI can be reported for more than one reason
Source: House of Commons Sessional Returns (annual)

The impact of the JCSI

The JCSI has a far greater impact on the process of delegated legislation than the 10 per cent of those that are reported by it would indicate. The likely reaction of the JCSI is in the minds of those that draft any SI, since what they draft will eventually be referred to it. Where the SI is almost an exact copy of an older SI there is some confidence that it will pose no problems with the Committee, but even this cannot be guaranteed. Even the well-worn Construction Board Levy Order attracted the Committee's attention, according to one civil servant:

> Last year the [two separate] Engineering Construction Board Levy and the Construction Board Levy Orders were compared and the Minister had to explain the significance of the differences in drafting. The Minister was angry about the pressure he was put under.

Inaction is not an option when the JCSI asks for information or clarification.

The impact of the JCSI is pervasive despite the fact that it is widely appreciated that the Committee is overworked and some items to which it may want to raise objections are likely to get through unnoticed. Most lawyers who have been drafting SIs for a few years are able to find examples of ones that got away:

> One of my first major gaffes . . . [was when] . . . I forgot to change the date on a very straightforward order updating the rate of levy on one sector of industry. This meant that there was a negative levy. This had to be revoked and remade—once signed it is the law. Some things can slip through the Joint Committee.

Not all of the ones that slip through are as innocent as that:

> Look at the NHS and Community Care Act 1990 on fundholding . . . I don't think anyone in their wildest dreams would have thought we would take fundholding as far as was done under that section. All sorts of fundholders were derived from that . . . We ended up with three or four different types of fundholder. Some of them stretched the *vires* of the legislation very much.

Moreover, the impact of the JCSI is pervasive despite the fact that JCSI criticism does not actually force departments to take swift remedial action, or indeed any remedial action. We can see this in departmental responses to JCSI reports. In 1997 the Joint Committee instituted a system of monitoring progress on the SIs they reported. Thus it is possible to see what was done in response to the criticisms. Table 8.2 shows the number of points reported in 1997 still to be resolved in 1998 ('points outstanding'), those that remained outstanding at the end of 1998 ('remaining outstanding') and those on which the department and the JCSI simply disagree. Table 8.2 also shows the SIs reported in 1998 and those that had criticisms still outstanding by the end of the year. The Joint Committee uses different categories to describe the data on its returns to those given in the sessional statistics, and so Tables 8.1 and 8.2 are not comparable.

Some criticisms require no further action anyway. Some aspects of defective drafting with, as the JCSI puts it, 'no harmful effect' or 'superfluous recital of power', and even some 'unexpected use of *vires*' do not require the relevant department to take any remedial action. With others, such as an 'incomplete explanatory note' or some requests for 'further elucidation', the JCSI can be satisfied without a new SI. Other aspects of defective drafting, some 'unexpected use' criticisms as well as those alleging 'dubious *vires*', require changes to legislation. Failing this the department can simply disagree with the JCSI.

If we take the most serious criticism that the JCSI might make of an SI, that it is either *ultra vires* or the *vires* are in doubt, five such points were outstanding in 1997. In three cases the department indicated that a replacement SI was envisaged for 1999, and in two cases the Government indicated it was giving itself the *vires* by primary legislation. In 1998, of the five SIs reported on the same grounds, the department indicated it was introducing new primary legislation giving it powers to do what it wanted in two cases and was planning a new SI to address the problem in one case. In a fourth case the department reported it was 'considering alternative approaches', and in the fifth it said '[t]he Secretary of State [will] write to [the] Joint Committee'. While departments make very strong efforts to remedy defects in legislation identified by the JCSI, it is ultimately possible for a department to ignore the JCSI's reports.

While the impact of the JCSI was pervasive, lawyers tended to have different views about the value and effect of its comments on their handiwork. Some officials pointed to the fact that their requests for memoranda and the issues on which they report SIs can be picayune. The lawyer who argued that the Committee had not noticed a coach and horses being driven through the *vires* concerning fundholding in the NHS and Community Care Act 1990 added 'these are the sorts of things the joint Committee should be picking up, instead of saying that a word should be spelled with a small "s" rather than a capital'. Another, whose SI was reported by the JCSI, complained: 'I thought what they [the JCSI] did was not far short of frivolous. I'm surprised they have the time for it.' Another explicitly distinguished between different types of JCSI query:

Table 8.2: The Consequences of SIs being reported by the JCSI

Grounds for reporting	SIs from 1998 with points outstanding			SIs from 1997 with points outstanding	
	raised 1998	end 1998	disagree	start 1997	end 1998
Defective drafting	97	67	7	119	93
Dubious vires	5	3	2	5	4
Elucidation	29	5	1	1	1
Unusual use	7	3	1	4	2
Failure proper practice	3	1	1	2	2
Explanatory Note	1	0	0	3	2
Other	12	2	2	3	1
TOTAL	154	81	14	137	105

Source: JCSI First Special Report 1998–9

I used to get excited about Joint Committee memorandums, but now I couldn't care less. Sometimes you feel points are raised just to keep people in a job. If it's a *vires* problem, we'll correct it immediately. If not, we give an undertaking to change it at the next available opportunity—six months or so later.

Another summed up his reactions to different criticisms of a long and complex SI for which he was responsible:

Seven points were taken up in its report . . . Some were about proof-reading errors. Otherwise it took up points on drafting which, in our defence, came from the undue haste in which we had to work . . . The comments are of all types. Some are exercises in pedantry. There are some general points—ones you want to stash away for future occasions. And there are details and points of substance that need attention.

Given that the JCSI is frequently perceived as having a tendency to split hairs, how can we say its impact is pervasive? Its influence can be seen in the drafting of SIs which use the powers of the parent primary legislation in ways that have not been done before. Here those who draft SIs are more likely to face the most important and potentially damaging criticism by the Committee—that the legal powers either were not there or were being in some way misused. The impact of the JCSI is most visible in the efforts that officials put into making sure that their SIs are not challenged by the Committee. In some cases lawyers reported informal contacts with the officials servicing the JCSI for an opinion.[3] A Scottish Office lawyer, for example argued:

It is handy to keep in with people like him [referring to a former Speaker's Counsel]. You could have problems with *vires* and he is useful to keep on side. When we were doing the Poll Tax [SIs] my colleague wanted to keep him on side because he wanted to use some rather novel instruments.

In a regulation making inventive use of existing primary legislation, the lawyer from a London-based department ruled out seeking informal advice from Speaker's Counsel since he was 'confident that this is the only way to do it'. He wanted to make sure that the Joint Committee had no objection to this and added 'you notice the long statement of powers at the start of the SI—I cited more powers than I really needed to show the Joint Committee that we had them'. He added, 'I had no problem with the Joint Committee . . . My view is that it was too complex for them'. His administrator had another explanation for it—the list of powers was 'sleight of hand' as only one of them was truly relevant.

The fact that lawyers seek to avoid JCSI attention affects the way they approach their drafting. One obvious strategy is not to draft things in ways that are known to have caused problems with the JCSI in the past, since 'some things they are especially hot on—power of entry into domestic premises, liberty of the

---

[3] All lawyers assured me this was exceptionally rare. However in at least four of the SIs in the sample, lawyers admitted that they had sought informal advice from JCSI officials. While this is not a random sample, it still suggests that such informal contacts may not be particularly rare.

subject and all that'. Lawyers find out what the JCSI dislikes through a variety of means: their own immediate experience, discussion with colleagues, reading JCSI reports,[4] departmental instructions for drafting (e.g. Department of Health 1995), the Cabinet Office guidance on drafting (Cabinet Office 1987) as well as the related circular series Statutory Instruments Practice. In addition there are courses on SI drafting at the Civil Service College. A lawyer who drafted one of the SIs in the sample happened to be a tutor at the College: 'that's one thing we tell our students . . . they have to read JCSI reports'. Moreover, those drafting SIs can look at the debates on the primary legislation to see whether their proposals go against the intentions of Parliament. In *The Social Security (Welfare to Work) Regulations 1998*:

> there were questions about whether the relevant power [in the primary legislation] . . . would allow us to do what we wanted [extend the linking period for benefits from eight weeks to a year]. When the power was being taken out, the then opposition put in an amendment to make the eight weeks two years straight away. So if Parliament was being asked to do that then, it seems to be in the realms of possibility to do it now.

That officials drafting SIs make considerable efforts to avoid attracting the attention of the JCSI can be seen in the reaction of two such officials in the sample—one from the Welsh Office and the other from the Lord Chancellor's Department—to the known problems associated with 'designating'. This problem is best explained with an example. *The Conditional Fee Agreements Order 1998* was made under a provision of the 1990 Courts and Legal Services Act (section 58(4)), which allows 'no-win-no-fee' arrangements in 'proceedings of a description specified by order made by the Lord Chancellor'. In the Order, the Lord Chancellor's Department wanted to specify *all* proceedings as subject to conditional fees. The Committee has in the past, as it did with this SI (JCSI 1998), reported to Parliament regulations which stipulate that the *totality* of any class of items can be 'specified' (in this case it is legal proceedings but in other regulations it could be schools or areas of the country). To 'specify', according to the JCSI, means to say that only *some* are separated out for distinctive treatment, not all. In this case 'the issue which concerns the Committee is whether Parliament intended the power to specify a description of proceedings to be used to specify all the proceedings not covered by section 58(1) (a)' (JCSI 1998: para. 2). The Welsh Office wanted to 'specify' all of Wales as a rural area in *The Non-Domestic Rating (Rural Settlements) (Wales) Order 1998* and, like her counterpart in the Lord Chancellor's Department, the lawyer knew this was likely to pose a problem with the JCSI.

The strategies used were slightly different in each case when this problem was raised. The Welsh Office decided to 'designate' as rural areas all of Wales except for a few small areas. The lawyer involved explained:

---

[4] The 1996 First Special Report of the Joint Committee lists some of the more common failings of SIs it examined in the preceding ten years (Joint Committee on Statutory Instruments 1996).

The administrators set down lists of areas to be designated as rural. We had problems. They wanted to designate the whole of Wales as a rural area except for one or two very small areas. Even Cardiff and Swansea. I thought that we might have a *vires* problem here . . . We ended up defining 22 counties and county boroughs as rural areas and excepted some parts . . . We heard nothing from the JCSI, surprisingly.

With the conditional fees issue, the Lord Chancellor's Department was bolder. Informal contacts with JCSI officials had confirmed what was already known: that the Department was going to have a problem with this one. One strategy was to designate all legal proceedings and then make a token exemption:

> We had an exemption all ready in case they insisted on it. We deliberately tried to find something odd, which would work as an exemption but not remove anything significant from the scope of conditional fee agreements and we identified a provision in the Marriage Act 1949 which allows County Courts to give permission to those aged under 18 to marry where the parents have withheld consent.

In the event, the department decided against this strategy and submitted a memorandum to the JCSI (JCSI 1998), more or less refusing to go through the charade of token exemptions. The JCSI, as expected, reported the Order. Officials in the Lord Chancellor's Department were not unduly worried. As one put it, '[w]ithin the division we were confident that this did not have any *real vires* problems and that we had sound arguments to back us up'. The Order (an affirmative instrument) was eventually passed by resolution of both Houses of Parliament. Although there was a major debate on this, and a division in the House of Lords, the debate did not touch on the JCSI's objections.

Such episodes illustrate that the JCSI hovers over the shoulder of lawyers drafting SIs in the same way that the Judge Over Your Shoulder pamphlet (Cabinet Office 1995) issued to civil servants was supposed to remind non-legal officials that a court could pick them up on anything they did, and that they should act as if everything was going to be tested in court. Apart, however, from a brief and unsustained period in the early 1990s (in the 1992/3 and 1993/4 sessions) when the number of SIs reported each week was double the average number reported in adjacent years,[5] it is by no means a certainty that errors will be detected. Most lawyers responding seemed to understand there was often an element of chance in being picked up by a Committee dealing with such a large volume of legislation with such a small staff. Moreover there is an ambivalence among many legal officials about the institution. It affects SI drafting practices profoundly, yet the same officials who point to its profound importance may also allege a degree of prolixity, inconsistency and inefficacy. One official who stressed its importance throughout the interview nevertheless pointed out that a few years ago the JCSI was:

---

[5] Reasons for this may include the clearing of a substantial backlog as well as the transition from one Speaker's Counsel to another in 1994.

in a shambles. The reports came out three years after the SIs. The backlog is not so bad now, but the reports come in well after it is too late to do anything, so it is water off a duck's back.

The reaction of a lawyer in a large department responsible for a wide range of public services captures this mixture of respect and mild irritation:

> We had to include things such as the provision that 'copies of the directions shall be provided'. We knew that everyone who wanted them would have them anyway, but I included that because the Joint Committee is very keen on that sort of thing. They get hung up on the niggling, technical sort of thing.

So how may one explain its pervasive presence over the shoulder of those drafting SIs?

The impact of the JCSI can be put down to four main factors. First, and most obviously, there is the question of the status of an SI which is deemed defective in some sense. If the SI reflects a misuse of primary powers, or a law passed in the absence of proper primary powers, then it can face litigation, and the JCSI's judgement may be taken as an indicator of the legal soundness of the measure. As the Department of Health (1995: 5) reminds its officials:

> It is worth bearing in mind that even if the SI survives the parliamentary process, there is always a risk of challenge in the courts. Interested persons or pressure groups can start proceedings in the courts to challenge an SI for lack of *vires* even where it has been 'passed' by the JCSI.

The fear of possible litigation has to be tempered by the observation that courts have tended not to challenge SIs 'where political judgements are at issue and the House of Commons has approved the instrument' (Baldwin 1995: 72), and that JCSI judgements do not play a prominent part in court cases challenging SIs.

Secondly, there is the potential embarrassment of having an SI reported by the Joint Committee. As an administrator pointed out:

> No minister likes to have the accusation that what he is doing exceeds his *vires* or does something 'novel and unusual' with them. What terrible epithets they use!

Yet the main impact of the JCSI is on the lawyers. Having something reported is widely regarded as a sign that you have done it wrong or badly. For one lawyer 'all hell breaks loose if they complain about a regulation'. Another put it more moderately:

> The main aim as a draftsman and lawyer is that you don't want to have a memorandum from the Joint Committee. It shows there is something wrong with your draft . . . Yes, it is a badge of infamy to have a memorandum from the Joint Committee.

Concern with the possibility of embarrassment is not uppermost in the mind of every lawyer. One official who did an unusually large amount of SI drafting was more sanguine and viewed the 'odd point' being picked up by the Committee as entirely to be expected, although best avoided. Several others argued it depended on the nature of the report. If it was a clear question of JCSI 'nitpicking', then no blame would attach to the lawyer. However, none of the lawyers actually dismissed a report by the JCSI as inconsequential. One lawyer related how he once stood firm against the Committee:

> [One of the current Speaker's Counsel's predecessors] once pulled me up on a set of regulations, and I refused to accept the changes they recommended, so they reported me. I told them to bog off. They are used to people kow-towing to them, so they reported me. Even said I was offensive. The newspapers even picked this up. The Committee said the order was drafted imprecisely. It was drafted exactly the same way as the previous order.

Nevertheless, the same official went on to point out that being summoned in person to the JCSI to explain the SI, a rare occurrence (only four officials were summoned in 1997/8), 'is pretty traumatic'.

The third reason for the pervasive impact of the JCSI is the pride legal officials have in doing a good job. The belligerent lawyer who told the JCSI to 'bog off' went on to say:

> The Committee is much better now. The current Speaker's Counsel, Stephen Mason, was a drafter and has a good understanding of the constraints under which we work. They do a valuable job of picking things up—perhaps things that slipped through our system or things that we have got wrong.

Doing a bad job is to be avoided and the JCSI helps avoid it. So much so that one lawyer shopped himself to the Committee following an Archimedean revelation:

> The Joint Committee did not notice my error. There were two in fact. One of them was a reference to 'before, during or after' the date of July 2nd when the SI was actually made on the 16th. The date of making the SI was brought forward and I omitted to change the date in the text. I wrote to the Joint Committee and told them. This had been bothering me for a while, and I was rather upset with myself. I was just about to go away for the weekend, and I was soaking in the bath and I thought about it. 'It is not an error, it is an anomaly' I thought, I even shouted it out. There was another drafting error—the reference to section 18A should be to section 24A. I got an email from an administrator saying that a 'picky journalist', would you believe, has picked this up. We propose to renumber them at the first opportunity.

In the words of another official, 'the JCSI is a lawyer's thing'. Getting something through the JCSI is not necessarily the major objective, rather doing a good job is.

A fourth reason for the broad impact of the JCSI is the amount of work that could be involved in dealing with it. As many legal drafters stressed, the best SI is one that you never see again. An SI which attracts the attention of the Committee means more work: drafting a memorandum in reply, explaining what is going wrong to your boss (draft memorandums to the Committee generally have to be approved by senior lawyers) and possibly appearing at the Committee. A Scottish Office lawyer's reaction on an SI implementing EU legislation borrowed from an English template illustrates this well:

The Scottish SI was commented on by the JCSI, but the [identical] English one was not. We got a letter saying 'why have you got this provision in?' The answer was 'because the Directive requires us to'. The identical provision was not picked up in the English regs. So only the Scottish Office had to do a memorandum. [Was it a black mark against me?] I thought 'couldn't you have picked this up in the English regulations?' It would have saved me the trouble of having to write a letter . . . It just meant another piece of work for me, writing the letter. That's all I was bothered about.

While it is possible to shrug off a critical report from the Joint Committee, a lawyer nevertheless has to do extra work addressing the problems raised.

SCRUTINY OF POLICY

Scrutiny of policy can be achieved in two ways: through debating the merits of an SI on the floor of either House, and through discussion in the House of Commons Standing Committee on Statutory Instruments. Some types of instrument, 'affirmative resolution' SIs, can only come into effect or, for some types of affirmative SIs, remain in effect if they have been positively approved by the House of Commons (or, in some cases, both Houses of Parliament). A detailed account of scrutiny and how it works (along with a discussion of the JCSI) can be found in the Report of the Select Committee on Procedure (1996). However, for our purposes policy scrutiny appears to be academic: debates rarely take place and they never directly prevent an SI from becoming law. Let us present the available quantitative information that leads to this conclusion.

According to Table 8.3, despite large numbers of prayers (see p. 27), usually between four and six a week, with most prayers signed by the leader of the opposition party, relatively few of those SIs prayed against become the object of a parliamentary debate (between 1 and 7 per cent of all prayers are debated). While around one tenth of SIs are taken in the Standing Committee on Delegated Legislation, a smaller percentage, between 6 and 8, are taken on the floor of the House of Commons. In both cases these are predominantly SIs needing an affirmative resolution. Of those SIs taken on the floor of the House, the majority are agreed without debate in most years. The percentage of SIs debated on which there was a division on the floor of the House has steadily declined from 34 per cent in 1992/3 to 5 per cent in 1997/8.

The House of Lords takes a relatively small percentage of total SIs on its floor, but is more thorough since it only rarely agrees to them without a debate (between 0 and 3 per cent of SIs taken on the floor of the House of Lords were agreed without debate). One group representative pointed out that 'the Lords is a very thoughtful place' and went on to describe a speech by Lord Newton, adding 'would you get a speech like that—thoughtful and of that quality—in the Commons? Never!' Divisions are also rare in the House of Lords' consideration of SIs—between 2 and 6 per cent of SIs debated go to a division.

Table 8.3 Prayers and debates 1992–1998

	1992–3	1993–4	1994–5	1995–6	1996–7	1997–8
N of SIs†	2,000	1,400	1,490	1,508	1,054	1,816
House of Commons						
Prayers	196	147	183	130	59	301
prayers per week (average)	4.8	5.4	6.1	4.5	3.7	6.3
% prayers signed by opposition leader	80	69	87	81	80	93
% prayers debated	7	1	4	5	3	1
Statutory Instruments						
taken in Standing Committee (as % of all SIs)	10	5	8	9	10	10
taken on floor (as % of all SIs)	8	6	6	7	6	6
agreed without debate (as % of SIs taken on floor)	59	42	57	73	73	83
debated (as % of SIs taken on floor)	41	58	43	27	27	17
subject to divided vote (as % of SIs debated on floor)	34	31	26	18	9	5
House of Lords						
Statutory Instruments						
taken on floor (as % of all SIs)	6	5	5	7	6	7
agreed without debate (as % of SIs taken on floor)	1	3	1	3	0	3
debated (as % of SIs taken on floor)	99	97	99	97	100	97
subject to divided vote (as % of SIs debated on floor)	4	7	4	6	2	2

No motions to annul on the floor of the House of Commons or of the House of Lords were agreed to in 1995–6 and 1994–5, and the POLIS database contains no records of successful motions to annul in the sessions since 1995–6 up to 1998–9 (House of Lords Written Answer, 14 December 1996). Affirmative resolution SIs are simply passed; the biggest difficulty for these SIs is finding parliamentary time to get them approved. Again there was no record on the POLIS database of SIs failing to be approved in the sessions since 1995–6 up to 1998–9.

Lawyers know that their SIs have been prayed against—their parliamentary offices tell them so. They are advised not to do anything else until a debate has been scheduled. In 1997 and 1998 there were period when, according to many lawyers interviewed, the opposition was praying against everything. William Hague tabled 279 prayer motions in 1997–8. A common reaction of indifference to prayers came from a Home Office official:

> All of the 1997 Police Act SIs were prayed against. The opposition seems to have taken a decision to pray against everything. I'm not sure why. We had a note round telling us to expect everything to be prayed against.

A similar reaction came from a DSS official:

> They prayed against this—there were prayers against a number of regulations. They objected as a matter of course. There was no way they would get a debate. The whips would never have approved a discussion of something as uncontentious as this.

Debates in the Standing Committee, around four-fifths of which are debates on affirmative resolution SIs guaranteed a parliamentary hearing, are rarely negated (see Select Committee on Procedure 1996: 41). I came across none in this research. Where negative instruments are defeated in Standing Committee, it makes no difference. One respondent recalled his involvement in an SI which had been voted down in the Standing Committee in April 1996. Two Conservatives were absent for the vote and the Major government was defeated on division by nine votes to eight (see *Guardian*, 1 May 1996). At issue were charges for dental, medical and optical services:

> The Tories were slow off the mark in getting their people back into the committee when the prayer motions were being discussed and the prayers against the SIs were carried. We were miffed, but to his credit Malone [the Secretary of State for Health] was unruffled—he stood his ground and said there was no problem. When you pray you ask the House to take notice. Since the motion was defeated, the House has not taken notice. But since it is a negative resolution SI the measure still stands. This shows the artificial nature of the whole thing. Negative resolution gives the executive total power. That was the lesson I learned.

The two SIs (*The National Health Service (Charges for Drugs and Appliances) Amendment Regulations 1996* and *The National Health Service (Optical Charges and Payments) Amendment Regulations 1996*) had already, in fact, come into effect before they were debated and remained in effect afterwards.[6]

---

[6] The point that a Committee defeat on an SI has no substantive consequences was recognised by the Select Committee on Procedure (2000: para. 16):

> 'A further criticism of the existing system is that debate on instruments in committee is meaning-less because it does not take place on a substantive motion. If a Delegated Legislation Committee votes against the motion, "That the Committee has considered the instrument", the Chairman's report to the House is couched in the same terms as if the motion had been agreed to, and no pro-cedural consequences follow from the Committee's vote.'

Nevertheless, officials whose SIs are being discussed in Parliament attend the debates. Several remarked on the tendency of officials to over-prepare. The debates do not last as long as they thought they might and they do not get generally into matters of detail for which they have prepared. For example, one official observed:

> The SI was prayed against. I cannot say I know for sure why. When we went to the debate we discovered the debate was very short. The amount of work we did to brief ministers was disproportionate. We found that the opposition said they prayed against it 'for information'—to find out what was included [in the SI]. You know how these politicians are—all matey with each other. They got the answers to the question before the debate began.

Few officials were impressed with Members of Parliament who frequently 'get the wrong end of the stick', as one put it, or simply blustered away to no real effect. A lawyer describes his experience with one of the 46 in the sample:

> The opposition realised they had made a mistake, in a way, by praying against a beneficial change [i.e. one which everybody agreed was a good thing]. When it came to the debate, [the opposition spokesman] started off saying they were in favour and were only seeking 'clarification'. It was all over in under 20 minutes. I'm rather sceptical about Parliament's role. I remember my first visit to the Commons [many years ago] . . . I thought they would go through the regulation I wrote then line by line. But the opposition just spoke about general stuff. If they had pressed on detail they would have turned up something [the legislation was internally inconsistent] and showed that the legislation could not have gone through. I am not impressed with them.

And a long-serving lawyer lamented the declining quality of MPs.

> The first SI I did was on [a highly technical legal issue]. It was taken on the floor of the House. I went and sat in the well where we civil servants go and sit and listen. Enoch Powell was the only one who understood it. This shows how you have to have a first class brain in Parliament. You just don't have that now.

To go along to the House of Commons or the House of Lords is a good excursion for most officials, and one for which they prepare conscientiously. But they know there is not the remotest chance that it will change anything in the SI. As we shall see, even where governments have been forced to retract, it has not been directly through parliamentary defeat.

In fact, while many officials may express disappointment over the quality of parliamentary scrutiny and debate, they nevertheless show respect for parliamentary procedure and accept willingly the need to secure tacit or explicit parliamentary approval. One official spoke of the lengths he went to to avoid any accusation of discourtesy towards Parliament:

> The order was going to be laid in the recess, so we had to plant a PQ [Parliamentary Question] to warn Parliament that these regulations were coming. It is not good form to lay something during the recess. So to avoid the accusation that we are seeking to avoid scrutiny we plant a PQ. With a . . . change like this one it should pose no

problems, but we have the defence, if it comes up, that we told them about it before. It was critical that it came into force before Parliament returned. We could not even have got an adjournment debate on it, though. So we got a PQ down the day before Parliament rose.

Parliamentary scrutiny of the policy issues involved in SIs appears to be much weaker than the scrutiny of technical issues. SIs are prayed against, but few are discussed. The Standing Committee on Delegated Legislation 'serves no real purpose' (Hayhurst and Wallington 1988), because even where defeated in a vote, Statutory Instruments are not blocked. And governments with majorities in Parliament are no more likely to be defeated on SIs than on Acts of Parliament in debates in the House. However, as Norton (1993) has argued, the influence of parliaments cannot be assessed by the quantitative indicators of the numbers of laws that have been initiated, blocked or amended. Bagehot argued in 1867 that legislation is a minor function of Parliament (Bagehot 1964). Where parties are disciplined and form a majority, the executive can control the legislature. Rather the role of Parliament has to be understood as affecting behaviour through the anticipation of actions. The JCSI offers a clear example of this. Its formal powers are never used to force a change to the SI through debate on the report in the House. Rather officials devote considerable effort to not attracting its attention in the first place, and, where reported, will generally seek to accommodate JCSI views. Where the department believes the JCSI is wrong, it can say so. On the occasions where officials interviewed had been involved in SIs disputed in this way, they made sure that their Cabinet ministers supported their position.

Outside the technical scrutiny offered by the JCSI, Parliament remains nevertheless important as a potential check on delegated legislation since, as with unpopular primary legislation, discontent among backbenchers on secondary legislation is also avoided. Getting backbenchers, preferably government backbenchers, to raise issues through an Early Day Motion, or much better through a Parliamentary Question, is an important strategy to challenge government action. Let me cite three examples here.

Only one of these comes directly from the 46 SIs examined in the sample. *The Jobseeker's Allowance (Amendment) Regulations 1998* which were later reversed, sought to extend the period that applicants had to wait before they were eligible to receive JSA benefit (see above Chapter 5). On 28 January 1998, four days after the regulations were laid, an Early Day Motion (EDM) attracted the signatures of over 50 MPs, on 6 February the government announced, in answer to a parliamentary question, that it was going to 'reconsider . . . as part of the Prime Minister's Welfare State Review'. On 10 February another EDM welcoming the government's decision to reconsider was signed by 50 MPs and the same day the government announced, again via Parliamentary Question, its decision to revoke the SI. 'Ministers took fright' at the scale of parliamentary disquiet about this measure, as one observer interviewed described it. There is little doubt among any of those involved that Labour backbench parliamentary opposition to the measure killed it off.

A second example comes in the vexed area of supported housing. The government wanted to limit the amount of Housing Benefit that would be received by, largely elderly, people in housing where additional services were provided—including not only concierge services but also personal services such as counselling and benefits advice. The Conservative Secretary of State for Social Security decided against it, after having laid the SI. Peter Lilley's justification was:

> I have concluded that the sudden removal of this source of income may cause significant difficulties for many vulnerable people in supported accommodation. I have therefore decided to withdraw the draft regulations, and I am commissioning an urgent inter-departmental review of the arrangements for funding supported accommodation [DSS Press Release, 8 July 1996].

An inside observer interviewed put the reason for the about turn more bluntly:

> Although it was a negative resolution SI [i.e. did not necessarily have to be raised in Parliament], the decision not to go ahead was a conscious political one. Abbeyfield [the pressure group] did it for a couple of nervy backbenchers who managed to persuade the Government that it was risky.

The third example was similar except that it came under the Blair government. The Labour administration wanted to limit Council Tax Benefit payable to those who lived in larger houses. An interest group managed to get a Labour MP to pray against the measure, and the Liberal Democrats forced a parliamentary division on it. Although the SI was passed, the pressure was maintained and three months later the effect of the SI was partially reversed before it came into force—a 'climbdown on council tax benefit cuts' as the *Guardian* of 28 March 1998 put it.

However, it is difficult to assess precisely the impact of potential parliamentary opposition to SIs. Commenting on the Major government, one group official said that with a small majority in Parliament 'you just need one backbencher and you can cause a hue and cry'. Moreover, knowing that significant opposition is a possibility could prevent measures ever seeing the light of day: 'on issues where we know they could be defeated, we pointed out they could be defeated and this must have stopped a few things'. Officials from several interest groups interviewed argued that 'opening up debate' on an issue was a means of modifying government plans for SIs, and one of the best ways of doing this was through MPs. One group official described collaborating with another group in mobilising MPs:

> We cooperate with other groups—we help ensure access of other groups to departments. One time I knew that a letter from X [a prominent and respected activist]

would have a big impact so I rang him up. 'We need you' I said. 'Here are the MPs that will listen to you, so write to them'. He was terribly overworked.

She elaborated on this in another case:

> In the 1980s we got sophisticated. On the Council Tax issue we got together with the Local Government Association and we saw an opening with the Minister. The LGA came in with the hard act, and we were the soft ones. We all try to draw on our strengths. You don't only get through to the 'right on' people. Different people listen to different voices so you need to know who to approach them through. We use the different networks.

The collaboration need not be particularly strongly choreographed. A representative of a motorcycling organisation pointed out that another motorcycling organisation was 'a lobby which specialises in PR and MPs . . . it can get members on the streets quickly' while his was better at the 'political/legal/technical' case. Since they both tended to have similar views on some issues, such as crash helmet regulations and the banning of right-hand sidecars, they worked in their own ways without close co-ordination.

MPs' support can backfire in a number of ways. One way is by entrenching the minister in a policy position:

> You have to chose the right time to bring in politicians, party people, because it can rebound. Your MP writes to the minister, the minister's official replies (i.e. you will get a reply from the person working on the proposal you are objecting to), then the minister becomes committed to this line because he cannot change it without losing face. So even if there is no firm draft, the minister's view can be frozen and cannot be changed.

A different type of problem resulted from well-meaning but misguided forms of support by (then) opposition Labour MPs to a welfare reform introduced under the Conservatives:

> One time we had been told in advance that the minister had prepared to back down during the debate—we knew he had a backdown position and speech prepared. But one after another Labour MP got up and went on about the poverty of their early years and did not give him time to back down. I tried to get a message to someone to stop them going on like this. I could have strangled them.

This highlights the observation made by one representative of a social welfare interest group that party is a poor guide to whether an MP will support you. 'We ditched the "all Tories are bastards" idea ages ago.'

CONCLUSIONS

Parliament has a crucial and pervasive impact on the technical, but not the policy, aspects of the delegated legislative process. Most lawyers try to draft regulations as if the JCSI is looking over their shoulder, and this carries through into the advice they give those administrators who draw up their instructions. An incredibly overworked group of lawyers supporting the Committee does its best to find not only drafting errors but more serious faults, above all where the government is making laws without the authority to do so.

The scrutiny role of Parliament appears to be at first sight rather weak. Debates are rare and defeats all but unheard of. However, avoiding embarrassment, or the prospect of embarrassment, rather than defeat is the main objective of seeking parliamentary support. While the executive controls Parliament, Parliament nevertheless offers significant opportunities for moving issues out of the obscure world of everyday politics and into a more familiar world of inter- and intraparty political conflict. By considering this world's relationship with everyday politics, we understand both better.

9

Everyday politics and high politics

This study has not been primarily about Statutory Instruments as a tool of government. Statutory Instruments are the focus of the study since they provide windows through which we may look at the obscure world of everyday policy-making. Delegated legislation has allowed us to see how issues such as the grubbing up of apple and pear orchards, the warehousing of cider and perry products, the voucher scheme for reimbursing optometrists and the role of postal services in Housing Benefit fraud have been handled. Through the same windows, however, we also catch a glimpse of another world, although perhaps not as clearly. The other world involves ministers pitted against each other, the mobilisation of parliamentary majorities to force issues through the House and personal interventions by the Prime Minister to head off embarrassing rebellions. Statutory Instruments are overwhelmingly about everyday politics, but they are also about high politics too.

There is no perfect match between the instrument of government and the importance of the issue at stake. Perhaps the most important single development in post-war British education was set in motion by lowly Ministry of Education Circular 10/65, when such quasi-laws are probably even more likely to deal with questions of routine than Statutory Instruments. Conversely, instruments associated with high politics frequently do mundane and technical things. Most obviously, Parliament frequently concerns itself with legislation which merely consolidates—tidies bodies of legislation—such as the Petroleum Act 1998.

How can we tell the difference between these two worlds of everyday politics and high politics? Cutting social security benefits amid protests from opposition parties as well as from backbenchers in the government party are clearly high politics. The annual updating of compensation rates for statutory maternity pay is not. To pursue some definition of this distinction is not primarily a quest for guidance on how to interpret different events. Rather, by defining what is characteristic of high politics we have a clearer idea of the nature of the world of everyday politics. So it is worth devoting some attention to seeing if there is a more satisfactory way of distinguishing between high politics and everyday politics that does not rely entirely on simple common sense.

Consider the case of the Lycra Louts. In 1998 Alun Michael, then a junior minister in the Home Office, announced his intention to make cycling on the pavement a more serious offence than it already was. In the tabloid papers this got as much, if not more, coverage than the cuts in benefit brought in by the lengthening of waiting days for Jobseeker's Allowance. The *Daily Mail*

(13 January 1998) published a report under the headline '£20 Spot Fines for Lycra Lout Cyclists' pointing out that reckless cyclists will be given £20 on-the-spot fines:

> Home Office Minister Alun Michael said last night that it was intended to make cycling on pavements a fixed penalty offence later this year. This will be done by Statutory Instrument under provisions contained in the Road Traffic Offences Act.[1]

This proposal, however, would not be classed as high politics in a common-sense understanding of the term. Although it was covered in the press, possibly because it was likely to be supported by a section of *Daily Mail* readers and received the endorsement of a minister, it was not high politics. Publicity alone does not make an issue high politics, so what does?

It has already been established that a policy cannot be deemed important or significant simply because of intrinsic characteristics such as the number of people affected, or the amount of public money committed. Rather, what is or becomes a matter of high politics is partly a question of perceptions. However the simple perception that something is intrinsically important does not make it high politics. *The Daily Mail* and Alun Michael might well have been right to think that Lycra louts were important to the public, but that does not make it an issue of high politics. In domestic policy-making, high politics is about *issues which affect the mobilisation of party support*. At the core this means controversial issues, which generate partisan opposition and require mobilisation of party majorities to secure their passage into law or guarantee their status as government policy. It is also about issues where partisan support has to be mobilised to defeat intra-party threats to policy initiatives.

However, high political issues cannot be defined only in terms of *successful* mobilisation of party support. Where the government's ability to mobilise party support is threatened, or appears to be threatened, by patterns of political support over an issue, we may also term this high politics. Also included in such an understanding of the term would be issues over which governments retreat in the face of substantial opposition, actual or anticipated, from within the governing party. Moreover, partisan controversy is a sufficient but not necessary precondition of high politics. Issues which affect perceptions of the ability to mobilise significant public support for the party may also be high politics, where politicians (whether from governing or from opposition parties) feel compelled to support a policy because of the perceived loss of public support that would result from opposition.

In short, once an issue enters the world of the democratic politician, and once the question of political support becomes significant either for the fate of the issue or for the strategy of a major political party, it becomes a matter of high politics. This is a refinement of the earlier definition of obscurity as lack of public exposure (Chapter 1) by defining obscurity in political terms. Public exposure

---

[1] The pledge was eventually honoured through *The Fixed Penalty Offences Order 1999* which came into effect in August 1999.

is usually associated with high politics, but not all public exposure makes something a matter of high politics. Public exposure reflects high politics only when the exposure forms part of a broader party political conflict in which political support is used to advance or hinder a proposal, or where a proposal itself seeks to generate party political support. Thus Lycra louts were not high politics since the issues they raise were neither controversial in party terms nor likely to generate support for New Labour. The struggles surrounding Jobseeker's Allowance or Council Tax Benefit cuts outlined in Chapter 8 are high politics because they were reversed owing to internal party political opposition.

This elaboration of the meaning of high politics enables us to understand the nature of everyday politics. As our empirical discussion of Statutory Instruments has brought us into contact with *high* politics, care needs to be taken when reviewing what SIs tell us about the nature of *everyday* politics, to exclude those aspects of the SIs discussed here which involve the mobilisation of party majority. However, there is a crucial empirical relationship between high and everyday politics; elevating everyday political issues to high politics or keeping them in the arena of low politics is an important strategy in managing political conflicts (see Chapter 1). Defining high politics in this way thus allows us some clarity in exposition of the relationship between everyday and high politics and how issues may move between the two.

UNDERSTANDING EVERYDAY GOVERNMENT

Chapter 1 set out our expectations about the character of politics beyond the range of public vision. In particular it pointed to specific characteristics of the participants, the process and the bias in policy-making in everyday government. Most of these expectations have been met in the elaboration of the delegated legislative process. However, the theoretical introduction was not set out simply to forward hypotheses which could be supported or falsified. More important even than establishing whether the theory was right or wrong was investigating empirically the way in which the participants, the process and the bias in everyday politics appear to differ from those involved in high politics.

Participants

It was argued in Chapter 1 that those involved in everyday politics are more likely to be placed lower in the organisational hierarchy than those involved in high politics. This may seem self-evident, but some of its implications are less obvious. Junior ministers have generally been assumed to have an essentially political role: offering political support to the Cabinet minister, providing a channel of political communication between MPs, parties and groups and government and representing the government at important meetings when the

Cabinet minister is unable to attend. The focus on everyday government has shown an extremely important executive role for junior ministers. In 40 of the 46 SIs in this study junior ministers were responsible for giving political approval to the SI and, where necessary, steering it through the drafting as well as parliamentary process. This role appears to be exercised without any direct approval from the Cabinet minister or any formal and clear division of labour between Cabinet and non-Cabinet ministers. For the most part, the civil servants as well as the junior ministers rely on their understanding of the folkways of the political world they inhabit to assess the level of political approval required for any particular measure. In everyday politics the level of approval is nearly always the that of the junior minister.

The involvement of officials several ranks below the most senior ones is another striking feature of everyday politics. While senior officials, say, at grade 5 and above, are certainly copied in to correspondence documenting what is going on in the world of everyday politics, in no case I examined did senior officials take a particularly active role. While the grades of administrative officials who did what is termed the 'policy work' on the SIs varied, most were Higher Executive Officers. These officials, ranging from HEO to around grade 7, are the unsung efficient secret of everyday government. They develop a strong expertise in their areas of responsibility and apply it to concrete issues of public policy with sensitivity to the political and constitutional constraints within which they have to operate. We know far too little about this group of officials and their world. Many have come from posts in operational divisions within the department. The importance of this background for the type of work involved in writing SIs was suggested by one interest group representative who observed that 'policy people come to meetings and clam up when you talk about problems, but operations people try to glean something from the different views and come up with ways through the problems'.

It is worth elaborating on precisely how important this group, from around HEO to grade 7, is in the world of everyday politics. Their practical expertise is indispensable within government departments. One relatively senior official in the Radiocommunications Agency pointed out how he came to be in his job:

> When the DTI took over radio regulatory work from the Home Office it wanted people who knew something of radiocommunication but with some knowledge of how Trade and Industry worked.

They can be put in charge of even the most important pieces of government legislation. When the Blair government set up its New Deal for the Disabled project group to develop policy to bring the disabled into work, it created a cross-departmental group, jointly between DSS and DfEE, with a total of 16 people. The project manager was a Grade 6, but an exceptionally able HEO was given the responsibility, as he put it:

> for the benefits side of the job, along with a couple of other colleagues to see if there were any ways we could reverse or reduce the barriers to disabled people getting into

work . . . [What is my title?] We don't have fancy titles around here—only the big grades have them. I'm just the HEO with responsibility for the disability angle of welfare to work.

In one episode related by a Grade 7, an SI (not among the 46 in the sample) became a question of intense political controversy, passing out of the realm of everyday into high politics:

> The issue went quite high. It went to the PM/Treasury—that was where the decision would have come from . . . The Government agreed to revoke it . . . When the regs were laid, there was every intention that they should continue. But in a short two-week period there was a huge amount of activity—submissions, briefings—the Press Office would have kept itself in on it . . . Most of the work on this was done by an HEO . . . I'd suggest changes, but she did all the work on what the regs should say and on dealing with the solicitors . . . When the [politicians] came along our Grade 5 would get involved and we would tell him what we were doing and he would sign off on the important stuff, as it is sensitive and he would like to make sure we were giving good advice. He would keep his eyes on what was happening. I am sure S [the HEO] would do most of the work, but he [the Grade 5] took charge. Grade 5s tend to clear the Parliamentary Questions (although not always, but they tend to like to clear the sensitive ones). Most of the paperwork on the submission and the briefing would be done by the HEO. The Head of Policy Group might have got involved. The Permanent Secretary would not have got much involved. Our Grade 5 is good and would have handled it. All submissions would be copied to senior people including the Permanent Secretary who could see what was going on. But I'd be surprised if he had intervened in what had happened. The Head of Information and the special advisers will have got involved. But you have to remember *in policy terms* this was not a very big issue . . . This was not a major policy issue—there are lots of bigger things. *Politically* it was very big. It can be that these small things have a disproportionate effect. In this department the vast majority of things are done at HEO level. There is a lot of detail—[this area of legislation] is so technical.

Even when higher grades became involved, the most senior civil servant actively involved was a Grade 5 and technical policy work was still carried out by an HEO.

Returning to the expectation set out in the introduction that everyday politics is likely to involve actors lower down in the hierarchies of the organisations involved, one area where this does not apply is among interest groups. Very few groups have the luxury of allowing tasks such as representing group views to government departments on an SI to a junior employee. Either the group is a very small one, with only one person effectively responsible for all lobbying, or among the larger groups the lobby sections tend to be 'flat' in organisation, with responsibilities allocated in functional terms rather than on the basis of the importance of the issue or the instrument of policy involved. Nevertheless, the hypothesis set out in the introduction is supported in so far as one feature of the nature of the interest group involvement in delegated legislation is the rather specific nature of many of the interests involved. While major groups such as the

Local Government Association, the National Farmers Union and the Law Society were involved in many of the SIs discussed in Chapters 4 to 6, most of the associations and groups were small and highly specific. Some, such as the Association of Mental Health Act Administrators, appear in no major directories of groups. Others are relatively small and reflect highly specialised interests such as the National Association of Cider Makers and the British Casino Association.

One of the curious aspects of the world of interest-group politics as far as SIs are concerned is that a substantial portion of it appears to be a cottage industry. Instead of being conducted from offices in London or provincial centres close to the officials who make regulations, many groups appear to operate from private homes. It is not possible to offer a clear estimate of the degree to which this is the case. Of the 600 questionnaires sent out it was not possible to identify which addresses were private addresses. Moreover, some employees of interest groups encountered in the research used offices as a contact addresses rather than places of work. However, among the interviews conducted with interest-group representatives at their places of work was one looking out over a beautiful Surrey garden with a retired civil servant who had gone to work for the industry he had previously been regulating. Another meeting with a group representative took place in a cluttered terraced house in Hertfordshire, with his pet cat sleeping on top of a pile of letters in a tray marked 'drink driving', while a telephone conversation was conducted with another ex-civil servant working at home in Gloucestershire for a London-based organisation. All three were well connected with the departments with which they interacted, two of them being closely involved in working groups within the European Union.

Correspondingly, our expectation that 'networks' of policy-making, in so far as the term simply defines who participates in the decision-making process, are relatively sparsely populated also appears to be supported by the evidence of previous chapters. Many of the SIs aroused the interest of only one or two specialist interests each. Moreover, many public consultations were 'disappointing' in the sense that they yielded few responses.

Strategies based upon trust

How do people secure outcomes favourable to themselves in this process of everyday politics? According to the characterisation of everyday politics advanced in Chapter 1, we would expect cases based on trust to be the most effective since, by definition, it is not possible to mobilise a wider public and apply that form of political pressure resulting from popular support to sustain an argument. Instead, who wins and loses may be expected to be based on who can be trusted. As will be discussed below, in the actual world of everyday policy-making it is possible, under some circumstances, to move an issue out of the everyday arena and into a high politics arena. However, concentrating at this stage on those issues that remain in the sphere of everyday politics, dependability, reliability and trust may be expected to be important in civil servant relations with interest groups in the same way that trust featured prominently in the 'private government of public money' as presented in Heclo and Wildavsky's (1981) study of the Treasury-centred public expenditure community.

Trust, in the sense of strong and positive interpersonal relations between group members and civil servants, could be found. For example, representatives of some interest groups were one-time civil servants operating in the policy areas of the groups which they now represent. One representative of an equipment manufacturing group was a former ministry official who retired and after his retirement (but before taking the post in the interest group) had been commissioned by his former employers to draft consolidating legislation in the field. Two former civil servants in the Lord Chancellor's Department were leading officials in groups consulted on the certificated bailiffs regulations (Chapter 4). Since this interpersonal linkage was not systematically explored, it is not possible here to say precisely how many of the 382 interest groups responding to the questionnaire (Chapter 7) employed former civil servants in key lobbying positions. One interest group representative pointed out that her group was especially trusted by one of the junior ministers in one department because 'we were [his] unofficial civil service for years' while Labour was in opposition.

Evidence of a different type of trust came up in the interviews. This relied less on interpersonal relations and more on the nature and character of the organisation—a 'track record' of interest in an area or of providing level-headed views and evaluations. One rather extreme incidence of reliance on interest groups was mentioned by one interest group respondent whose organisation enjoyed close contacts with both major parties: '[j]ust before the [1997] election we had the strange phenomenon of civil servants coming up to us to find out the view of the *Labour Party* on X, Y or Z. A very odd thing.'

Trust in the *organization*, as opposed to any individuals in the group, is especially important in everyday politics since those who are likely to evaluate the comments of interest groups and other consultees are usually relatively junior. They also tend to move on to other posts fairly frequently, so institutional trust is likely to be a force for continuity in everyday policy-making. A group representative attributed the influence his group had on an SI to the fact that:

> We had spent the previous 18 months in discussion with the department on the primary legislation. We were respected for having sat through all the debates on it. They saw we were committed.

In one case a group official argued that:

> here we established a track record as an authoritative and important voice. If we had parachuted into an area where we did not have a track record, we'd have been ignored. But [this] . . . is something we have been in for 70 years.

Another argued that they were listened to because they employed the only person who understood a particular area of social security administration. This should not be interpreted as any form of exclusivity or favouritism in an approach to groups, or even in paying attention to what they say. In many cases a group consulted is the only one in a particular area, so the question of favouring one over another does not come up. It is possible to build up a reputation for soundness, but this does not necessarily guarantee influence.

Trust and reputation work both ways: groups make distinctions between civil servants who are likely to listen and those who are not. The basis on which such distinctions are made also differs. It may vary according to the job they do—the fact that one group representative argued that 'operational' officials are more likely to listen than 'policy' officials has already been discussed. Another mentioned that 'the arrogance of the Employment Service has to be seen to be believed. There are a couple of good souls there.' Or the variation among civil servants may be on a person-to-person basis. One group representative pointed out that 'some civil servants are awful and hide behind the neutrality thing. Others are much more open', and went on to describe how a senior official acted as a form of 'mole' within the department, lobbying wherever he could for it and passing on bits of information. Another interest group respondent made a distinction between types of officials: the 'cynical' civil servants who care little about how the legislation affects their group and the 'regular' officials who are 'ashamed' if perfectly good proposals are ignored by the department for political convenience.

FORMS OF BIAS

There is little doubt that the executive dominates the process of delegated legislation. The initiative to legislate comes overwhelmingly from within the executive, either from the minister or from other parts of the department or its cognate agencies. Civil servants remain very much in control in the process of development. As one official commented:

> On the whole delegated legislation is good news for us civil servants; we get to implement our ministers' wishes without having to go through primary legislation. There is always a large queue to get things in for primary legislation. This is especially a big issue now because of what the New Labour government wants to do—it wants to do a lot.

While it is possible for groups to make their points in the process of consultation, what civil servants listen to is filtered through their general confidence that what they are doing is right and for the general good. From their perspective, while the interests may have perfectly valid points that need to be taken into account to improve legislation, they may be assumed to be grinding their own particular axes. As one civil servant turned interest group activist put it, 'as a civil servant you decide what you want to do and consult once you are clear. You change things only if there are very strong arguments to do so'.

However, the idea that this constitutes a particular executive bias in *delegated* legislation cannot be accepted without reservation. There is a bias in primary legislation as well; the executive dominates the parliamentary agenda. Where governments have majorities virtually no items are passed in Parliament, and no amendments carried, unless they have the active or tacit support of the government. Thus to ascribe bias to delegated legislation may be of little more use than describing the environment in which fish live as 'wet'.

Within the constraints of an executive-dominated system, however, the bias needs to be modified by three observations. First, the obligation to consult is in some cases mandatory. As was discussed in Chapters 2 and 7, it is possible for legislation to be challenged successfully in the courts on the basis of inadequate consultation, and government departments take consultation exceptionally seriously. Not every SI is the subject of external consultation, even though it is possible to envisage that external interests may have some stake in the SI. For example the SI discontinuing the Home Office register of addicts was not consulted on even though those who might have been expected to have had an opinion included doctors. In this case academic health researchers also later appealed to the Home Office to have the register continue as a means of maintaining valuable time-series data.

A second qualification to the idea that everyday politics is an executive-dominated process is that group consultation can produce changes, even though it does not invariably do so. To defeat the principle (usually described as 'policy') behind an SI requires stifling the proposed regulation at a very early stage or convincing officials and/or politicians that the reaction they may anticipate would be sufficiently powerful or embarrassing to render pursuit of the regulation unattractive. The research design of this project does not allow us to say very much about these largely unobservable forms of interest-group influence. Although not directly observable, the corollary of the impact of anticipated reactions was alluded to by group representatives who knew that stopping the proposed regulations was impossible, so they focus their attention on ameliorating, from their perspective, its detailed provisions (see p. 147). However in two cases out of the 46 there was clear evidence that the SI was brought into existence by groups, and in a third it was rescued from potential oblivion by group pressures. Furthermore several SIs were designed to give groups what civil servants thought the groups wanted, and they largely turned out to be correct (see Chapter 4).

Thirdly, the relative obscurity of delegated legislation means that diverse interests can be accommodated without causing the government major problems of face saving. Interest groups can argue about issues such as charging for skips to take away rubble, or deals for more cash to help relieve the extra burdens of keeping young people at school for some extra weeks or months, without the presentational problems of how to handle an about-turn or a climbdown. The everyday political process is usually constructed so that climbdowns are hard to detect and few people are likely ever to notice. As one group representative put it, 'the PR campaign trying to topple legislation has no effect, but they think about it with the SI. SIs are easier to bend—they are less public and less exposed'. The big exception to this, in the case studies as well as some other SIs raised in interviews (Chapter 5) are those that acquired a much higher profile (e.g. the amendments to Jobseeker's Allowance). These left the world of everyday politics and entered the world of high politics. The relationship between the two is important for understanding policy making in Britain more generally and the world of everyday politics in particular.

THE RELATIONSHIP BETWEEN EVERYDAY AND HIGH POLITICS

One characterisation of the place of everyday politics in the overall policy-making system, derived from traditional criticisms of delegated legislation, is that things are done by Statutory Instrument to avoid going through the process of creating an Act of Parliament. One reason for this may be logistical. Relatively little primary legislation can be passed in a parliamentary session, on average around 60 Public and General Acts. Another reason may be political. It is possible to manage potentially damaging or awkward political conflicts by moving them out of the arena of high politics. When an issue is turned into a Statutory Instrument, or possibly divided up and turned into a variety of SIs, it can be safely, quietly and swiftly handled in an obscure political arena.

Traditionally the increasing use by government of SIs has been criticised on the ground that they offer a way for the executive to enact what Parliament should be called upon to decide (see Chapters 1 and 2). Laws can be passed more easily by decree than by primary legislation, and governments thus avoid the inconvenience and embarrassment of having to mobilise a possibly unwilling parliamentary majority to get their measures passed through Parliament. Such questions, important though they are, cannot be answered directly here because of the way high politics is defined (as something which is directly related to political support). There is no *a priori* characteristic of an issue that makes it a matter of high politics, as has been already explained. Therefore, whether awkward political questions are broken up into smaller, less exposed, items of legislation is primarily a normative question: are there types of issue handled by SI that really *should* be handled through less obscure forms of legislation because of their nature? An answer is not, however, possible within the confines of a political science study of the subject, and probably cannot be answered other than on a case-by-case basis.

If we concentrate on more general questions of the *empirical* relationship between the world of high and everyday politics, some matters are actually transferred out of high politics and moved to the everyday arena. The argument put forward by the government to groups that no major concessions can be made on the framing of primary legislation but that it would see what it could do in the implementing regulations was mentioned by several interest-group respondents—a clear and conscious move by the government to take an issue out of the more exposed arena of parliamentary debate and leave discussion until the delegated legislation. One said:

> We table amendments to primary legislation, the minister says 'it is inappropriate to deal with this using primary legislation and we will respond to the issue later on in the SI'.

Another social security group pointed to a similar trade off of influence in primary versus secondary legislation:

> We had been pushing against this [Social Security Act]. The next thing is that officials decided to call a meeting of lobbyists who would come in to talk under Chatham House rules. The whole thing was based on trust. It was an incredible innovation before the Bill got the Royal Assent to get us talking about regulations early. If what had been said had got out, it would have put the Minister in a difficult position. They brought together all sorts of people.

Moreover, consultation can be extended to cover other 'soft law' instruments which are associated with delegated legislation such as codes of practice, circulars and directions. *The National Health Service (Proposals for Pilot Schemes) and (Miscellaneous Amendments) Regulations 1997* were, as one official said, framed so as 'not to allow the health authorities to block the legislation' passed under the last Conservative administration; the government limited their role and strengthened that of GPs in the subsequent delegated legislation as well as the directions to health boards connected with the regulations.

Moving an issue out of obscurity into the exposed party political arena of high politics can be a crucial strategy pursued by interest groups. To get any wider support the issue has to be raised in an arena where that support can be attracted and where that support counts. The most common way of moving an issue out of everyday politics is through MPs. With a negative SI you need an MP to pray against the regulation; with affirmative and negative SIs you need MPs to give enough support to make the government take any objections seriously. However, as one group representative put it, MPs are 'hard to get fired up'. Another underlined the difference between affirmative and negative SIs:

> On affirmative resolution regulations we brief the opposition on what to object to. You can get your points across with affirmative resolution . . . Negative resolutions are more difficult. the opposition has got a limited number of chances to debate a prayer, and you don't want them to use them all up.

Debates are not guaranteed even where the legislation is affirmative and there is evidence of substantial support for a debate among MPs, even from government benches. As one respondent said, 'We tabled 100 amendments. We got MPs all geared up for the . . . debate. The government removed the debate and we had MPs coming up and asking—where's the . . . debate then? And it did not happen.' Although, as we have seen in the case of the Jobseeker's Allowance regulations, evidence of parliamentary dissatisfaction rather than a debate or the exceptionally remote chance of defeating government in a debate appears to be most decisive in moving an issue out of everyday politics.

The early years of the New Labour administration were a particularly difficult time for groups seeking to move issues onto the agenda of high politics. The slim majority of the last years of the Conservative government gave way to a Labour administration with a comfortable cushion of 179 which was discussed in Chapter 8 as a particular difficulty. Moreover, the Conservatives found it hard to oppose many Labour initiatives, in regulations as well as parliamentary Bills. One respondent argued:

> It is especially difficult with the change of government to get MPs to speak up. We used to get MPs to speak up. We used to be able to go up to them and say 'this is what they are doing, will you do a PQ'? Now with the Conservatives in opposition it is not convincing when they raise an objection to something the same as what they were doing 18 months before when they were in government. The government just says 'why are you objecting now?' Maybe we will be able to use MPs a bit more in future as Labour is in power longer.

In addition, one group representative, not generally associated with a pro-Conservative stance, voiced a general problem with getting Parliament to widen involvement in political issues raised by SIs under the New Labour administration:

> The Tories are pissed off with the contempt of the current government for Parliament—following protocols and allowing debate is not what they like. Betty Boothroyd [then Speaker of the House of Commons] issued a warning against the Government over its contempt for Parliament. You are faced with these arrogant young researchers who don't appreciate what happens to people when you take money away from them.

The apparent disregard for Parliament, mentioned by several group representatives, makes it all the more difficult to find parliamentarians, certainly from the Labour benches, prepared to use Parliament as a means of opening up debates on issues raised by delegated legislation.

While some of the interest-group literature tends to suggest that there is a distinction between 'insider' strategies and 'outsider' strategies for interest-group influence, with 'outsider' strategies referring to the use of public opinion and public campaigns and 'insider' tactics aimed at calm dialogue within Whitehall (see Grant 1995), there was little evidence that interest groups made a clear strategic choice that affected their general mode of operation. As one group official put it, 'the insider track works sometimes, yelling at government from newspaper headlines works sometimes. It's horses for courses'. There is no difficulty with government departments switching between strategies—no evidence that using public channels to move an issue into the world of high politics will harm the prospects of a group participating in everyday politics. There is, one group representative said:

> No problem about using both strategies simultaneously. We put our case through 'lunch', shouting through the headlines and technical notes. The ministry is quite

understanding. They know where we come from and don't mind us campaigning alongside the other channels.

Another suggested that while 'consultation status' was a big privilege for a group in European Union policy-making, and one that could be removed if the group was seen engaging in public protests against EU proposals, in the UK such status was neither difficult to attain nor ever likely to be taken away.

The cusp between everyday politics and high politics is where unusual things happen. It is here that individuals seek to gain support outside the obscure world of everyday politics. They seek to broaden or narrow the scope of conflict and gain support in the wider political arena. Pursuing the objective of moving an issue into the world of high politics, or keeping it in the world of everyday politics, can involve abandoning conventional beliefs and behaviour. The most obvious of these is the government backbenchers abandoning traditional support for their government to pray against an SI they oppose. However, this book has contained several other examples of remarkable episodes of individuals and groups seeking to raise or lower the political stakes involved in a piece of delegated legislation: junior ministers ranged in acrimonious opposition to their ministerial superiors, Prime Ministers publicly overriding Cabinet ministers, Conservatives espousing the rights of trade unions and the unemployed and Labour ministers offering principled defences for cutting Jobseeker's Allowance, a Lord Chancellor of one government defending his policy with arguments the previous government used against him (and *vice versa*). One official from a social welfare group criticised the New Labour administration's 'appalling' treatment of the Conservative ex-Minister John Redwood's 'valid and probing' amendments to an SI in Standing Committee. Ministers 'rung the press directly, unbeknown to the Department, to rubbish him as he sought to mobilise opposition to the proposed regulations'. He was unsuccessful.

In everyday politics, what matters is what works. The Conservatives' strategies for widening the conflict during the period in which most of this research was conducted (1997–1999) were hampered by the fact that their attempts to mobilise support for the poor and downtrodden lacked conviction. Some of the measures they contemplated opposing, such as cuts to Jobseeker's Allowance, were either old Conservative policies or close to policies the Conservatives had pursued in office. The Labour government managed, in some cases where an SI might possibly have entered the world of high politics, such as the local authorities' transport charges and conditional fees regulations, to contain the issue. In one case, on Jobseeker's Allowance, it gave way rather than risk offending backbench support.

Devolution to Scotland and Wales, not introduced until after the research on which this book is based was largely completed, might offer additional possibilities for widening conflicts that previously would have remained initially confined to small groups of politicians and officials. Some of the discussion in Chapters 4 to 6 highlighted the (frequently rather cursory) internal consultation between Whitehall-based departments and the pre-devolution Scottish and Welsh Offices. Since issues of secondary legislation are one of the major concerns of the Welsh Assembly and Scottish Parliament, it is quite possible that such issues may be projected into the world of high politics. Under devolution decisions taken within the executive are more exposed to party-political debate within Scotland and Wales (one of the basic points behind devolution), moreover the issues they raise may become related to questions of the power of the centre and the autonomy of the devolved bodies. To object to a regulation initiated in London (or to propose a regulation likely to be opposed in London), one is not confined to arguing the merits and demerits of the case among the small number of people involved. One may also have the option of seeking to involve a wider range of participants by raising the desirability of following English legislation.

In this sense, autonomy from London might prove to be an important concept for, in Schattschneider's terms, socialising formerly privatised conflicts. One early sign of this possibility came in 1999 when an end to the beef on the bone ban (following *The Beef Bones Regulations 1997*) was being mooted in the United Kingdom. The question of the ban had always been a party political issue, but after devolution it took on a number of extra dimensions: the dimension of the trust in English administrative and technical procedures (since the Welsh and Scottish counterparts did not want to move as fast as the English Chief Medical Officer and lift the ban in September 1999); whether the different parts of the United Kingdom should seek to maintain distinctive laws in these areas and, in Scotland, whether the Liberal Democrats, in coalition with Labour in the Scottish Executive, were reneging on manifesto commitments and acting as a subordinate of Labour. While this example refers to an already socialised conflict, it is quite possible to envisage devolution as a means of socialising formerly privatised conflicts. In fact, this is precisely what devolution was intended to achieve: to expose to the scrutiny of a territorial legislature decisions taken largely within the executive branch of government, and explicitly decisions leading to delegated legislation. Viewed from the perspective of their constitutive Acts of Parliament, almost all the powers of the Welsh Assembly and a large portion of the powers of the Scottish Parliament relate to control over issues handled in England by delegated legislation.

GOVERNING IN A NETHER WORLD

Discussion of parliamentary battles and *twilight zones* or cusps between two worlds where strange things happen is important to see how the world of everyday politics links with the wider political world. Yet to enter this world of high politics is a privilege or fate that rarely befalls an SI. Most are stuck in the nether world of everyday politics. Improbable or unforeseen events can conspire to make issues suddenly capable of making the transition to high politics. This includes events, say, of the character of the discovery that a kidney donor's family insisted that the kidneys only be given to a white recipient, making *The United Kingdom Transplant Support Service Authority Regulations 1991* as well as the various Human Organ Transplants regulations possible candidates for the transition, at least temporarily, to high politics. Yet for the most part those involved with, for example, grubbing up orchards, upgrading compensation for statutory maternity pay, closing obscure loopholes in European Community transit law, administering forms for patients under mental health care, redefining animal pathogens and raising the Industrial Training Board Levy, might be dealing with important issues, but they will be hard pressed to involve anyone else in taking up cudgels for them in a wider political arena.

The subject of the overwhelming majority of SIs discussed in this book hardly makes them capable of being turned into the sort of stuff that breeds parliamentary rebellion or makes and breaks electoral support. There are other issues that might make more promising material for high political conflict—abandoning registers of drug addicts, getting rid of height and eyesight requirements for firefighters as well as what information the Bank of England should be allowed to demand from banks—but few appear to have had much motivation to move these issues through the twilight zone and into high politics. The reasons for this could be, among other things, lack of strong opposition even within the world of everyday politics to many of the measures proposed by government, or an ability by those opposed to them to let go of a lost cause. The press is not very active in pursuing detailed investigations of matters covered in SIs and publishing them unless there are eye-catching leaks on which to base a story. All of this means that for most issues handled by SI, they will be subject to the dynamics of the world of everyday politics. When a certificated bailiff is told that he cannot get a penny more than £10 for writing a single letter to a poor soul who has incurred a traffic fine, he is unlikely to be able to appeal over the head of the Lord Chancellor directly to the court of public opinion.

The world of everyday politics is not completely different from the one with which we are familiar through text books on British policy-making. The institutions are the same as those that appear in all general descriptions of British government—the ministry, Parliament and interest groups. Most of the laws of gravity in this world are the same as those of the high political world with which we are more familiar—governments win votes, control the executive and the executive dominates the policy process. The stakes can be every bit as high as in the world of high politics. For example, delegated legislation can make the difference between boom and bust for big firms in an industry like telecommunications.

Yet the world of everyday politics is different in many important respects. The leading figures in this world are not Cabinet ministers, permanent secretaries and big 'corporatist' interest groups, but junior ministers, HEOs, legal advisers and lobbyists from often tiny groups working from home. Parliament, and especially the House of Lords, instead of being a largely peripheral institution, is crucial to those drafting and writing laws. The politics in this world is surreptitious. By the time you hear that a regulation is going to be passed, there is generally little you can do about it except try to make it less bad for you or your organisation. For the government, what can be done in this world is constrained by what is doable within the confines of existing legislation. The relationships between those involved display some characteristics, admittedly not necessarily commonplace, which could probably only be found in this world. They include lawyers widening the scope of social security provisions, lawyers telling civil servants what legislation they should be asking the lawyers to draft, civil servants telling Members of Parliament to 'bog off' and senior officials asking members of interest groups what the policy of the incoming government is likely to be.

The picture painted here is one in which the executive dominates, but without any strong sign of substantial alienation or resentment among the groups and individuals most affected by the delegated legislation it produces. If critics of delegated legislation are correct that statutes are increasingly leaving important issues to ministerial discretion exercised through Statutory Instrument, this is probably more a matter for concern than alarm. The cause for concern is that the system of scrutiny is sound and capable of supporting the apparently ever-increasing number of rules, and here the JCSI is certainly straining under the burden of work which it faces, doing an impressive job with so few resources.

Alarm is probably a misplaced response to the apparent growing importance of delegated legislation for a variety of reasons. It is not necessarily the case that the inclusion of detail in the primary legislation will give greater opportunities for participation to those interested in shaping it. A single detailed provision in a Bill containing a whole mass of other detail is no more likely to be subjected to serious scrutiny than, say, an SI is likely to be prayed against. A busy Bill team of civil servants is unlikely to have as much time to listen to the concerns of a part-time representative of a group affected by one small aspect of a particular clause in the Bill, and the representative has probably no better chance of getting an MP to offer support on a Bill than on an SI. A Bill team is probably even less likely to get the detail right than if it had time to develop the delegated legislation. Moving more detail into a Bill could remove two features of everyday politics that appear to make it easier for a wider range of groups to shape policy at this level—time and twilight.

It would be hopelessly pious, and run counter to what we know about how politics and the media work, to expect politicians and the press suddenly to develop an appetite for the sort of detail that makes up the world of everyday politics. As the theory which has underpinned this book suggests, there is a limit to the number of conflicts in which the public can remain interested—when you find a new fight to observe, you tend to lose interest in an older one (Schattschneider 1960). However, this does not excuse the extreme reluctance of most observers, academic and otherwise, as well as politicians to monitor what is going on in this world. If the cliché about the devil being in the detail is correct, we need to understand it and its political implications. This means pursuing the diabolically unprepossessing task of delving into its micro-level depths. Otherwise our understanding of the specific ways in which what is usually con-descendingly described as 'low politics' works will remain small in comparison to our obsessive preoccupation with political high jinks, and infinitessimal in comparison to its effects on the daily lives of citizens.

Appendix A: The Medicines (Control of Substances for Manufacture) (Revocation) Order 1997

STATUTORY INSTRUMENTS

1997 No. 1728

MEDICINES

The Medicines (Control of Substances for Manufacture)
(Revocation) Order 1997

Made	*18th July 1997*
Laid before Parliament	*21st July 1997*
Coming into force	*11th August 1997*

The Secretary of State concerned with health in England, the Secretaries of State respectively concerned with health and with agriculture in Scotland and in Wales, the Minister of Agriculture, Fisheries and Food, the Department of Health and Social Services for Northern Ireland and the Department of Agriculture for Northern Ireland, acting jointly, in exercise of the powers conferred by sections 105(1)(a) and 129(4) of the Medicines Act 1968(a) and now vested in them(b) and of all other powers enabling them in that behalf, after consulting and taking into account the advice of the Veterinary Products Committee(c) in accordance with section 129(7) of that Act and after consulting such organisations as appear to them to be representative of interests likely to be substantially affected by the following Order in accordance with section 129(6) of that Act, hereby make the following Order:—

(a) 1968 c. 67; "the Ministers" referred to in section 105 is defined in section 1: see also the following footnote.

(b) In the case of the Secretaries of State concerned with health in England and in Wales by virtue of S.I. 1969/388, in the case of the Secretary of State concerned with agriculture in Wales by virtue of S.I. 1978/272 and in the case of the Northern Ireland Departments by virtue of the Northern Ireland Constitution Act 1973 (c. 36), section 40 and Schedule 5, and the Northern Ireland Act 1974 (c. 28), section 1(3) and Schedule 1, paragraph 2(1)(b).

(c) A committee established under section 4 of the Medicines Act 1968 by virtue of the Medicines (Veterinary Products Committee) Order 1970 (S.I. 1970/1304).

Title and commencement

1. This Order may be cited as the Medicines (Control of Substances for Manufacture) (Revocation) Order 1997 and shall come into force on 11th August 1997.

Revocation of the Medicines (Control of Substances for Manufacture) Order 1982

2. The Medicines (Control of Substances for Manufacture) Order 1982(a) is hereby revoked.

Signed by authority of the Secretary of State for Health

Tessa Jowell
Minister of State for Public Health,
Department of Health

16th July 1997

Sewel
Parliamentary Under Secretary of State,
Scottish Office

14th July 1997

Signed by authority of the Secretary of State for Wales

Win Griffiths
Parliamentary Under Secretary of State,
Welsh Office

18th July 1997

Jeff Rooker
Minister of State,
Ministry of Agriculture, Fisheries and Food

15th July 1997

Sealed with the Official Seal of the Department of Health and Social Services for Northern Ireland this 18th day of July 1997.

(L.S.)

Jeremy Harbison
Under Secretary

1997

Sealed with the Official Seal of the Department of Agriculture for Northern Ireland this 18th day of July 1997.

(L.S.)

P. J. Small
Permanent Secretary

(a) S.I. 1982/425.

EXPLANATORY NOTE

(This note is not part of the Order)

This Order revokes the Medicines (Control of Substances for Manufacture) Order 1982 as part of the implementation by the Animals and Animal Products (Examination for Residues and Maximum Residue Limits) Regulations 1997 of Council Directive 96/22/EEC concerning the prohibition on the use in stockfarming of certain substances having a hormonal or thyrostatic action and of beta-agonists, and repealing Directives 81/602/EEC, 88/146/EEC and 88/299/EEC (OJ No. L 125, 23.5.96, p.3).

A Compliance Cost Assessment has been prepared and a copy has been placed in the library of each House of Parliament. Copies can be obtained from the Veterinary Medicines Directorate, Woodham Lane, Addlestone, Surrey KT15 3NB.

Appendix B Analysis of SIs on CD-ROM

The 27,999 Statutory Instruments analysed in Chapter 3 were downloaded from The Stationery Office's Statutory Instruments Database May 1997 supplied by Context Ltd. I am extremely grateful to Context Ltd and the Stationery Office for allowing me to download the data and perform my own analysis on them.

The data were downloaded as an ASCII text file and this large (over 150 MB) file was coded using the text analysis features of Transform Reports supplied by Access Informatics Ltd on a Macintosh SE30. Coded data were transferred to a UNIX main-frame and analysed using SPSS.

Appendix C: SIs examined in detail in Chapter 3

1991/1943	*The Protection from Eviction (Excluded Licences) Order 1991*	London Hostels Association, Limited does not have to provide notices to quit under 1977 housing legislation.
1992/476	*The Employment Code of Practice (Picketing) Order 1992*	Appoints a day on which a new code of practice on picketing comes into effect.
1993/1451	*The Harbour Authorities (Variation of Constitution) Order 1993*	Varies the constitution of five named harbour commissioners.

CONSEQUENTIAL SIS

1994/2812	*The Local Government (Magistrates' Courts etc.) (Amendment) Order 1994*	Revokes legislation rendered obsolete by changes in the law.
1994/3255(S.183)	*The Local Government (Transitional Election Arrangements) (Scotland) Order 1994*	Makes short term provisions (1 year) for vacancies to new local councils in Scotland.
1996/1034	*The North Eastern Sea Fisheries District (Constitution ofCommittee and Expenses) (Variation) Order 1996*	Changes the constitution of this body following the reorganisation of local government (Humberside and Cleveland).
1990/2613	*The Land Registration (Charges) Rules 1990*	Tidy up the scheme, to take account of the change in style of mortgage documentation.

DEFINITIONS AND FORMS

1993/323(S.31)	*The Town and Country Planning (Hazardous Substances) (Scotland) Regulations 1993*	List hazardous substances under the Act, deals with consent and exemptions as well as enforcement of regulations.
11993/2182	*The Right to Purchase (Application Form) (Scotland) Order 1993*	A new form for those applying to buy their homes under right to buy legislation.
1988/2069(S.199)	*The Assured Tenancies (Tenancies at a Low Rent) (Scotland) Order 1988*	Specifies how low a rent has to be to avoid being an assured tenancy.
1990/1276(S.140)	*The Corn Returns (Scotland) (Variation) Regulations 1990*	A new form for Corn Returns.
1992/1704	*The Housing (Right to Buy) (Mortgage Limit) Regulations 1992*	Define the tenant's eligibility to a mortgage under right to buy legislation.
1992/2645	*The Child Support (Maintenance Arrangements and Jurisdiction) Regulations 1992*	Make provision as to the effect that making a maintenance assessment on a maintenance order or a maintenance agreement.
1993/169	*The Special Road Schemes and Highways Orders (Procedure) Regulations 1993*	Regulations setting out how to draw a centre line on plans for roads.
1993/1691	*The Football Spectators (Designation of Football Matches in England and Wales) Order 1993*	Designates association football matches for the purposes of the Football Spectators Act 1989.
1993/2181	*The Right to Purchase (Loan Application) (Scotland) Amendment Order 1993*	Makes a minor correction to the right to purchase loan form for public housing.
1994/1821	*The Air Passenger Duty (Connected Flights) Order 1994*	Sets out when two flights shall be treated as 'connected' for the purposes of exemption from air passenger duty.
1994/2318	*The Income Tax (Authorised Unit Trusts) (Interest Distributions) Regulations 1994*	Specify some conditions under which interest payments from unit trusts are tax exempt.

1994/3278	*The Overseas Life Assurance Fund (Amendment) Order 1994*	Defines which assets of a company are the assets of its overseas life assurance fund.
1996/1311	*The Personal Pension Schemes (Tables of Rates of Annuities) Regulations 1996*	Make provision for the basis on which the Government Actuary is to prepare tables of rates of annuities for personal pension schemes.
1996/3204	*The Homelessness (Suitability of Accommodation) Order 1996*	Gives legal definitions concerning some aspects of what people may reasonably be expected tolive in for homelessness legislation.

PROCEDURES AND MACHINERY OF GOVERNMENT

1987/1422	*The Revenue Appeals Order 1987*	Allows some tax cases to be referred direct to the Court of Appeal instead of to the High Court.
1987/465	*The Transfer of Functions (Immigration Appeals) Order 1987*	Transfers responsibility for immigration appeals from the Home Secretary to the Lord Chancellor.
1988/1169	*The Vaccine Damage Payments (Amendment) Regulations 1988*	Define arrangements for appointment and training of members, officers and staff of Vaccine Damage Tribunals.
1989/336	*The Water Resources (Licences) (Amendment) Regulations 1989*	Specify some procedures for consultations on extraction orders in the Norfolk and Suffolk Broads.
1989/480	*The CSCE Information Forum (Immunities and Privileges) Order 1989*	Confers privileges and immunities upon the representatives of the sovereign Powers at the May 1989 Conference on Security and Co-operation in Europe (CSCE).
1990/1330	*The Family Health Services Authorities (Membership and Procedure) Regulations 1990*	Make provisions relating to the constitution of Family Health Service authorities and to their meetings and proceedings.

1990/2236	*The Land Registration (Solicitor to H M Land Registry) Regulations 1990*	Specify the acts of the Chief Land Registrar which may be done by a legally qualified registrar.
1991/1688	*The Returning Officer's Charges (Northern Ireland) Order 1991*	Sets out expenses that can be claimed by a returning officer.
1991/2699	*The Tribunals and Inquiries (Specified Tribunals) Order 1991*	Brings bodies (e.g. Forestry Committees Building Societies Act tribunals) under the supervision of the Council on Tribunals.
1991/894	*Representations Procedure (Children) Regulations 1991*	Establish a procedure for considering representations (including complaints) made to local authorities about children in care or fostered.
1992/1314	*The Transfers of Functions (Energy) Order 1992*	Divides up functions of Minister of Energy, mainly passing to DTI.
1992/1732	*The Parliamentary Corporate Bodies (Crown Immunities etc.) Order 1992*	Puts the Corporate Officer of the House of Lords and the Corporate Officer of the House of Commons in a corresponding position to that of the Crown for some planning permission purposes.
1993/1823	*The Offshore Safety (Repeals and Modifications) Regulations 1993*	Make minor procedural changes to legislation on oil rigs (e.g. the 1987 Petroleum Act) connected with health and safety at work.
1993/434	*The Education (PCFC and UFC Staff) Order 1993*	Shifts 153 named staff from PCFC to UFC following reorganisation of higher education funding.
1994/1894	*The Civil Service (Management Functions) (Northern Ireland) Order 1994*	Empowers the Department of Finance and Personnel to delegate the power to make appointments.
1994/2023	*The Police Authorities (Selection Panel) Regulations 1994*	Provisions for the conduct of selection panels for magistrate members of police authorities.

1995/3192	*The Retirement Age of General Commissioners Order 1995*	Sets maximum retirement age of General Commissioners at 70.
1995/686	*The Justices' Chief Executives and Justices' Clerks (Appointment) Regulations 1995*	Set out procedure to be followed when magistrates courts submit candidates for the posts of justices' chief executive or justices' clerk to the Lord Chancellor for approval.
1994/2736	*The Welsh Language (Names for Police Authorities in Wales) Order 1994*	Gives Welsh names to existing police authorities.
1996/273	*The Transfer of Functions (Registration and Statistics) Order 1996*	Arrangements for the creation of an Office of National Statistics.
1997/45	*The Local Housing Authorities (Prescribed Principles for Allocation Schemes) (Wales) Regulations 1997*	Regulations covering the allocation of council houses (e.g. councillors taking decisions cannot be councillors for the area and officers can take decisions too).
1997/536	*The Disability Discrimination (Abolition of District Advisory Committees) Order 1997*	Abolishes committees, set up in 1944, which used to advise the Secretary of State whether to prosecute an employer for not employing a disabled person.

PERMISSIVE

1989/1329	*The Visiting Forces (Designation) Order 1989*	Designates Spain as a country to which the Visiting Forces Act 1952 applies.
1990/1989	*The Education (Grant) Regulations 1990*	The Secretary of State may pay education grants to persons other than local education authorities for approved items.
1991/1593	*The Hormonal Substances (Food Sources) (Animals) Regulations 1991*	Give ministry powers and outlines powers of inspection and destruction of animals with prohibited hormonal substances.

1989/538	*The African Development Bank (Further Subscription to Capital Stock) Order 1989*	Provides for the payment to the African Development Bank of a further subscription to the authorised capital stock of the Bank.
1996/2900	*The Residuary Body for Wales (Levies) Regulations 1996*	Provide for the Residuary Body for Wales issue a levy on local authorities.

REGULATORY

1987/1280	*The Occupiers' Liability (Northern Ireland) Order 1987*	Allows owners of land to exclude liability for people (e.g. rock climbers) using it.
1987/1629(N.I.17)	*The Limitation (Amendment) (Northern Ireland) Order 1987*	Amends the law of limitation of actions in negligence cases, libel actions and defamation actions (alters length of time under some circumstances).
1987/2061	*The Uniform Laws on International Sales Order 1987*	Specifies the contracting states for the purpose of the Hague Convention of 1964 relating to a Uniform Law on the International Sale of Goods.
1987/2078	*The Air Navigation (General) (Second Amendment) Regulations 1987*	Diverse air safety rules including weight of passengers, flying times and such like.
1987/2196	*The Mink (Keeping) Order 1987*	Prohibits keeping of mink except in some places and under licence (mainly renews an old SI which was due to expire).
1987/2198	*The Criminal Jurisdiction (Offshore Activities) Order 1987*	Applies UK criminal law to offshore installations in UK territorial waters.
1987/2236	*The Meat Inspection Regulations 1987*	Re-enacting with some changes the regime of meat inspection (changes include allowing heads and penises of some animals to be discarded immediately after slaughter).
1989/1852	*The Medicines (Prescription Only, Pharmacy and General Sale) Amendment Order 1989*	Amends the lists of prescription only medicines.

1989/112	*The Poisons (Amendment) Rules 1989*	Allow people longer to submit signed orders for transporting poisons in an emergency.
1989/2406(N.I.20)	*The Education Reform (Northern Ireland) Order 1989*	Minor provisions tidying up major education reform in Northern Ireland.
1989/2449	*The Anglerfish (Specified Sea Areas) (Prohibition of Fishing) Order 1989*	Prohibits fishing for anglerfish by specified British vessels in some areas.
1989/504	*The Testing of Poultry Flocks Order 1989*	Regulates the process of testing poultry flocks.
1990/2605	*The Merchant Shipping (Dangerous Goods and Marine Pollutants) Regulations 1990*	Give effect to provisions concerning the carriage of dangerous goods of the International Convention for the Safety of Life at Sea 1974.
1992/1142	*The Patents (Amendment) Rules1992*	Make major changes to rules on inventions.
1992/2671	*The Pharmaceutical Services (Northern Ireland) Order 1992*	Makes small change in the law to allow for the provision of drugs prescribed by nurses and midwives.
1993/1685	*The Diseases of Animals (Seizure) Order 1993*	Extends the powers of inspectors to seize things (other than live animals) by means of which diseases may be spread (including BSE).
1993/208	*The Coal and Other Safety-Lamp Mines (Explosives) Regulations 1993*	Cover use of explosives and associated material and equipment in safety-lamp mines.
1993/439(S.50)	*The Bankruptcy (Scotland) Amendment Regulations 1993*	Make amendments to bankruptcy regulations in Scotland.
1994/1646	*The Social Security (Cyprus) Order 1994*	Extends sickness and maternity benefit provisions to the Sovereign Base Areas in Cyprus.
1994/1748	*The Race Relations (Interest on Awards) Regulations 1994*	How interest on awards made by industrial tribunals under Race Relations Act is to be handled.

1994/1758	*The Prevention of Terrorism (Temporary Provisions) Act 1989 (Crown Servants and Regiulators etc.) Regulations 1994*	Apply money laundering legislation to Directors of Savings and exempts some institutions (e.g. Bank of England) from it.
1994/1922	*The Monopoly References (Alteration of Exclusions) Order 1994*	Allows the Director General of Fair Trading to make monopoly references for some forms of milk.
1994/3064	*The Coal Mining Subsidence (Land Drainage) Regulations 1994*	Prescribe how questions of subsidence damage affecting land drainage, arising between persons responsible for such damage are to be determined.
1994/73	*The Water Enterprises (Merger) (Modification) Regulations 1994*	Uprate the amount of joint assets required to trigger reference under the Fair Trading Act in the merger of water companies.
1995/2015	*The Children (Short-term Placements) (Miscellaneous Amendments) Regulations 1995*	Make clear that the prohibition on voluntary organisations placing a child outside the British Islands applies even where local authority is responsible for the child (and makes other changes).
1995/2550	*The Video Recordings (Labelling) (Amendment) Regulations 1995*	Alter the labelling regime for videos for young children.
1996/1333	*The Disability Discrimination (Sub-leases and Sub-tenancies) Regulations 1996*	Establish that the disabled are to deal with immediate landlords rather than superior landlords when looking for alterations to rented property.
1996/1645	*The Police (Conduct) (Senior Officers) (Scotland) Regulations 1996*	Change regulations governing the handling of disciplinary offences by chief officers.
1996/1661	*The Value Added Tax (Anti-avoidance (Heating)) Order 1996*	Makes importations of heated water chargeable to VAT at the standard rate (previously zero rated).

1996/1664	*The Education (Disability Statements for Further Education Institutions) Regulations 1996*	Disability statements are a requirement for receipt of Further Education Funding Council money—the regulations set out what should be in them and how often they should be published.
1996/1855	*The Anthrax (Amendment) Order 1996*	Extends the powers of veterinary inspectors in dealing with suspected cases of anthrax.
1996/1925	*The Recovery Abroad of Maintenance (Convention Countries) Order 1996*	Extends the list of countries with mutual arrangements with the UK covering maintenance of dependants.
1996/221(S.15)	*The Police (Promotion) (Scotland) Regulations 1996*	Simplify arrangements for promotion above the rank of constable.
1996/2348	*The Stamp Duty (Production of Documents) (Northern Ireland) Regulations 1996*	Specify the conditions under which documents governing land transactions have to be shown and to whom.
1996/3259	*The Refuges for Children (Scotland) Regulations 1996*	Set out requirements for establishments to be approved as children's refuges and set out conditions for extending the maximum stay from 7 to 14 days.
1997/31	*The Trading Schemes (Exclusion) Regulations 1997*	Extricate some trading schemes from legislation designed to limit pyramid selling.
1997/57	*The Electronic Lodgement of Tax Returns Order 1997*	Makes provision with respect to the electronic lodgement of tax returns and documents required in connection with tax returns.

DISTRIBUTIVE

1987/157	*The Police Cadets (Pensions) (Amendment) Regulations 1987*	Allow pension payments to dependents of police cadets killed in the execution of duty.
1987/1699	*The Police Cadets (Pensions) (Scotland) Amendment Regulations 1987*	Scottish application of English SI allowing pension payment to dependents of police cadets killed in the execution of duty.

1988/1328(L.15)	*The Matrimonial Causes (Costs) Rules 1988*	Make new provision for the taxation of costs in matrimonial proceedings in the High Court and county courts.
1988/568	*The War Pensions (Chinese Seamen and Indian Seamen) (Revocations) Order 1988*	Removes provisions under which the rate of war pension payable to certain non-British seamen employed on British ships is lower than that payable to British seamen.
1989/417	*The Pensions Increase (Local Authorities' etc. Pensions) (Amendment) Regulations 1989*	Provide for the payment of increases under the Pensions Increase Act 1971 on Scottish Homes pensions and secure that the cost of such increases is to be borne by that body.
1989/483	*The Social Security (Isle of Man) Order 1989*	Gives effect to a reciprocal agreement permitting periods of presence in the Isle of Man to be treated as if they were periods of presence in the United Kingdom for the purposes of entitlement to mobility allowance.
1990/990	*The Marshall Scholarships Order 1990*	Increases number of Marshall (university) scholarships from 30 to 40.
1992/1690	*The Street Works (Sharing of Costs of Works) Regulations 1992*	Make provision for the sharing of costs between the highway, bridge or transport authority and the undertaker where the undertaker's apparatus in a street is affected by major high-way, bridge or transport works.
1992/620	*The Collection Fund (England) (Amendment) Regulations 1992*	Make minor changes in treatment of interest on collection funds of charging authorities under Part VI of the Local Government Finance Act 1988.
1994 /2564	*The Coal Mining Subsidence (Blight and Compensation for Inconvenience During Works) Regulations 1994*	Owners of houses blighted by mining subsidence can be compensated *inter alia* by requiring mine owners to buy blighted houses at unblighted market value.

1992/1598 (S.153)	*The Housing (Percentage of Approved Expense for Repairs Grants) (Lead Plumbing and Radon Gas Works) (Scotland) Order 1992*	Increases the grant that can be paid for housing improvements in the case of removing lead plumbing or radon gas.
1991/1995	*The Employment Action (Miscellaneous Provisions) Order 1991*	People under employment Action Programme will get benefits as if they are in training.
1988/1483(S.145)	*The Housing Benefit (Social Security Act 1986 Modifications) (Scotland) Regulations 1988*	Allow Community Charge rebate and cover the conditions governing entitlement to such rebates and how such rebates are to be calculated.

PUBLIC SERVICES

1994/351(S.11)	*The Self-Governing Schools (Application and Amendment of Regulations) (Scotland) Regulations 1994*	Apply general school regulations (class sizes etc.) to self-governing schools.
1995/302	*The Approved Probation and Bail Hostel Rules 1995*	Regulate the running of bail hostels.

Appendix D: Selection of 46 SIs for detailed case studies

The SIs were selected on a number of criteria. First, they had to be recent. First approaches to government departments were made between September 1997 and December 1998, and the selection of SIs reflected the recent output of the department being approached. Secondly, they had to cover a range of the department's activity— while it is not possible to have a sample covering all, or even all major, functions carried out by a department, SIs were selected which spread across the department's interests and SIs covering the same policy areas were avoided. Over and above these two criteria it is difficult to select SIs in advance on any other basis since it usually only becomes clear to a non-specialist what an SI actually does only when one speaks to someone closely involved in its development, whether an official or a member of an interest group. SIs that looked straightforward from reading their content and relating it to the parent legislation rarely were quite that straightforward in practice. Overtly controversial SIs that had already made headlines were avoided on the grounds that I could not expect officials to talk openly about them. Yet it is generally impossible to say in advance simply on the basis of scrutinising the content of the SI whether it was controversial among those involved in generating it or those affected by it. As will be seen below, several SIs which appeared innocuous and routine were the subject of immense controversy, and others which might be expected to generate some controversy proved to be entirely unproblematic. To be able to identify controversy in advance in all cases would have required an intimate knowledge of the development of detailed policy issues across a broader range of government activity than is likely to be held by any one scholar. Only twice did departments suggest that I examine an alternative SI to the one I had originally proposed—one of these reflected an area of extreme sensitivity within one department; the other, from a different department, was currently the subject of a court case.

The list of SIs examined in Chapters 4 to 7 is set out below in alphabetical order for ease of reference. From the government officials' perspective the history of each of these SIs was generally traced by first approaching the official who actually wrote the SI (usually in the legal adviser's office of the relevant department) who would then put me in touch with the administrator responsible. Within government, therefore, there would generally be two interviews per SI.

The Action Programme for Nitrate Vulnerable Zones (Scotland) Regulations 1998	Scottish Office	1998/2927	25.11.98
The Aircraft Operators (Accounts and Records) (Amendment) Regulations 1998	Customs and Excise	1998/63	20.1.98
The Apple and Pear Orchard Grubbing Up Regulations 1998	Agriculture, Fisheries and Food	1998/1131	23.4.98

The Bank of England (Information Powers) Order 1998	Treasury	1998/1270	19.5.98
The Bread and Flour Regulations 1998	Agriculture, Fisheries and Food	1998/141	22.1.98
The Broadcasting (Percentage of National Radio Multiplex Revenue) Order 1998	Culture, Media and Sport	1998/189	28.1.98
The Channel 4 (Application of Excess Revenues) Order 1997	Culture, Media and Sport	1997/3019	17.12.97
The Cider and Perry (Amendment) Regulations 1997	Customs and Excise	1997/659	7.7.97
The Cod (Specified Sea Areas) (Prohibition of Fishing) Order 1998	Agriculture, Fisheries and Food	1998/1195	8.5.98
The Conditional Fee Agreements Order 1998	Lord Chancellor's Department	1998/1860	29.7.98
The Contracting Out (Functions Relating toNational Savings) Order 1998	Treasury	1998/1449	11.6.98
The Crime (Sentences) Act 1997 (Commencement No. 2 and Transitional Provisions Order 1997	Home Office	1997/2200	8.9.97
The Dual-use and related Goods (Export Control) (Amendment) Regulations 1998	Trade and Industry	1998/272	11.2.98
The Education (Amount to Follow Permanently Excluded Pupil) Regulations 1997	Education and Employment	1997/680	6.8.97
The Education (School Inspection) Regulations 1997	Education and Employment	1997/1966	6.98.97
The Education (School Leaving Date) Order 1997	Education and Employment	1997/1970	8.8.97
The Enforcement of Road Traffic Debts (Certificated Bailiffs)(Amendment) Regulations 1998	Lord Chancellor's Department	1998/1351	22.5.98
The Environmental Protection (Prescribed Processes and Substances) (Amendment) (Hazardous Waste Incineration) Regulations 1998	Environment, Transport and the Regions	1998/767	12.3.98

The Excise Duty Point (External and Internal Community Transit Procedure)(Amendment) Regulations 1998	Customs and Excise	1998/202	
The Fire Services (Appointments and Promotion) Amendment Regulations 1977	Home Office	1997/959	19.3.97
The Gaming Duty Regulations 1997	Customs and Excise	1997/2196	9.9.97
The Government of Wales Act 1998 (Commencement No. 2) Order 1998	Welsh Office	1998/2789	10.11.98
The Grants for Improvements in School Education (Scotland) Regulations 1998	Scottish Office	1998/3051	2.12.98
The Industrial Training Levy (Construction Board) Order 1997	Education and Employment	1997/407	18.2.97
The Jobseeker's Allowance (Amendment) Regulations 1998	Social Security	1998/71	15.1.98
The Jobseeker's Allowance (Workskill Courses) Pilot (No. 2) Regulations 1997	Education and Employment	1997/1909	29.7.99
The Local Authorities (Transport Charges) Regulations 1998	Environment, Transport and the Regions	1998/948	31.3.98
The Local Government Act 1988 (Competition)(England)(No. 2) Regulations 1997	Environment, Transport and the Regions	1997/2732	17.11.97
The Mental Health Act (Hospital Guardianship and Consent to Treatment) Amendment Regulations 1997	Health	1997/801	13.3.97
The Merchant Shipping (Small Workboats and Pilot Boats) Regulations 1998	Environment, Transport and the Regions	1998/1609	02.7.98
The Misuse of Drugs (Supply to Addicts) Regulations 1997	Home Office	1997/1001	20.3.97
The National Crime Squad Service Authority (Levying) Order 1997	Home Office	1998/2283	19.9.97
The National Health Service (Optical Charges and Payments) Amendment Regulations 1997	Health	1997/2488	17.10.97
The National Health Service (Pharmaceutical Services) (Scotland) Amendment Regulations 1998	Scottish Office	1998/3031	2.12.98

The National Health Service (Proposals for Pilot Schemes) and (Miscellaneous Amendments) Regulations 1997	Health	1997/2289	22.9.97
The Non-Domestic Rating (Rural Settlements)(Wales) Order 1998	Welsh Office	1998/2963	25.11.98
The Nurses, Midwives and Health Visitors (Supervisors of Midwives) Amendment Rules Approval Order 1997	Health	1997/1723	16.7.97
The Pensions Appeal Tribunals (England and Wales)(Amendment) Rules 1998	Lord Chancellor's Department	1998/1201	8.5.98
The Restrictive Trade Practices (Non-notifiable Agreements) (Turnover Threshold) Amendment Order 1997	Trade and Industry	1997/2944	6.12.97
The Social Security (Welfare to Work) Regulations 1998	Social Security	1988/2231	10.9.98
The Social Security Administration (Fraud) Act 1997 (Commencement No. 6) Order 1998	Social Security	1998/2779	12.11.98
The Specified Animal Pathogens Order 1998	Agriculture, Fisheries and Food	1998/463	27.2.98
The Statutory Maternity Pay (Compensation of Employers) Amendment Regulations 1998	Social Security	1998/522	3.3.98
The Telecommunications (Interconnection) Regulation 1997	Trade and Industry	1997/2931	9.12.97
The Wireless Telegraphy (Control of Interference from Videosenders) Order 1998	Trade and Industry	1998/722	10.3.98

Appendix E: Survey of interest groups

The survey was sent to the executive directors or equivalent of 639 groups set out in the Combined British Directories and the PMS Guide to Pressure Groups (CBD 1996; PMS 1997). While the CBD source contains over 6,300 entries and the PMS 500, questionnaires were sent to trade associations and interest groups which might be expected to have an *interest* in shaping government decisions. This excluded predominantly self-help groups, appreciation societies and those which exist to provide services for members which do not generally include lobbying government. Thus groups such as the 'Followers of Rupert' (the Bear) and the 'Foot Lovers Admiration Society' were excluded: included were trade unions, professional associations and promotional groups, including many that might on *a priori* grounds be expected to be 'outsiders' (such as Surfers Against Sewage, the Towpath Action Group and the National Union of Mineworkers).

A total of 639 questionnaires were sent out in March 1998 and 382 replies were received, a response rate of 60 per cent. The questionnaires were anonymous, and while around one half of the respondents chose to identify their groups by name, it is not possible to determine how many apparent 'outsider' groups actually replied. Moreover, the assurance of anonymity means that no individual groups can be identified even if they did chose to reveal their names.

Question 1

With which government department(s) do you tend to have contact? Please tick as many as apply.

Response	N	%
Culture	55	14.6
Education	116	30.8
Health	117	31.0
Development	13	3.4
Soc Sec	57	15.1
Environment	191	50.7
Trade	184	48.8
Foreign	37	9.8
Treasury	67	17.8
Home	132	35.0
Law Off	16	4.2
Lord C	51	13.5
Agriculture	95	25.2
Defence	23	6.1
NIO	43	11.4
Scottish	96	25.5
Welsh	58	15.4
Other	27	7.2
None	4	1.1
Total	1,382	366.6

Question 2
How often does your contact with government departments involve consultation or discussion concerning particular Statutory Instruments (and proposed Statutory Instruments)? Please tick ONE only.

Response	N	%
Most of the time	26	7.1
Some of the time	184	50.3
Only rarely	102	27.9
Never	54	14.8
Total	366	100.1†

† Percentages in this and some subsequent tables do not add up to 100.0 due to rounding.

Question 3
Which ONE department tends to be responsible for the largest number of Statutory Instruments affecting your organisation and its members? Please tick ONE only.

Response	N	%
Culture	6	1.9
Education	18	5.7
Health	36	11.4
Soc Sec	18	5.7
Environment	92	29.0
Trade	48	15.1
Treasury	3	0.9
Home	34	10.7
Lord C	2	0.6
Agriculture	31	9.8
NIO	2	0.6
Scottish	21	6.6
Welsh	1	0.3
Other	5	1.6
Total	317	99.9

Question 4
How would you describe your contact with this department? Please tick ONE only.

Response	N	%
Frequent	100	31.2
Steady	109	34.0
Occasional	59	18.4
Intermittent	46	14.3
No contact	7	2.2
Total	321	100.1

Question 5
Does this department ask your organization for its views on all relevant Statutory Instruments before they are published?

Response	N	%
Most of the time	172	53.9

Some of the time	99	31.0
Rarely	30	9.4
Never	18	5.6
Total	319	99.9

Question 6

When this department asks for your views on proposed Statutory Instruments does it give you enough time to digest the implications and formulate a response?

Response	N	%
Most of the time	134	44.2
Some of the time	125	41.3
Rarely	35	11.6
Never	9	3.0
Total	303	100.1

Question 7

How often do you or colleagues in your organisation raise objections to proposed Statutory Instruments with the department? Please tick ONE.

Response	N	%
Majority of proposals	64	21.5
About half	81	27.3
Minority of proposals	103	34.7
Very rarely	32	10.8
Never	7	2.4
Dont know	10	3.4
Total	297	100.1

Question 8

Are these objections usually

Response	N	%
Predominantly substantive	62	21.4
Predominantly technical	74	25.5
Half substantive	154	53.1
Total	290	100.0

Question 9

And which of the following would best describe the most common response of this department to your objections to proposed Statutory Instruments? Please tick ONE only.

Response	N	%
Usually make changes	15	5.1
Sometimes make chang	192	65.5
Rarely make changes	77	26.3
Don't listen	9	3.1
Total	293	100.0

Question 10
Would you say that persistence in making known your objections to proposed Statutory Instruments with this department produces the desired result?

Response	N	%
Most of the time	31	10.9
Some of the time	199	70.1
Rarely	45	15.8
Never	9	3.2
Total	284	100.0

Question 11
Does your own organisation initiate proposals for Statutory Instruments to this department? Please tick ONE only.

Response	N	%
Several times a year	15	4.9
Total	46	15.1
Once every few years	70	23.0
Never	174	57.0
Total	305	100.0

Question 12
Here are some statements that we have heard about Statutory Instruments. Please indicate whether you think each one a) always or nearly always true b) frequently true c) rarely true or d) never true

a) Statutory Instruments which affect us are published before we get to hear about them.

Response	N	%
Nearly always true	40	11.5
Frequently true	109	31.3
Rarely true	174	50.0
Never true	25	7.2
Total	348	100.0

b) The government uses Statutory Instruments to get things through that might cause problems if opened up to full parliamentary scrutiny.

Response	N	%
Nearly always true	24	7.4
Frequently true	164	51.4
Rarely true	117	36.7
Never true	14	4.4
Total	319	99.9

c) Consultation on Statutory Instruments offers groups like ours a better chance to shape legislation than consultation on parliamentary Bills.

Response	N	%
Nearly always true	44	13.1
Frequently true	139	41.5
Rarely true	123	36.7
Never true	29	8.7
Total	335	100.0

d) Statutory Instruments are technical and raise no contentious political issues.

Response	N	%
Nearly always true	20	5.8
Frequently true	117	34.0
Rarely true	181	52.6
Never true	26	7.6
Total	344	100.0

e) SIs are well drafted.

Response	N	%
Nearly always true	17	5.4
Frequently true	192	61.3
Rarely true	95	30.4
Never true	9	2.9
Total	313	100.0

Appendix F: SIs cited in text

Bibliography

ALLEN, C. K. (1950), *Law and Orders. An Inquiry into the Nature and Scope of Delegated Legislation and Executive Owers in English Law* (London, Stevens & Sons Ltd.)

BAGEHOT, W. (1963), *The English Constitution* (Glasgow, Collins)

BALDWIN, R. (1995), *Rules and Government* (Oxford, Clarendon Press)

BATES, T. ST. J. N. (1998), 'The Future of Parliamentary Scrutiny of Delegated Legisation: Some Judicial Perspectives', 19(3) *Statute Law Review* 155–76

BAUMGARTNER, F.R. (1989), 'Independent and Politicised Policy Communities: Education and Nuclear Energy in France and the United States', 2(1) *Governance* 42–66

BENNETT, A. F. (1990), 'The Uses and Abuses of Delegated Legislation', 11(1) *Statute Law Review* 23–7

BLOM-HANSEN, J. (1997) 'A "New Institutional" Perspective on Policy Networks', 75 *Public Administration* (Winter) 669–93

BOOKER, C., and NORTH, R. (1996), *The Castle of Lies: Why Britain must get Out of Europe* (London, Duckworth)

BOULTON, C. J. (1989), *Erskine May's Treatise on the Law, Privileges, Proceedings and Usage of Parliament* (21st edn., London, Butterworths)

BRADLEY, A.W., and EWING, H.D. (1993), *Constitutional and Administrative Law* (11th edn., London, Longman)

CABINET OFFICE (1987), *Statutory Instruments Practice* (London, HMSO)

—— (1995), *Judge Over your Shoulder. Judicial Review: Balancing the Scales* (London, HMSO)

—— (1997), *Bringing Acts of Parliament into Force* (London, HMSO)

CANE, P. (1986), *An Introduction to Administrative Law* (Oxford, Clarendon Press)

CAMPBELL, A. I. (1987), 'Statutory Instruments. Laying and Legislation by Reference' [1987] *Public Law* 328–34

CARR, C.T. (1921), *Delegated Legislation: Three Lectures* (Cambridge, Cambridge University Press)

CARR, C. (1952), 'Delegated Legislation' in L. Campion, L. Amery, D. Brogan *et al.*, *Parliament. A Survey* (London, Allen and Unwin)

CLARK, A. (1994), *Diaries* (London, Phoenix Press)

CARROLL, A. (1998), *Constitutional and Administrative Law* (London, Pitman)

COMBINED BRITISH DIRECTORIES (CBD) (1996), *Directory of British Associations Edition 13* (London, CBD Research Ltd.)

COMMITTEE ON MINISTERS' POWERS (1932), *Report* (Cmd 4060, London, HMSO)

CONSERVATIVE PARTY (1997), *You can only be sure with the Conservatives*, The Conservative Manifesto 1997 (London, Conservative Party (also http://www.psr. keele.ac.uk/area/uk/man/con97.htm))

CRAIG, J. T. (1946), 'The Working of the Statutory Instruments Act 1946', 36 *Public Administration* 181–91

DAINTITH, T., and PAGE, A. (1999), *The Executive in the Constitution. Structure, Autonomy and Internal Control* (Oxford, Clarendon)

DELL, E. (1998), 'Controversies in the Early History of Channel 4', 12(4) *Contemporary British History* 1–52

DEPARTMENT OF HEALTH (1995), *Preparation and Making of Statutory Instruments* (London, Department of Health)

DEPARTMENT OF SOCIAL SECURITY (1998), *The Jobseeker's Allowance (Amendment) Regulations 1998 (SI 1998 No 71). Report by the Social Security Advisory Committee under Section 174(1) of the Social Security Administration Act 1992 and the statement by the Secretary of State for Social Security in accordance with Section 174(2) of that Act* (Cm 3829, London, HMSO)

DEREGULATION TASK FORCE (1996), *Deregulation Task Force Report* (London, Cabinet Office)

DICEY, A.V. (1952), *The Law of the Constitution* (9th edn., London, Macmillan)

FALLON, P. (1999), *Report of the Committee of Inquiry into the Personality Disorder Unit, Ashworth Special Hospital* (Cm 4194, London, HMSO)

FIELD, B. (1995), 'Above Party Politics?', *The Parliamentary Monitor*, December, 16

FINER, S. E. (1958), *Anonymous Empire. A Study of the Lobby in Great Britain* (London, The Pall Mall Press Ltd)

FOULKES, D. (1986), *Administrative Law* (London, Butterworths)

FURLONG, P. F. (1994), *Modern Italy: Representation and Reform* (London, Routledge)

FURLONG, S. (1997), 'Interest Group Lobbying: Difference between Legislative and Executive Branches'. Annual Meeting of the American Political Science Association, Washington DC

GANZ, G. (1997), 'Delegated Legislation: A Necessary Evil or a Constitutional Outrage?' in P. Leyland and J. Woods (eds.), *Administrative Law: Facing the Future. Old Constraints and New Horizons* (London, Blackstone Press)

GORDON, R. (1996), *Judicial Review: Law and Procedure* (London, Sweet and Maxwell)

GORDON, S. (1943), *Our Parliament* (London, Hansard Society)

GRADE, M. (1999), *It Seemed Like a Good Idea at the Time* (London, Macmillan)

GRANT, W. P. (1995), *Pressure Groups, Politics and Democracy in Britain* (Brighton, Harvester Wheatsheaf)

HAYHURST, J. D., and WALLINGTON, P. (1988), 'The Parliamentary Scrutiny of Delegated Legislation' [1988] *Public Law* 255–72

HECLO, H., and WILDAVSKY, A. V. (1981), *The Private Government of Public Money* (London, Macmillan)

HEWART (LORD HEWART OF BURY) (1929), *The New Despotism* (London, Benn)

HIMSWORTH, C. (1995), 'The Delegated Powers Scrutiny Committee' [1995] *Public Law*, 34–44

HINDMOOR, A. (1998), 'The Importance of Being Trusted: Transaction Costs and Policy Network Theory', 76(1) *Public Administration* 25–43

HMSO (1946), *Statutory Instruments Act 1946* (London, HMSO)

HOME OFFICE (1997), 'Height Requirements for Fire Service Recruitment', *Fire Service Circular 5/1997*, 8 April

HOOD, C. C. (1983), *The Tools of Government* (London, Macmillan)

——, DUNSIRE, A., and THOMPSON, K.S. (1978), 'So You Think You Know what Government Departments Are . . .?', 27 *Public Administration Bulletin* 20–32

HOWELL, M. A. (1994), *Women Firefighters: The Inequality Gap*, unpublished dissertation for MBA, University of Hertforshire

JCSI (1996), *First Special Report*, Session 1996–6 HC34 (London, HMSO)

—— (1997), *Fourteenth Report*, Session 1997–8, HL42 (London, HMSO) (also available at http://www.publications.parliament.uk/pa/jt199798/jtselect/jtstatin/042/si1401. htm)

—— (1998), *Forty-Second Report*. Session 1997–8, HL42 (London, HMSO) (also available at http://www.publications.parliament.uk/pa/jt199798/jtselect/jtstatin/134/ 13401.htm)

JENNINGS, W. I. (1932), 'The Committee on Ministers' Powers', 10(4) *Public Administration* 333–51

—— (1933), 'Ministers' Powers', 11(1) *Public Administration* 109–14

JORDAN, A. G., and RICHARDSON, J. J. (1987), *British Politics and the Policy Process* (London, Allen and Unwin)

JOWELL, J., and LE SUEUR, A. P. (1999), *de Smith, Woolf amd Jowell's Principles of Judicial Review* (London, Sweet and Maxwell)

KERWIN, C. M. (1999), *Rulemaking. How Government Agencies Write Law and Make Policy* (Washington DC, Congressional Quarterly Press)

LASKI, H. (1938), *Parliamentary Government in England* (London, George Allen and Unwin)

LIJPHART, A. (1984), *Democracies: Patterns of Majoritarian and Consensus Government in Twenty-one Countries* (New Haven, Conn., Yale University Press)

LOGIE, J. (1989), 'The Social Security Advisory Comittee', 23(3) *Social Policy and Administration* 248–61

LORD CHANCELLOR'S DEPARTMENT (1998). *Access to Justice with Conditional Fees. A Consultation Paper* (London, Lord Chancellor's Department)

—— (1998), *Summmary of the Responses to the Consultation Paper 'Access to Justice with Conditional Fees'* (London, Lord Chancellor's Department)

LOVELAND, I. (1996), *Constitutional Law: A Critical Introduction* (London: Butterworth)

M.D.C. (1893), 'Statutory Rules and Orders (review)', VIII *Law Quarterly Review* 165–7

MIERS, D. R., and PAGE, A. C. (1990), *Legislation* (2nd edn., London, Sweet and Maxwell)

NORTON, P. (1993), *Does Parliament Matter?* (London, Harvester Wheatsheaf)

OGUS, A. (1998), 'SSAC as an Independent Advisory Body: Its Role and Influence on Policymaking', 5(4) *Journal of Social Security Law* 156–74

PARLIAMENTARY MONITORING SERVICES (PMS) (1997), *PMS Guide to Pressure Groups, Issue 2* (London, PMS Publications Ltd)

PAGE, A. (1995), 'The Deregulation and Contracting Out Act 1994' [1994] *Current Law Statutes Annotated* c. 40

PAGE, E.C. (1998), 'The Impact of European Legislation on British Public Policy Making: A Research Note', 76(4) *Public Administration* 803–9

—— (1999), 'The Insider/Outsider Distinction: An Empirical Investigation', 1(2) *British Journal of Politics and International Relations* 205–14

PAPWORTH, N. (2000), *Constitutional and Administrative Law* (London, Butterworths)

POLSBY, N.W. (1980), 'Empirical Investigations of Mobilizationn of Bias in Community Power Research', XXVII(4) *Political Studies* 527–41

REID, C. T. (1987), 'A Deluge of Legislation', 137 *New Law Journal* 682

RHODES, R., and MARSH, D. (1992), 'New Directions in the Study of Policy Networks', 21 *European Journal of Political Research* 181–205

RICHARDSON, J. J., (ed.) (1982), *Policy Styles in Western Europe* (London, Allen & Unwin)

—— and JORDAN, A. G. (1979), *Governing under Pressure* (Oxford, Martin Robertson)

RIPPON, L. (1989), 'Henry VIII Clauses', 10(3) *Statute Law Review* 205–7

ROSE, R. (1974), *The Problem of Party Government* (London, Macmillan)

—— (1980), *Do Parties Make a Difference?* (London, Macmillan)

SCHATTSCHNEIDER, E. E. (1960), *The Semisovereign People: A Realist's View of Democracy in America* (New York, Holt, Rinehart and Winston)

SCOTT, R. (1996), *Report of the Inquiry into the Export of Defence Equipment and Dual-Use Goods to Iraq and Related Prosecutions*, HC 115 Vol 1 (London, HMSO)

SELECT COMMITTEE ON AGRICULTURE (2000), *Fourth Report Environmental Regulation and Farming Volume I—Report and Proceedings* HC 212-I (London, HMSO)

SELECT COMMITTEE ON DELEGATED LEGISLATION (1953), *Report HC 310* (London, HMSO)

SELECT COMMITTEE ON PROCEDURE (1996), *4th Report Delegated Legislation HC–152* (London, HMSO)

—— (2000), *1st Report Delegated Legislation HC–48* (London, HMSO)

SHEPPARD, D. (1996), 'Learning the Lessons. Mental Health Inquiry Reports Published in England and Wales between 1969 and 1996 and their Recommendations for Improving Practice' (2nd edn., London, The Zito Trust)

SHRIMSLEY, R. (1995), 'Victims offered up for bonfire of controls' *Financial Times*, 20 September

SIEGHART, M. A. (1950), *Government by Decree. A Comparative Study of the History of the Ordinance in English and French Law* (London, Stevens and Sons Ltd)

SMITH, M. J. (1999), *The Core Executive in Britain* (London, Macmillan)

TULLO, C., and PAWSEY, A. (1998), 'The Role of HMSO in the Legislative Process', 29(3) *The Law Librarian* 149–52

WAARDEN, F. (1992), 'Dimensions and Types of Policy Networks', 21 *European Journal of Political Research* 29–52

WALKLAND, S. A. (1968), *The Legislative Process in Great Britain* (London, George Allen and Unwin Ltd)

WEST, W. (1988), 'The Growth of Internal Conflicts in Administrative Regulation', 4 *Public Administration Review* 773–82

WILLIS, J. (1933), *The Parliamentary Powers of English Government Departments* (Cambridge, Mass., Harvard University Press)

Index

Pages in italics refer to notes and tables.